Routledge Revivals

The Empire of the East

This book, first published in 1908, is a result of Helen Barrett Montgomery's visits to Japan, and the way in which she experienced Japanese life and culture. This book thoroughly examines aspects such as religion, language, trade and education in Japan at the beginning of the twentieth century. This book will be of interest to students of Asian Studies.

I0895754

The Empire of the East

H. B. Montgomery

Routledge
Taylor & Francis Group

First published in 1908
by Methuen & Co.

This edition first published in 2015 by Routledge
4 Park Square, Milton Park, Abingdon, Oxon OX14 4RN
605 Third Avenue, New York, NY 10017

Routledge is an imprint of the Taylor & Francis Group, an informa business

© 1908 H. B. Montgomery

All rights reserved. No part of this book may be reprinted or reproduced or utilised in any form or by any electronic, mechanical, or other means, now known or hereafter invented, including photocopying and recording, or in any information storage or retrieval system, without permission in writing from the publishers.

Publisher's Note
The publisher has gone to great lengths to ensure the quality of this reprint but points out that some imperfections in the original copies may be apparent.

Disclaimer
The publisher has made every effort to trace copyright holders and welcomes correspondence from those they have been unable to contact.

A Library of Congress record exists under LC control number: 47042545

ISBN 13: 978-1-138-91968-6 (hbk)
ISBN 13: 978-1-315-68772-8 (ebk)
ISBN 13: 978-1-138-91969-3 (pbk)

A STAR OF THE EAST

FROM A PRINT BY TOSHIKATA

THE
EMPIRE OF THE EAST

BY

H. B. MONTGOMERY

"THIS NATION IS THE DELIGHT OF MY SOUL"
ST. FRANCIS XAVIER

WITH NINETEEN ILLUSTRATIONS

METHUEN & CO.
36 ESSEX STREET W.C.
LONDON

First Published in 1908.

PREFACE

ON my return from another visit to Japan a few months ago I found those persons in this country with whom I was brought into close association extremely curious and strangely ignorant regarding that ancient Empire. Despite the multitude of books which have of late years been published about Japan and things Japanese a correct knowledge of the country and the people is, so far as I can judge, altogether lacking in England. Indeed the multiplicity of books may have something to do with that fact, as many of them have been written by persons whose knowledge, acquired in the course of a flying visit, was, to say the least, perfunctory, and who had no opportunities for viewing the life of the people from within and forming a sound judgment on many matters upon which the writers have dogmatically pronounced. I, accordingly, came to the conclusion not only that there was room for one more book on Japan, but that another book was greatly needed—a book not technical, historical, abstruse or recondite, but a book describing in simple language Japan as it was, is, and will be. This is the task I set before myself when I commenced to write this volume, and the reader must be the judge to what extent I have been successful in the accomplishment thereof. I have touched but lightly on the material development of the country of recent years. I know from experience that though statistics are the fad of a few they are caviare to the great mass of the public. Nor have I dealt at all with politics or political parties in new Japan. It is, I think, unfortunate that the Japanese people, in adopting or adapting English institutions, should have introduced the political party system so much in evidence in Great Britain and other European countries. Whether that system works well in the West, where it has been in existence for centuries and is not always taken over-seriously by party politicians themselves, is a question upon which I shall express no opinion. But I think it is problematical whether such a system is well adapted for an Oriental people, possessed of and permeated by an ancient civilisation—a people whose feelings, sentiments, modes of thought, prejudices and passions are so essentially different from those of Western nations. Be that as it may, Japanese politics find no place in this work.

The morality or otherwise of the Japanese is a matter which has been much discussed and written about. The views of speakers and writers in regard thereto, so far as I have been able to ascertain them, have been largely affected by their prejudices or the particular standpoint from which they have regarded the matter. The result, in my opinion, has been that an entirely erroneous conception of the whole subject of Japanese morality has not only been formed but has been set forth in speech or writing, and a grave injustice has been done to the Japanese in this matter, to say nothing of the entirely false view of the whole question which has been promulgated. In this book I have endeavoured to deal with this thorny subject, so far as it can be dealt with in a book, free from prejudice or preconceived ideas of any kind. I have simply confined myself to facts, and have endeavoured to represent the whole matter as it appears to the Japanese and to morality according to the Japanese standard.

I have deemed it necessary to deal at some length with the various phases of Japanese art, which it is no exaggeration to say has permeated the whole nation so that the Japanese may truthfully be termed the most artistic people in the world. Of course it is impossible to deal exhaustively in a work of this kind with Japanese art. I have, however, endeavoured to describe the principal art industries of the country and to set forth what I may term the catholicity of art in Japan. I have also dealt with the question how far art has been affected by the Europeanising of the nation which has taken place of recent years, and the effect thereof.

The religion of the Japanese, the Constitution, the home life of the people, the Army and Navy, the financial position of the country are all subjects treated as fully as possible, inasmuch as they are matters essential to be understood in order to realise the Japan of to-day. The Japan of the future I have attempted to forecast in two final chapters.

But the Japan of to-day and the Japan of the future can neither be understood nor realised unless the reader have in his mind some idea as to the Japan of the past—not the barbaric or uncivilised Japan brought into contact with civilisation and suddenly discarding its barbarism, which is, I fear, the conception many persons still have, but, as I have sought to show, a highly civilised country holding itself aloof from European influences and excluding, so long as possible, the European invasion of its shores just because it had convinced itself by painful experience that European ideas and manners and methods were undesirable and unsuitable for a great island nation which possessed and cherished a civilisation of its own, had high artistic ideas and ideals, had its own code of morals, its own conception of chivalry, and was, on the whole, undoubtedly happy, contented, and prosperous. I trust the chapter I have written on this subject will tend to dispel many erroneous ideas.

The book is the result of my own investigations, and the opinions expressed therein are entirely my own. I have, however, read nearly every work on Japan that has appeared in recent years, and when the views put forward in any of these have not coincided with my own I have endeavoured, by impartial investigation and inquiry, to arrive at a correct conclusion in the matter. No doubt some of my views and opinions will be questioned and criticised, but I claim to have written this book with a mind free from prejudices of any kind. I have sought to depict Japan as it really is, not the Japan seen through glasses of various colours, of which, I think, the public has had enough.

H. B. M.

CONTENTS

LIST OF ILLUSTRATIONS

THE EMPIRE OF THE EAST

CHAPTER I

A GLIMPSE AT THE PAST

I HAVE seen it stated in a popular handbook that Japan possesses a written history extending over two thousand five hundred years, while its sovereigns have formed an unbroken dynasty since 660 B.C., but that the "authentic history begins about 400 A.D." "Authentic history" is, I consider, not a very apt phrase in this connection. Most Japanese history is legendary, and authenticity in history, Japanese or European, even much later than 400 A.D., is hopeless to look for. I have no intention of leading my readers into, as I should find a difficulty in extricating them from, the mazes of Japanese history at any date. I simply propose to give them a glimpse of Japan as it has appeared to Europeans since it was first "discovered" by three storm-tossed Portuguese sailors about the year 1542. I say "discovered" with full knowledge of the fact that Marco Paolo, as early as 1275, dictated to a friend when imprisoned at Genoa that stirring narrative, "Maravigliose Cose," which, by the way, was not printed for nearly two centuries later. That narrative was read by and, it is stated, so fired the imagination of Christopher Columbus as to lead him to set out on that voyage of exploration which ended in the discovery of America. Marco Paolo's narrative must, however, be received with caution. I regard it as largely legendary. He never himself visited Japan, and his glowing description of the "Isles washed by stormy seas and abounding in gold and pearls" was founded on what he had been told by the Chinese he had met during his Eastern travels.

The commencement of European intercourse with Japan may, as I have said, be taken to be 1542, when three Portuguese adventurers in a Chinese junk were driven by stress of weather on a part of the Japanese coast under the authority of the Prince of Bungo. The Portuguese were kindly received by the natives, and a treaty or arrangement seems to have been entered into whereby a Portuguese vessel was to be annually despatched to Japan laden with "woollen cloths, furs, silks, taffetas," and other articles. Some years later a Japanese noble, Hansiro by name, murdered another Japanese and fled the country. He found his way to Goa, where he came under the influence of some Portuguese priests, and was eventually converted to Christianity and baptized. He was, if the records of his career are correct, desirous to bring to his fellow-countrymen not only the knowledge of the Christian religion but many articles of European commerce. The great Apostle of the East and disciple of Ignatius Loyola, St. Francis Xavier, had then recently arrived in Goa, where he appears to have taken up with ardour the project of converting Japan. Both enterprises, the material and the spiritual, seem to have been organised about the same time. A ship was loaded with articles likely to be in demand in Japan, and Francis Xavier embarked in another vessel, with the Japanese refugee and a number of Jesuit priests as missionaries.

The vessels in due course arrived at Bungo, and both priests and traders were cordially, not to say enthusiastically, received. Foreigners were evidently not then excluded from Japan, and no objection whatever was made to the Christian propaganda in any part of the country. The efforts of the Jesuit missionaries were crowned with remarkable success. All ranks and classes, from priest to peasant, embraced the Catholic faith. Churches, schools, convents, and monasteries sprang up all over the country. The only opposition came from the Bonzes, or native priests, who felt their influence and power declining. They appealed to the Emperor to banish the Roman Catholic priests, but the imperial edict simply was, "Leave the strangers in peace." For forty years or thereabouts Catholicism not only flourished but was triumphant. Indeed, a Japanese mission of three princes was despatched to Pope Gregory XIII. laden with valuable presents. The arrival of this mission was acclaimed as a veritable triumph throughout Catholic Europe. By a stroke of irony its advent there was almost contemporaneous with not only the overthrow but the almost total extinction of Christianity in Japan. The edict for the banishment of the missionaries was published in 1587. It was followed by persecutions, martyrdoms, and the rasing of all the Christian churches and buildings—the destruction, in a word, of Christianity in Japan. This was in due course followed by not only the expulsion of all foreigners from the country—with the exception of the Dutch, who were allowed to have a factory at Nagasaki—but the enactment of a law, rigidly observed for two and a half centuries, that no Japanese should leave his country on any pretence whatever, and no foreigner be permitted to land therein. Prior to this edict the Japanese had been enterprising sailors and had extended their voyages to many distant lands. What, it might be asked, was the reason of or occasion for this violent change in the attitude of the Japanese to Christianity and the presence of Europeans in their midst? It is impossible, at this length of time, to arrive at a correct answer to this question, largely mixed up as it has been with the *odium theologicum.* We have been told that the result was greatly or altogether due to the pride, arrogance, and avarice of the Roman Catholic priests; to the pretensions of the Pope, which came to be regarded with suspicion by the feudatory princes of Japan, as also to the cupidity and cunning of the traders. How far any or all of these alleged causes were responsible for the change in Japanese opinion I shall not venture to pronounce. Suffice it to remark that, whatever the cause, there must have been some powerful, impelling influence at work to induce the nation not only to cast out the stranger within its gates, but to exclude him for two and a half centuries, and veto any inhabitant of Japan leaving its shores and thus being brought into contact with, and stand the chance of being contaminated by, the foreigner. We may regret the destruction of Christianity in Japan, but at the same time we may, I think, accept the fact that the uprising of Japan against the foreigner at the close of the sixteenth century was simply the result of the gorge which had arisen in the nation against the foreigner's manners, methods, and morals, his trampling underfoot of national prejudices and ideas, his cupidity, his avarice, his cruelty, and his attempt to impose on Japanese civilisation a veneer which it did not desire and deemed it was much better without. It must be remembered that the missionaries and the traders had a common nationality, and that the Japan of the sixteenth century did not find it possible to differentiate between them.

Down to the nineteenth century we have to rely for our knowledge of Japan and the Japanese on the narratives of the few travellers who managed to visit that country more or less by stealth, or from the information derived from Europeans serving in the Dutch factory at Nagasaki. Every Englishman has heard of Will Adams and his Japanese wife, but though his career was romantic and interesting it has added but little to our knowledge of Japan at the time of his visit thereto. In 1727 Dr. Kaemfer's work on Japan was published. Kaemfer had been physician to the Dutch factory at Nagasaki, and, accordingly, had some opportunities of studying Japanese life and character. His book in the original form is rare, but I am glad to say that a cheap edition, a reprint of the English edition produced by the Royal Society in 1727, has recently been published in this country. Kaemfer's work is spoiled and its utility or reliability largely impaired by the fanciful theories put forward by the author respecting the origin of the Japanese. Much of his information is, of course, mere hearsay, and a great deal of it, by the light of what we now know, is not only misleading but nonsensical. A considerable amount of space is devoted by Kaemfer to chimerical animals, and he dilates upon the awful sanctity that surrounds the person of the Emperor. "There is," he remarks, "such a Holiness ascribed to all the parts of his Body that he dares not cut off neither his hair, nor his beard, nor his nails. However, lest he should grow too dirty, they may clean him in the night when he is asleep; because they say that what is taken from his Body at that time had been stolen from him, and that such a theft does not prejudice his Holiness or Dignity." In a notice of this new edition of Kaemfer's work I have seen it asserted that the book is the foundation of nearly all that was known or written of Japan till the last twenty-five years. How such a statement as this came to be published I quite fail to comprehend. There was plenty of literature in reference to Japan far more reliable than Kaemfer's whimsical "yarns" at a much earlier period than twenty-five years back. Sir Rutherford Alcock's "The Capital of the Tycoon" was, I think, published in 1863. Sir Rutherford was the first resident British Minister in Japan, and his book remains a stirring and, making allowance for the author's prejudices on various matters, on the whole a vivid picture of Japan as it was in the early sixties. Alcock's book was followed by many others, and twenty-five years ago the world was so far from being dependent on Kaemfer for its knowledge of Japan that, as I have said, it had even then quite a library of recent and reliable books in regard to that country.

Following Kaemfer, a little later in the eighteenth century, a Swedish physician, Thunberg by name, who also had been attached to the Dutch factory at Nagasaki, wrote a book undoubtedly interesting and of great value. That country, he remarks, is "in many respects a singular country, and with regard to customs and institutions totally different from Europe, or, I had almost said, from any other part of the world. Of all the nations that inhabit the three largest parts of the globe, the Japanese deserve to rank the first, and to be compared with the Europeans; and although in many points they must yield the palm to the latter, yet in various other respects they may with great justice be preferred to them. Here, indeed, as well as in other countries, are found both useful and pernicious establishments, both rational and absurd institutions; yet still we must admire the steadiness which constitutes the national character, the immutability which reigns in the administration of their laws and in the exercise of their public functions, the unwearied assiduity of this nation to do and to promote what is useful, and a hundred other things of a similar nature. That so numerous a people as this should love so ardently and so universally (without even a single exception to the contrary) their native country, their Government, and each other—that the whole country should be, as it were, enclosed, so that no native can get out, nor foreigner enter in, without permission—that their laws should have remained unaltered for several thousand years—and that justice should be administered without partiality or respect of persons—that the Governments can neither become despotic nor evade the laws in order to grant pardons or do other acts of mercy—that the monarch and all his subjects should be clad alike in a particular national dress—that no fashions should be adopted from abroad, nor new ones invented at home—that no foreign war should have been waged for centuries past—that a great variety of religious sects should live in peace and harmony together—that hunger and want should be almost unknown, or at least known but seldom,—all this must appear improbable, and to many as impossible as it is strictly true, and deserving of the utmost attention." He goes on to say, "If the laws in this country are rigid, the police are equally vigilant, while discipline and good order are scrupulously observed. The happy consequences of this are extremely visible and important, for hardly any country exhibits fewer instances of vice. And as no respect whatever is paid to persons, and at the same time the laws preserve their pristine and original purity, without any alterations, explanations, and misconstructions, the subjects not only imbibe, as they grow up, an infallible knowledge of what ought or ought not to be done, but are likewise enlightened by the example and irreproachable conduct of their superiors in age.

"Most crimes are punished with death—a sentence which is inflicted with less regard to the magnitude of the crime than to the audacity of the attempt to transgress the hallowed laws of the empire, and to violate justice, which together with religion they consider as the most sacred things in the whole land. Fines and pecuniary mulcts they regard as equally repugnant to justice and reason, as the rich are thereby freed from all punishment—a procedure which to them appears the height of absurdity.

"In the towns it often happens that the inhabitants of a whole street are made to suffer for the malpractice of a single individual, the master of a house for the faults of his domestics, and parents for those of their children, in proportion to the share they may have had in the transaction. In Europe, which boasts a purer religion and a more enlightened philosophy, we very rarely see those punished who have debauched and seduced others, never see parents and relatives made to suffer for neglecting the education of their children and kindred, at the same time that these heathens see the justice and propriety of such punishment." Dealing with agriculture, the Swedish physician remarked : "Agriculture is in the highest esteem with the Japanese, insomuch that (the most barren and untractable mountains excepted) one sees here the surface of the earth cultivated all over the country, and most of the mountains and hills up to their very tops. Neither rewards nor encouragements are necessary in a country where the tillers of the ground are considered as the most useful class of citizens and where they do not groan under various oppressions, which in other countries have hindered, and ever must hinder, the progress of agriculture. The duties paid by the farmer of his corn in kind are indeed very heavy, but in other respects he cultivates his land with greater freedom than the lord of a manor in Sweden. He is not hindered two days together at a time, in consequence of furnishing relays of horses, by which he perhaps earns a groat and often returns with the loss of his horses; he is not dragged from his field and plough to transport a prisoner or a deserter to the next castle; nor are his time and property wasted in making roads, building bridges, almshouses, parsonage-houses, and magazines. He knows nothing of the impediments and inconveniences which attend the maintenance and equipments of horses and foot soldiers. And what contributes still more to his happiness, and leaves sufficient scope for his industry in cultivating his land is this—that he has only one master, viz., his feudal lord, without being under the commands of a host of masters, as with us. No parcelling out of the land forbids him to improve to the least advantage the portion he possesses, and no right of commonage, belonging to many, prevents each from deriving profit from his share. All are bound to cultivate their land, and if a husbandman cannot annually cultivate a certain portion of his fields he forfeits them, and another who can is at liberty to cultivate them. Meadows are not to be met with in the whole country; on the contrary, every spot of ground is made use of either for corn-fields or else for plantations of esculent-rooted vegetables: so that the land is neither wasted upon extensive meadows for the support of cattle and saddle-horses, nor upon large and unprofitable plantations of tobacco; nor is it sown with seed for any other still less necessary purpose; which is the reason that the whole country is very thickly inhabited and populous, and can without difficulty give maintenance to all its innumerable inhabitants."

Let us now take a step, a long step, forward in time from the Swedish physician relating his impressions in the seventeenth century, to an American in the eighteenth century delivering his opinions on Japan and the Japanese as viewed from the American standpoint at that period. "The sitter is the same, and, what is more, he sits on his heels to-day just as his grandfather did to Thunberg, yet it is hard to see any points of resemblance—a lesson to all theologians and politicians who still indulge the dreams that uniformity of opinion on the plainest matters of fact and observation can ever be attained among men, however honest and conscientious they may be in their efforts after unity. The Chinese proverb with more wisdom declares, 'Truth is one, but opinions are many.'

"All officials serve in pairs, as spies upon each other, and this pervades the entire polity of Japan. It is a government of espionage. Everybody is watched. No man knows who are the secret spies around him, even though he may be and is acquainted with those that are official. The emperors themselves are not exempt; governors, grand councillors, vassal princes, all are under the eye of an everlasting unknown police. This wretched system is even extended to the humblest of the citizens. Every town is divided into collections of five families, and every member of such a division is personally responsible for the conduct of the others ; everything which occurs, therefore, out of the ordinary course in any one of these is instantly reported by the other four to save themselves from censure. The Ziogoon (Tycoon) has his minions about the Mikado and the Grand Council have theirs about the Ziogoon. And the cowardice engendered by such ceaseless distrust necessarily leads to cruelty in penalties. When an official has offended, or even when in his department there has been any violation of law, although beyond his power of prevention, so sure is he of the punishment of death, that he anticipates it by ripping up his own body rather than be delivered over to the executioner and entailing disgrace and ruin on all his family. There cannot under such a system be anything like judicious legislation founded on enquiry and adapted to the ever-varying circumstances of life. As Government functionaries they lie and practise artifice to save themselves from condemnation by the higher powers : it is their vocation. As private gentlemen they are frank, truthful, and hospitable."

Taking a further step and coming down to the year 1877, I have before me, as I write, the private letter of a naval officer of an impressionable age visiting Japan for the first time and giving his opinions thereof, at a period when Japan was just beginning to feel really at work the distinct influences of estern civilisation—the beginning, in fact, of the extraordinary metamorphosis which has been witnessed of recent years. He remarks : "Probably to the traveller seeking the marvellous and desiring the beautiful, there is no more interesting country to pay a visit to than Japan. In something under a decade that country astonished, and, at first, rather amused the civilised world by emerging from the acme of barbarism to the extremes of civilisation. It was but a very few years ago that a foreigner could not land in the country unless accompanied by a Government escort. But now that is all changed. The foreigner is welcomed, his habits and religion are not alone tolerated but respected ; his dress is copied to an extreme that indeed proves imitation to be the sincerest flattery, and but for the olive complexion, flat nose and dark hair, a Japanese gentleman of the period is very little different from his English contemporary. There is a tendency I find among a good many persons, whose ideas on the subject of race and geography are slightly mixed, to confound the Japanese with the Chinese, and to imagine that the two names indicate no greater difference than at present exist between an Englishman and an Irishman. The fact, however, is that a greater difference exists among these two nationalities than can be either imagined or described, and, considering their contiguity, it is indeed surprising that they have scarcely a habit or a pursuit in common. The mind of the modern Japanese is progressive and acquisitive. The mind of the Chinaman of the nineteenth century, as far as he allows it to be seen, is as torpid and retrogressive as his ancestors of the Confucian period.

"Up to the year 1868 Japan was governed jointly by a Tycoon and a Mikado together with a council of the Daimios, or great feudal princes, in whose hands all real power rested. The spiritual sovereign was the Mikado, nominally the chief ruler, the Tycoon being considered his first subject. All enactments required his sanction. The office of the Tycoon was hereditary and he gradually absorbed all the powers of the State. In 1868 a revolution occurred which culminated in the overthrow of the spiritual head and the seating of the Tycoon on the throne as an hereditary prince with the title of Mikado. There is now no such person as a Tycoon in Japan. The insurrection of 1868 also saw the downfall of the Daimios or feudal princes of Japan. These princes had each standing armies of their own, and administered justice in their own territories. Their retainers were the famous two-sworded men so long a terror to Europeans, and who strongly objected to any intercourse with foreigners, probably foreseeing its inevitable result. In 1868 the whole of these ferocious men were disarmed, and a standing army modelled on the French fashion established for the defence of the Empire. The Japanese Navy was organised about the same time by an English officer, and at first consisted of a few obsolete American and English men-of-war. That, however, is now a thing of the past, the Japanese Government having during the past few years spent many millions in purchasing modern ironclads and other vessels of the most approved type, and the Japanese Navy bids fair before long to become a power in the Far East.

"Concerning the oft-debated question of Japanese morality I can say little. Their ideas on the subject are, to put it mildly, somewhat lax, and would no doubt shock any one strongly imbued with morality as it is in vogue (theoretically) in European countries. That there is not that privacy between the sexes which prevails in other countries may be indicated by the fact that men and women make their ablutions together in the public wash-houses. Nevertheless the Japanese have a code of morality peculiar to themselves, and any infidelity on the part of a woman to her husband is punished with severity.

"The great drawback to the prosperity of Japan is a matter that prevails in some more ancient civilised lands, viz., an enormous issue of paper-money. Young Japan, finding it easy to print notes to pay its obligations, printed them to the extent of twenty millions sterling in all sizes from 5 cents to 100 dollars. The consequence is that this paper-money has depreciated in value to the extent of 15 per cent. The Government, however, have seen their mistake, and are gradually calling it in, and have established a very fine mint with a gold and silver coinage. Insurrections have also been a drag on Japan in its progress. The Prince of Satsuma, one of the most powerful of the ancient Daimios, has never acknowledged the present system of government and has periodically rebelled against it. This year a serious rebellion broke out at Kagoshima, and was not quelled without great loss of life and a heavy expenditure. His followers behaved with great fanaticism, many of them loading themselves with gunpowder rushing into the midst of the enemy and setting fire to the powder, killing themselves by so doing, but also, to the admiration of their less ardent comrades, killing numbers of the enemy.

"Against no ancient custom has the Japanese Government more set its face than tattooing. Any persons in Japan now either allowing themselves to be tattooed or performing the operation on any one else are liable to imprisonment. Blacking the teeth, a custom prevalent among the women on being married, is rapidly dying out, being discouraged by the authorities."

The glimpses of Japan shown us by Thunberg and the American I have quoted prove clearly enough, even were it not amplified by a host of other testimony I have not space to refer to, that the Japan of the sixteenth, seventeenth, eighteenth, and early part of the nineteenth centuries was a highly civilised country in which law and order reigned supreme, where respect for authority was marked, the standard of comfort, if not high, was at any rate sufficient, the domestic relations and family life were almost ideal, clean living was the custom, crime was at a minimum, education was universal, amusements were plentiful, the artistic feeling and instincts were not the cult of a class but were shared by the common people. This was the nation, self-contained and self-satisfied, that some persons, like the young naval officer from whom I have quoted, gravely affirm to have been steeped in barbarism until it came under Western influences and went in for frock-coats and silk hats for the men, Paris costumes for the women, and an Army and Navy on European lines. If these be the factors which constitute civilisation I admit that Japan has only recently been civilised. Being of opinion, however, that civilisation does not consist in costumery, but is a refining and educating influence, I prefer to regard Japan as a country of more ancient civilisation than Great Britain, which has of recent years determined to tack on to that civilisation some Western manners and customs and facilities. Many of Japan's greatest thinkers, a few Western philosophers who can look beyond a costume, the telegraph or the telephone, are strongly of opinion that in the process of modern development Japan has not improved either morally or materially, and that, regarded through the dry light of philosophy, her pretensions to be considered a highly civilised nation were greater half a century back than they are at the present moment. Upon that matter my readers must form their own opinion. It is a question, the answer to which largely depends upon the point of view from which it is regarded and the factors taken into or left out of account.

In the first year of the Meiji (1868) the Emperor, in an edict, laid down clearly and concisely the lines on which he and his advisers had determined that Japan should for the future be governed. "The old uncivilised way shall be replaced by the eternal principles of the universe," "The best knowledge shall be sought throughout the world so as to promote the imperial welfare." "The eternal principles of the universe" is a resonant phrase needing interpretation. The rulers of Japan to-day, if they were interrogated on the subject, would probably reply that the record of Japan for over thirty-eight years past is the practical interpretation of the Emperor's cryptic utterance. Be that as it may, the ink was hardly dry on the Imperial edict before Japan laid herself out with earnestness, not to say enthusiasm, to carry into effect the principles enunciated in the edict. The whole country was quickly in a positive ferment of energy. The brightest intellects among its youth were despatched to foreign lands to acquire knowledge and wisdom to be applied at home in due course, education was taken in hand, so also was the reorganisation of the Army and Navy, and railways, telegraphs, and various other accessories of European civilisation were introduced into the country. Japan, in a word, became quickly transformed and, being unable any longer to keep the foreigner out, she determined to utilise him and in the future fight him, should fighting be necessary, with his own weapons, intellectual rather than material, but not omitting the material. Thirty-eight years and more have elapsed since the issue of the Imperial edict referred to, and this book is designed to show what results have flowed therefrom, along what lines the development of Japan has proceeded, and what are the position and prospects of that country to-day.

CHAPTER II

THE COUNTRY—ITS PHYSICAL FEATURES—PRODUCTS—FAUNA—FLORA, ETC.

THE Empire of Japan (a corruption of Nippon, the native name) is composed of four large islands—Honshiu, Shikoku, Kiusiu, and Yesso, besides some thousands of smaller isles. The Kurile Isles, north of Yesso, and in the neighbourhood of Kamschatka, have been incorporated in the Empire since 1875, and the Loo-Choo Islands, some 500 miles south-west of Japan's southern extremity, since 1876. The great island of Formosa, situated off the coast of China, was ceded to Japan as the outcome of the Chino-Japanese War in 1895, while as the result of the recent conflict with Russia, Japan has obtained back the southern half of the large island of Sakhalin, which formerly entirely belonged to her, as well as Port Arthur and Dalny on the mainland, not to speak of the preponderating influence she has obtained in Korea, which is now practically under the suzerainty of Japan. The population of the Empire according to the last census was about forty-seven millions, and, like that of Great Britain, it is annually increasing. The proximity of Japan to the Asiatic Continent, despite the lessons in geography which the late war afforded, is not, I think, generally understood. The nearest point of the Japanese coast is only 100 miles distant from Korea, while between the two lies the important island of Tsu-shima, which Japan found so useful as a strategic position during the war with Russia. The island of Sakhalin, the southern portion of which, as I have said, has lately passed into the possession of Japan, is about 20 miles distant from the northern part of Yesso, while at some places the island is only separated from the Russian mainland by 5 or 6 miles of water. The distance between Hakodate, in Yesso, and the great Russian port of Vladivostock is somewhere about 200 miles. This contiguity of Japan to the Asiatic Continent has already had a marked effect on the politics of the world, and in the future, if I mistake not, is likely to be a preponderating factor therein. The area of Japan is about half as large again as that of the United Kingdom. The southern extremity of the country is in latitude 31° N., the northern in latitude 45½° N.

The Japanese islands are undoubtedly of volcanic origin, and many of the volcanoes in the country are still more or less active. The general conformation of the land leads one to suppose that the islands are the summits of mountain ranges which some thousands of years back had their bases submerged by the rising of the sea or else had by degrees settled down beneath the surface of the ocean. The general characteristic of the country is mountainous, and only about one-sixth of the total area is in cultivation. Fuji-yama, the loftiest mountain, for which the Japanese have a peculiar veneration and which has been immortalised in the art of the country, has an altitude of 12,730 feet. The next in height, Mount Mitake, ascends some 9,000 feet, and there are many others of 5,000 feet or more. Japan has from time to time been ravaged by, and indeed still is subject to, terrible earthquakes. These dire calamities seem to recur at regular intervals. The Japanese islands appear to be in the centre of great volcanic disturbances—a fact which probably accounts for those seismic outbreaks which periodically devastate considerable tracts of the country and cause tremendous havoc to life and property. The written records, extending back some 1,400 or 1,500 years, clearly prove that earthquakes even more terrible in their effects than any that have taken place in recent times were of frequent occurrence. It is, of course, possible that these records may be inaccurate or have been largely exaggerated, but they at any rate tend to show that those great cosmic forces which are popularly termed earthquakes have been constantly at work in Japan ever since any written records have been preserved and no doubt long anterior to that time.

As the islands are narrow and mountainous there are no great rivers and none available for important navigation. None of the rivers exceed 200 miles in length. Although Japan is situated much further south than Great Britain, its northern extremity being in about the same latitude as Cornwall, its climate is, on the whole, not unlike that of this country. Of course the climate of such a mountainous country and one extending over 14 degrees of latitude varies considerably. That of the island of Yesso, for example, is in winter rigorous to a degree, a fact in some measure caused by a cold current which flows down its eastern shores from the Sea of Okohotsk. Professor Rein, who has given great attention to the matter of the Japanese climate, has remarked in reference thereto: "The climate of Japan reflects the characteristics of that of the neighbouring continent, and exhibits like that two great annual contrasts—a hot, damp summer and a cold relatively dry winter; these two seasons lie under the sway of the monsoons, but the neighbouring seas weaken the effects of these winds and mitigate their extremes in such a manner that neither the summer heat nor the cold of winter attain the same height in Japan as in China at the same latitudes. Spring and autumn are extremely agreeable seasons; the oppressive summer heat does not last long, and in winter the contrast between the nightly frosts and the midday heat, produced by considerable insulation but still more by the raw northerly winds, causes frequent chills, though the prevailing bright sky makes the season of the year much more endurable than in many other regions where the winter cold is equal. As a fact the climate of Japan agrees very well with most Europeans, so that people have already begun to look upon certain localities as climatic watering-places where the inhabitant of Hong Kong and Shanghai can find refuge from the oppressive heat of summer and invigorate his health."

The mean annual temperature of Tokio is about 56°. The lowest temperature is in January or February, when the thermometer seldom falls below 25°, the highest in August, when it sometimes rises to 95° or 100° in the shade, the average being 82°. The Japanese suffer a good deal from the effects of the wintry weather, bronchial, chest, and rheumatic affections being prevalent. The dwellings of the people, somewhat flimsy in construction as they are, are not well adapted to withstand the effects of a low temperature. On the whole the people must be pronounced to be extremely healthy—a fact probably due to their scrupulous cleanliness, to the excellent ventilation of their houses, and, as regards those living in the towns, to the wide and well-kept streets where nothing offensive is allowed to remain. The country has, however, from time to time been subject to epidemics introduced from without, cholera and the plague having more than once carried death throughout the length and breadth of the land.

Those circular storms known as cyclones in the Indian Ocean and typhoons in further Eastern seas have from time to time wrought great devastation in Japan. Fortunately these revolving storms are of brief duration, and in the neighbourhood of Japan they do not so frequently occur as in the China Sea.

Japan is well provided with good harbours, that of Nagasaki in especial being one of the finest in the world. Sheltered completely by lofty and beautiful hills, with deep water throughout, it is an ideal anchorage. Until recently foreign trade was confined to the treaty ports; but as the country has now been completely thrown open, there is no doubt that the many fine harbours which Japan possesses, and which so far have hardly been utilised at all, will in due course become the centres of great commercial activity. The Inland Sea—the beautiful Mediterranean of Japan—abounds with excellent anchorages, most of which have hitherto been only entered by an occasional junk.

Regarding the mineral wealth of the country, it is impossible to speak with any precision. It was not until after the Revolution of 1868 that the mining industry assumed importance in Japan. At first the Government itself owned several mines, but these were not financially successful, and they were after a time disposed of to private owners. The old mining regulations have recently been superseded by a new mining law. In accordance with this the Minister of Agriculture and Commerce is the official who permits, approves, cancels, or suspends the right of mining, whether permanently or on trial. I may, however, at once remark that the Japanese Government has not up to the present held out much encouragement to the speculative prospector. Gold is believed to exist in considerable quantities in Yesso, and as a matter of fact, although the amount mined is still small, it is annually increasing. Coal is abundant in various parts of the country and the mines are extensively worked. In 1903 there were over ten million tons of coal produced, and the quantity is at the present time assuredly very much greater. The coal is not of such a good quality as either Welsh or North Country, but there is a large and growing demand for it in the East, and coal is undoubtedly a highly important part of Japan's latent wealth. Copper, a metal which is in increasing demand, exists in Japan in enormous quantities, and she promises at no very far-distant date to be the chief copper-producing country of the world. Iron and sulphur are also found, and there are many other minerals, some of which are more or less worked. The Japanese Mining Law, it may be interesting to relate, recognises the following minerals and mineral ores, which may accordingly be taken as existing in the country: Gold, silver, copper, lead, tin, hematite, antimony, quicksilver, zinc, iron, manganese and arsenic, plumbago, coal, kerosene, sulphur, bismuth, phosphorus, peat.

Whatever the mineral wealth of Japan—and the extent and variety thereof are probably yet not fully realised—there can be no question as to the value of its aboreal products. The lacquer-tree (*rhus vernicifera*), which furnishes the well-known Japanese lacquer, the paper mulberry, the elm, oak, maple, bamboo, camphor, and many other descriptions of trees, grow in abundance. The forests of Japan cover nearly 60 per cent. of the land. For some years after the Revolution there was a reduction in the wooded area, nearly four million acres having been cleared for occupation. Of late years, however, forestry has been scientifically taken in hand, and about one and a half million acres have been replanted in districts which have not been found suitable for farming. The climate of Japan varies so greatly that there is a corresponding variety in its trees. About eight hundred kinds of forest trees are suitable for cultivation in Japan, varying from the palm and the bamboo to the fir and many other trees with which we are familiar in this country.

The Japanese are above all things an agricultural people. The tobacco plant, the tea shrub, potatoes, rice, wheat, barley, millet, cotton, rape, and many cereals other than those I have mentioned are extensively cultivated. The great mass of the people of Japan live on the land, and though I think the tendency, as in Great Britain, is for the large towns to magnetically draw the dwellers in the country, nevertheless agriculture is still held in high esteem, and the peasant is content to dwell on the land and live by it. Rice is the staple food of the people, and it is grown everywhere ; indeed the yearly harvest of it affects the Japanese economy quite as much as, if not even more than, the wheat crop does that of Europe. The Japanese peasant is almost as dependent on rice as the Irish peasant used to be on potatoes. The water, so necessary for irrigating the land, is supplied by the streams and rivulets which are plentiful in the country. The Japanese agriculturist has long been famous for the admirable manner in which he keeps and tills his farm. The fields are clean as regards weeds, and order and neatness are perceptible everywhere. The labour is almost entirely manual, and men, women, and children all take part in the work.

Fruit is abundant in Japan, but it is for the most part

of an inferior quality. Grapes, apples, pears, plums, peaches, chestnuts, persimmons, oranges, figs, lemons, citrons, melons, and wild strawberries are all grown, but except as regards the grapes I cannot speak in laudatory terms of Japanese fruit. The flowers of many fruit trees seem more appreciated than the fruit itself.

The floral kingdom is rich, beautiful and varied. Probably in no other part of the world are flowers so greatly appreciated as in Japan. They enter largely into various popular festivals. The Japanese, as most people know, excel in the art of gardening and the dwarfing of trees and shrubs. The flower vendor is a familiar sight, and there is never any lack of buyers. The poorest householder will do without anything almost rather than deprive himself of flowers. These enter largely into the religious services of the people, and are also extensively placed on the graves of the departed. Flowers, indeed, play an important part in the lives of the Japanese. Japan has long been famous for the great number of its evergreens. A large number of the plants growing wild are of this class, so that even in winter the land has not the bare appearance characteristic of European countries at that time of the year. Coniferous plants are abundant, many of them being peculiar to Japan.

The coasts abound with fish of an excellent quality, and this, with rice, forms the staple diet of the people. Tea is, as I have said, largely cultivated, and indeed may be regarded as the national beverage. It has been cultivated in the country for over two thousand years. It is an article of faith in Japan that tea strengthens the body. It is drunk everywhere and at all times, without either milk or sugar—the true way, I think, in which to appreciate its flavour. The tea-house in Japan occupies the same position as the public-house in this country, but it has many advantages over the latter. In the towns and some other parts of Japan, saké—a spirit distilled from rice—is drunk, and when the Japanese has to any extent been Europeanised or brought into contact with Europeans, he affects a taste for European varieties of alcohol. On the whole, however, the people are distinctly a sober race.

The principal towns are Tokio, the capital, with a population of about one and half millions, Osaka, having a population nearly as great, Kyoto, the ancient capital, Nagoya, Kobé, Yokohama, and Nagasaki. Yokohama may be regarded as the European headquarters; indeed it is largely a European town, while Nagasaki has more than any other been under European influences, the Dutch having, as I have already stated, had a factory there, in the suburb of Decima, continuously ever since the expulsion of foreigners from the country in the sixteenth century.

Railway communication in Japan is a subject upon which much might be written. For many years there was only one line in the country—that between Yokohama and Tokio, about 22 miles in length. At the present time there are some 4,500 miles of railway open, and extensions are either in progress or in contemplation. Of the lines now being worked, about one-third are the property of the Government, the rest having been constructed by private enterprise. This dual system of ownership has its disadvantages, and it will doubtless not be permitted to last. Railway construction has already had a considerable effect on the opening up of the country, and as the construction is extended the development of Japan will doubtless proceed in an increasing ratio.

The scenery of Japan has provided a theme for so many pens that I do not feel inclined to do more than refer to it in passing. Much of the scenery is sublime but, truth to tell, its beauty, or perhaps it would be more correct to say the effect thereof on the sightseer, has been somewhat marred of recent years by the influx of those persons colloquially known as "globe trotters," the railway extensions to which I have referred, and the erection of large hotels run on European lines. Nikko, the incomparable, with its glorious scenery and its still more glorious temples, the meandering Daynogawa, the beauteous Lake Chiuzenji, on which a quarter of a century or so ago a European provided with a passport and having his headquarters at a neighbouring tea-house might gaze at his leisure, and meditate in a glorious silence broken only by the sound of the ripples of the water or the cry of the birds from the neighbouring woods, all are now vulgarised. The personally conducted tourist is there and very much in evidence. He wanders carelessly, often contemptuously, through the ancient temples, regarding temples, scenery, river, lakes, merely as "something to be done." The change was, I suppose, inevitable, but the change is one that I think is in some respects to be regretted. The tourist brings money and spends it freely, and the country no doubt reaps the advantage thereof, but the effect on the Japanese brought into contact with the European under such conditions is not, in my opinion, always, or often, beneficial.

I have not much to remark in regard to the fauna of Japan. The domestic animals are comparatively few. The fact of the inhabitants not eating animal food has led to their paying little or no attention to the breeding of those animals which are largely in request in foreign countries. Horses, however, are fairly plentiful, though small. Japan, as I have elsewhere remarked, has been handicapped in the organisation of her cavalry by the lack of a proper supply of suitable horses, and she has recently despatched a commission to Europe to effect purchases with a view of putting this matter right, and improving the breed of horses in the country. Oxen and cows were till recently entirely, and are still largely, used for purposes of draught only. Sheep and pigs have been introduced from abroad, but they have not been generally distributed, and in many parts of Japan have never been seen.

The wild animals of Japan are neither numerous nor important. The black bear and the wolf still exist, chiefly in the Northern Island, but it is certain that at no far-distant date they will, unless artificially preserved, go the way of all wild animals in civilised countries. The red-faced monkey is there, the only kind found in Japan, and snakes exist, but they are for the most part harmless. The art of the country will have familiarised Europeans with the presence of the crane and the stork, which play such a prominent part therein. Indeed the wild birds of the country are more numerous than the animals. I am not aware whether geological research in Japan has been sufficiently extensive or systematic to ascertain whether, and if so what, any species of animals have ever existed there other than those at present found in the country. It certainly is in some respects extraordinary that a country so close to the Asiatic Continent and possessing such a variety of climates should, as regards the animal kingdom from the standpoint of the zoologist, be put down as distinctly poor. The fact, or supposed fact, to which I have previously referred, that the Japanese islands are the summits of mountain ranges which many thousand years ago had their bases submerged by the rising of the sea or had gradually settled down beneath the surface of the ocean, may, of course, account for the poverty of Japan in regard to the animals therein. I must leave other pens than mine to descant on that interesting if highly speculative matter. Be that as it may, if the fauna of Japan is poor, the country certainly makes up for it by the variety and magnificence of its flora—a flora which deserves to be studied, and which has done so much to brighten not only the appearance of the country but the lives of its inhabitants.

CHAPTER III

THE JAPANESE RACE AND ITS LANGUAGE

THERE are, I have always thought, two ways in which any race should be considered if it is desired to form a correct idea in regard to it, viz., from an ethnological and philological standpoint. No race deserves to be closer studied in these matters than the Japanese. Indeed, I am of opinion that it is impossible to arrive at any clear or correct opinion concerning it without having, however slightly, investigated its racial descent and the language which, among Eastern dialects, has so long been as great a puzzle to the philologist as has Basque among the European languages. Respecting the origin of the Japanese we know practically nothing—at any rate nothing authentic. The native legends and histories afford us neither guide nor clue in the matter. These legends and histories tell us that the Japanese are descended from the gods, but I am quite certain that the modern Japanese receives that fact (?) with something more than the proverbial grain of salt. According to the old legend Ninigi-no-Nikoto was a god despatched by his grandmother the Sun-goddess to take possession of Japan, and the land was peopled by him and his entourage. This god-man, it is stated, lived over 300,000 years; his son, Hohoderni, attained to twice that period of longevity, while a grandchild, Ugaya by name, reached the respectable old age of 836,042 years. Ugaya was, it is stated, the father of Jimmu, the first Emperor. It is not necessary to seriously notice fables or legends or poetic imagery, or whatever these tales may be deemed to be, although I may remark that the divine descent of the sovereign of Japan has, so far as I know, never been formally repudiated, and it is still explicitly, if not implicitly, held.

Dr. Kaemfer, whose great work I have already referred to, propounded therein the somewhat fanciful theory that the Japanese are really the direct descendants of the ancient Babylonians, and that their language "is one of those which Sacred Writ mentions the all-wise Providence thought fit to infuse into the minds of the vain builders of the Babylonian Tower." According to his theory, which to me seems absolutely ludicrous, the Japanese came through Persia, then along the shores of the Caspian Sea and by the bank of the Oxus to its source. From there, he suggests, they crossed China, descended the Amoor, proceeded southwards to Korea, and found their way across the intervening sea to the Japanese islands. Another theory, which has found many supporters, is that the Japanese are descended from the Ainos, the hairy race still to be found in the island of Yesso. An advocate of this view seeks to bolster up his faith by the evidences of an aboriginal race still to be found in the relics of the Stone Age in Japan. "Flint arrows and spearheads," he remarks, "hammers, chisels, scrapers, kitchen refuse, and various other trophies are frequently excavated, or may be found in the museum or in homes of private persons. Though covered with the soil for centuries, they seem as though freshly brought from an Aino hut in Yesso.

THE SWEET SCENT OF THE CHERRY BLOSSOM

FROM A PRINT BY HIROSHIGE

In scores of striking instances the very peculiar ideas, customs, and superstitions of both Japanese and Aino are the same, or but slightly modified."

This seems to me to be no evidence at all. Flint arrows, spear-heads, hammers, and so on are to be found in every part of the world. Mankind all over the globe seems to have evolved its civilisation, or what passes for it, in very much the same way, viz., by process of experiment. Another authority has asserted that the short, round skull, the oblique eyes, the prominent cheek-bones, the dark, black hair, and the scanty beard all proclaim the Manchus and Koreans as the nearest congeners of the Japanese. This authority considers it positive that the latter are a Tungusic race, and that their own traditions and the whole course of their history are incompatible with any other conclusion than that Korea is the route by which the immigrant tribes made their entry into Kiushiu from their original Manchurian home. While accepting this theory with some reservations, I may remark that I altogether fail to see what the "whole course" of Japanese history has to do with the matter. Japanese history, as I have previously observed, is almost altogether legendary, and proves nothing except the credulity of those who have accepted it as statements of fact. Ethnology, I admit, is a most interesting field for speculation. It is one in which the mind can positively run riot and the imagination revel. The wildest theories have been put forward in regard to many of the world's races, and philological arguments of the thinnest possible kind have been used to bolster them up. For example, one very able writer on this matter has broached a theory respecting the origin of the Japanese, and supported it by what seems to be very plausible evidence. He assumes, on what grounds

I know not, that there was a white race earlier in the field of history than the Aryans, and that the seat of this white race was in High Africa. That it was from Africa that migrations were made to North, Central, and South America, as well as to Egypt, and subsequently to Babylonia and, apparently, to India. In due course, according to this authority, Syria and Babylonia were conquered by the Semites, while the Aryans became masters of Europe, Asia Minor, and India. The suggestion is that the conquerors of the Japanese islands and the founders of the Japanese language and mythology were of the Turano-African type. That these invaders intermarried with a mixed short race, and that the new dominating Japanese race maintained and propagated their dialect of the language and their sect of the religion, and displaced the pure natives. The same authority suggests that when the Pacific route to America was closed by the weakness of the Turano Africans and the rising of cannibals and other savages (where did they rise from ?) the Japanese were isolated on the east. On their west the Turano-African dynasties in China and Korea fell, and were replaced by natives, the same series of events taking place as in Egypt, Peru, Mexico, &c. The principal evidence in support of this somewhat startling theory is the similarity between the words in use in Japanese and in certain African languages. But if evidence of that nature is to be accepted in proof of somewhat improbable theories, it will be possible to prove almost anything in regard to the origin of races. I utterly reject all these far-fetched theories. Any unprejudiced man looking at the Japanese, the Chinaman, and the Korean will have no doubt whatever in his own mind as to their racial affinity. Differences there most certainly are, just as there are between the Frenchman and the Englishman, or even the Englishman and the Scotchman, but what I may term the pronounced characteristics are the same—the colour of the skin, the oblique eyes, the dark hair, and the contour of the skull. These people, whatever the present difference in their mental, moral, and physical characteristics, have quite evidently all come from the same stock. They are, in a word, Mongolians, and any attempt to prove that one particular portion of this stock is Turano-African, or something else equally absurd from an ethnological point of view, seems to me to be positively childish. There was probably originally a mixture of races, Malay as well as others, which has had its effect on the peculiar temperament of the Japanese as he is to-day compared with the Chinaman.

Of course language cannot be left out of account in the question of the racial origin of any people, and the Japanese language has, as I have said, long been a puzzle for the philologist. In the early times we are told the Japanese had no written language. The language in use before the opening up of communications with Korea and China stood alone. Indeed there is only one language outside Japan which has any affinity therewith, that is the language of the inhabitants of the Loo-choo Islands. Philologists have excluded the language from the Aryan and Semitic tongues, and included it in the Turanian group. It is said to possess all the characteristics of the Turanian family being agglutinated, that is to say, maintaining its roots in their integrity without formative prefixes, poor in conjunctions, and copious in the use of participles. It is uncertain when alphabetical characters were introduced into Japan, but it is believed to have happened when intercourse with Korea was first opened about the commencement of the

Christian Era. The warrior Empress, Jungu-kogo, is said to have carried away from Korea as many books as possible after the successful invasion of that country. In the third century the son of the Emperor Ojin learned to read Chinese works, and henceforward the Chinese language and literature seem to have been introduced into Japan. A great impetus was given to the spread of Chinese literature by the introduction of Buddhism and Buddhist writings in the sixth century, and the effect thereof is now apparent in the number of Chinese words in the Japanese language. The question as to the origin of the earliest written characters employed in Japan is one that has produced, and probably will continue to produce, much controversy. These are known as Shinji letters of the God Age, but they have left no traces in the existing alphabet. There is a remarkable difference between the written and spoken dialects of Japan. The grammars of the two are entirely different, and it is possible to speak the language colloquially and yet not be able to read a newspaper, book, or letter ; while, on the other hand, it is possible to know the written language thoroughly, and yet be unable to carry on a conversation with a Japanese. The spoken language, as a matter of fact, is not difficult except in regard to the complicated construction of the words. The difficulty is in reference to the written language. There are really three modes or systems of writing: the first consists of the use of the Chinese characters, the second and third of two different alphabets. Although the Japanese have adopted the Chinese characters and learned to attach to them the same meaning as obtains in China, the construction of sentences is sometimes so totally different that it is difficult for a Chinaman to read a book written by a Japanese in the Chinese characters, while the Japanese cannot read Chinese books unless he has specially studied Chinese. It is evident from what I have said that it is difficult to obtain a complete knowledge of the written language of Japan in its Chinese form. There is a certain school of thought in Japan which is enthusiastic for the replacement of the present complicated system by the introduction of a Roman alphabet, but I feel bound to say that this school has not made much progress, and it is not likely to be successful. Although the present system has its disadvantages, it has its advantages likewise. The written characters are those common to about 450 millions of the world's people, and I think that the use of the Chinese characters in Japan will be a factor of considerable importance in the future history of the world, because I am convinced that Japan is destined to exercise a preponderating influence in and over China, and that the exercise of that influence will be greatly facilitated by the written characters which both nations have in common.

I may at once candidly confess that I have no theory to broach in respect of the origin of the Japanese people or the language that they speak. In such matters theorising appears to me to be a pure waste of time. One has only to look round the world as it is to-day, or for the matter of that within the confines of one's own country, to see how rapidly the people living for long periods in a certain part of the country develop distinct characteristics not only in physiognomy but in dialect. It is only the existence of the printing press which has, so to speak, stereotyped the languages of nations and prevented variations becoming fixed, variations and dialects which in days prior to the existence of printing presses were evolved into distinct languages. Take the British Isles for example, any part of them, Yorkshire, Scotland, Ireland, London, and note the difference between the spoken language of certain classes and the language as printed in newspapers and books. Given a nation isolated, or comparatively isolated, for many hundreds of years, it is difficult to say to what extent its language might be evolved or in what degree the few chance visitors thereto may introduce words which are readily adapted to or adopted in the language and influence it for all time. Take, for example, a word which any visitor to China or Japan must have heard over and over again, viz., " Joss," as applied to God. This is, as most people know, simply a corruption of the Portuguese name for the deity. I hope some philologist a few thousand years hence who may trace that word to its original source will not adduce therefrom that either the Chinese or the Japanese sprang from a Latin race.

The most ancient Japanese writings date from the eighth century. These are Japanese written in Chinese characters, but the Chinese written language as also its literature and the teachings of the great Chinese philosopher, Confucius, are believed to have been introduced several hundreds of years previously. This contact with and importation from China undoubtedly had a marked effect in inducing what I may term atrophy in the development of the Japanese language as also the growth of its own literature, that is a literature entirely devoid of Chinese influences. Indeed it is impossible to speculate on what might have been the development of Japan and in what direction that development would have proceeded had she never come under the influence of the Chinese language, literature, religion, and artistic principles.

I have not the slightest doubt myself, as I have said before, that the Japanese are of the same stock as the

Chinese and Koreans. I have no theory in regard to the origin of the Ainos, who are most likely the aboriginal inhabitants. They are quite evidently a distinct race from the Japanese proper, although of course there has been some interbreeding between them.

The language of Japan naturally suggests some reference to its literature, of which there is no lack, either ancient or modern. I have dealt with this matter in some detail in a subsequent chapter. The old literature of Japan is but little known to Europeans, and probably most Europeans would be incapable of appreciating or understanding it. It abounds in verbal artifices, and the whole habits of life and modes of thought and conception of things, material and spiritual, of the Japanese of those days were so totally different to those of the European as to render it almost unintelligible to the latter. There are, however, scholars who have waded through this literature as also through the poetry of Japan and have found great delight therein. In the process of translating an Oriental language, full of depths of subtlety of thought and expressing Oriental ideas in an Oriental manner, much, if not most, of its beauty and charm must be lost. That is, I think, why the Japanese prose and poetry when translated into English seem so bald and lifeless. We know by experience that even a European language loses in the process of translation which is, except in very rare instances, a purely mechanical art. How much more so must be the case in regard to an Oriental language with its depths of hyperbole and replete with imagery, idealism, and flowery illustrations.

I have referred to the literature of modern Japan, the ephemeral literature, in a chapter on its newspaper press. The modern literature, whether ephemeral or otherwise, is distinctly not on Oriental lines. The influence of the West permeates it. Distinctive Japanese literature is, I imagine, a thing of the past, and I fear it will be less and less studied as time goes on. Young Japan is a "hustler," to use a modern word, and it has no time and mayhap not much inclination for what it perhaps regards as somewhat effete matter. It thinks hurriedly and acts rapidly, and it, accordingly, aspires to express its thoughts and ideas through a medium which shall do so concisely and effectively.

Whatever the origin of the Japanese race or the Japanese language, whether the former came from the plains of Babylon, the heights of Africa, or from some part of the American Continent, or was evolved on the spot, one thing is certain—that the Japanese race and the Japanese language have been indelibly stamped on the world's history. The ethnologist may still puzzle himself as to the origin of these forty-seven millions of people and feel annoyed because he cannot classify them to his own satisfaction. The philologist may feel an equal or even a greater puzzle in reference to their language. These are merely speculative matters which may interest or amuse the man who has the time for such pursuits, but they are, after all, of no great practical importance. The future of a race is of more concern than its past, and, whatever the origin of a language may have been, if that language serves in the processes of development to give expression to noble thoughts, whether in prose or poetry, to voice the wisdom of the people, to preach the gospel of human brotherhood, it matters little how it was evolved or whence it came. It is because I believe that the Japanese race and the Japanese language have a great future before them in the directions I have indicated that I have dealt but lightly, I hope none of my readers will think contemptuously, with the theories that have been put forward in reference to the origin of both.

CHAPTER IV

THE RELIGIONS OF JAPAN, THEIR INFLUENCES AND EFFECTS

MOST persons in this country if they were asked what was the religion of the Japanese people would probably answer Buddhism. As a matter of fact, though Buddhism was introduced into Japan from Korea as far back as 552 A.D., it is not and never has been the preponderating religion in Japan. At the same time I quite admit that it has had a marked effect on the religious life of the people, and that it again has been influenced by the ancient Shinto (literally, "The way of the gods") belief of the Japanese people. This belief, a compound of mythology and ancestral worship, was about the first century largely encrusted by Confucian doctrines or maxims, mostly ethical, imported from China. Of the precise doctrines of Shintoism but little is even now known. It has apparently no dogmas and no sacred book. I am aware that there are the ancient Shinto rituals, called Nurito, and that in reference to them a vast amount of more or less erudite commentary has been written. The result, however, has not been very enlightening. I think that Kaemfer succinctly summed up the Shinto faith in reference to the Japanese people when he remarked, "The more immediate end which they propose to themselves is a state of happiness in this world." In other words, if this assertion be correct, Shintoism preaches utilitarianism. As to the origin of this religion there is very much the same uncertainty and quite as large an amount of theorising as is the case in reference to the Japanese race and language. The most generally received opinion is that Shintoism is closely allied with, if not an offshoot of, the old religion of the Chinese people prior to the days of Confucius. Originally Shinto was in all probability a natural religion, but, like all religious systems, it has developed or suffered from accretions until the ancient belief is lost in obscurity. The author of a now somewhat out-of-date book, entitled "Progress of Japan," asserts that the religion of the Japanese consists in a "belief that the productive ethereal spirit being expanded through the whole universe, every part is in some degree impregnated with it and therefore every part is in some measure the seat of the Deity; whence local gods and goddesses are everywhere worshipped and consequently multiplied without end. Like the ancient Romans and Greeks they acknowledge a supreme being, the first, the supreme, the intellectual, by which men have been reclaimed from rudeness and barbarism to elegance and refinement, and been taught through privileged men and women not only to live with more comfort but to die with better hope." Such a religion, however it may be described, seems to me to be in effect Pantheism.

When Buddhism was introduced into Japan the Buddhist priesthood seems to have made no difficulty about receiving the native gods into their Pantheon. Gradually the greater number of the Shinto temples were served by Buddhist priests who introduced into them the elaborate ornaments and ritual of Buddhism. The result was a kind of hybrid religion, the line of demarcation between the ancient and the imported faith not being very clearly defined. Hence perhaps the religious tolerance of the Japanese for so many centuries, even to Christianity when first introduced by St. Francis Xavier. About the beginning of the eighteenth century there was something akin to a religious reformation in Japan in the direction of the revival of pure Shintoism. For a century and a half subsequently Shintoism held up its head, and eventually, as the outcome of the Revolution of 1868, which marked a turning-point in the history of Japan, Buddhism was disestablished and disendowed and Shinto was installed as the State religion. Simultaneously many thousand of Buddhist temples were stripped of their magnificent and elaborate ornaments and handed over to Shinto keeping; but the downfall of Buddhism was merely of a temporary nature. Nevertheless Shinto is, ostensibly at any rate, still the State religion. Certain temples are maintained from public funds and certain official religious functions take place in Shinto edifices.

Buddhism, acclimatised though it has been in Japan for thirteen centuries, is still a foreign religion, but it has played, and to some extent still plays, an important part in the life and history of the nation, and it has, as I have said, materially influenced the ancient faith of Japan and in turn been influenced by it. I have no intention of describing, much less tracing, the history of Buddhism, whether in Japan or elsewhere. It is a subject on which many writers have descanted and in regard to which much might still be written. There is no doubt whatever that Buddhism as it exists to-day, whether in Ceylon, India, China, or Japan, is widely different from the religion of its founder. Many of its original doctrines were purely symbolical and poetical. These have been evolved into something they were certainly never intended to mean. That the principles of the Buddhist religion are essentially pure and moral no one who has any knowledge of it can deny. It preaches above all things the suppression of self, and it inculcates a tenderness and fondness for all forms of life. According to Griffis, "Its commandments are the dictates of the most refined morality. Besides the cardinal prohibitions against murder, stealing, adultery, lying, drunkenness and unchastity, every shade of vice, hypocrisy, anger, pride, suspicion, greediness, gossiping, cruelty to animals is guarded against by special precepts. Among the virtues recommended we find not only reverence of parents, care of children, submission to authority, gratitude, moderation in times of prosperity, submission in times of trial, equanimity at all times, but virtues such as the duty of forgiving insults and not rewarding evil with evil." This is a pretty exhaustive moral code, and though Buddhism has often been taunted with the fact that its followers do not practically carry out its precepts and live up to the level of its high moral teaching, Buddhism is not, I would suggest, the only religion against which such taunts can be levelled.

The history of Buddhism ever since its introduction into Japan has been an eventful one. It has had its ups and its downs. It came into the country under royal auspices, it has nearly always enjoyed the royal favour, and I think its existence, during at any rate the first few centuries it was in the country, has been due to that fact rather than to any pronounced affection on the part of the mass of the people for it. One Emperor, Shirakawa by name, is recorded to have erected more than 50,000 pagodas and statues throughout the country in honour of Buddha.

Many of these works are still, after many centuries, in an excellent state of preservation, and are of deep interest not only to the antiquarian but to any student of the religious history of a nation. The Buddhist priests, like the Jesuits in European countries, during many centuries captured and controlled education in Japan and showed themselves thoroughly progressive in their methods and the knowledge they inculcated. Art and medicine were introduced under their auspices and, whatever one may think of, or whatever criticism may be passed on the religion itself, it is impossible, in my opinion, to deny that Buddhism on the whole has had a vast and, I venture to think, not an unhealthy influence on every phase of Japanese national and domestic life. The strength and weakness of Buddhism have undoubtedly lain in the fact that it possessed and possesses no dogmatic creed. It concerned itself almost entirely with self-mastery, self-suppression, the duty of doing good in this world without looking forward to any reward for the same in the next. It preached benevolence in the true meaning of that word in every shape and form. It taught that benevolence was the highest aspiration of a noble spirit. Benevolence was, indeed, the master virtue, the crown, the coping stone, of all virtues. As the term is used in Buddhist teaching, it may be regarded as the synonym of love and a close study of the teaching of Buddhism on this subject must impress any thinking man strongly with the idea that it was very much the teaching of Christ in reference to the love of one's neighbour. Buddhism in Japan at any rate has not been conservative; it has gone the way of most religious systems, has been subject to development and has evolved from time to time different sects, some of which have held and preached dogmas which would, I think, have astounded, and I feel certain would have been anathematised by, the founder of Buddhism. The principal of the sects now existing in Japan are the Tendai, Shingon Yoko and Ken, all of which, I may observe, are of Chinese origin. Besides these there are the Shin and the Nichiren evolved in Japan and dating from the thirteenth century. Respecting the metaphysics of Buddhism and their effect on the Japanese people I cannot, I think, do better than quote from that great authority on all things Japanese, Mr. Basil Hall Chamberlain, whose writings have done so much, not only to awaken an interest in Japan but to give correct ideas respecting the life of the people. He remarks, in this connection, "The complicated metaphysics of Buddhism have awakened no interest in the Japanese nation. Another fact, curious but true, is that these people have never been at the trouble to translate the Buddhist canon into their own language. The priests use a Chinese version, the laity no version at all nowadays, though to judge from the allusions scattered up and down Japanese literature they would seem to have been more given to searching the Scriptures a few hundred years ago. The Buddhist religion was disestablished and disendowed during the years 1871–4—a step taken in consequence of the temporary ascendency of Shinto. At the present time a faint struggle is being carried on by the Buddhist priesthood against rivals in comparison with whom Shinto is insignificant: we mean the two great streams of European thought—Christianity and physical science. A few—a very few—men trained in European methods fight for the Buddhist cause. They do so, not as orthodox believers in any existing sect, but because they are convinced that the philosophical contents of Buddhism in general are supported by the doctrine of evolution, and that this religion needs therefore only to be regenerated on modern lines in order to find universal acceptance."

The "Reformation" of 1868 in Japan followed much the same course in regard to religious matters as the Reformation in England. It laid vandal hands on Buddhist temples and ornaments of priceless value. The objective point of this religious Reformation was presumably very much the same as that which occurred in this country, viz., a reversion to simplicity in religion. The Shinto Temple which is invariably thatched is a development of the ancient Japanese hut, whereas the Buddhist Temple, which is of Indian origin, is tiled, and as regards its internal fittings and ornamentation is elaborate in comparison with the plain appearance of the Shinto edifice.

So far as the Japan of to-day is concerned these two religions may be regarded as moribund, although their temples are still thronged by the lower classes of the people. They exist because they are there, but they have no vitality, no message for the people, and it is questionable whether any of Japan's great thinkers or the educated classes in the country, whichever religion they may nominally belong to, have faith or belief in it. A man may have, or for sundry reasons profess, a creed in Japan as in other countries without believing in it. Custom and prejudices are as strong there as elsewhere, and it is often easier to appear to acquiesce in a religion than to openly reject it.

There are, I know, some optimistic persons who believe, or affect to believe, that Christianity is in due course destined to replace the ancient faiths in Japan. They point to what was effected by St. Francis Xavier in the sixteenth century, and they imagine that the Japan of the twentieth century is only waiting to finally unshackle itself from Shintoism and Buddhism before arraying itself in the garb of Christianity. Well, Christian missions have had a fair field in Japan for many years past, and though many members of those missions have been men of great piety, zeal, and learning, they have made comparatively little headway among and have exercised extremely little influence on the mass of the Japanese people. Indeed, the fair field that all Christian missions without distinction have had, in my opinion, accounts for the small amount of progress they have made Because all the leading Christian denominations are there—Roman Catholicism, Church of England, Greek Church, Congregationalists, Methodists, Baptists, Salvation Army, Society of Friends, and others—all preaching and proclaiming their own particular dogmas and all lumped together by the Japanese under the generic title of Christians. The Japanese may, I think, be excused if he fails to differentiate between them. He views and hears their differences in dogma. He observes that there is no bond of union, and frequently considerable jealousy among these numerous sects. Each claims to preach the truth, and the Japanese concludes that as they cannot all be right they may possibly all be wrong. It is only on this assumption that it is possible to account for the little headway made by Christianity in Japan in view of the labour and money devoted by different religious bodies to its propagation for many years past. There is, let me add, no marked hostility to Christianity in Japan—only indifference. The educated Japanese of to-day is, I believe, for the most part an agnostic, and he views Shintoism, Buddhism, Christianity alike, except in so far as he regards the first two as more or less national and the last as an exotic.

At the commencement of the seventeenth century the Japanese Christians are stated to have amounted in numbers to one million. At the present time it is doubtful if they total up to one hundred thousand. And this despite the splendid religious organisations that exist, the facilities that are given for the propagation of the Christian faith, and the opportunities which were certainly not in existence three hundred years ago. Into the causes of this comparative failure of Christianity in Japan to-day as compared with its marvellous progress in the sixteenth century, I do not propose to enter. The enthusiasm of a Francis Xavier is not an everyday event, and the Japanese of the sixteenth century was, mayhap, more impressed by the missionaries of those days, arriving in flimsy and diminutive vessels after undergoing the perils and hardships of long voyages, having neither purse nor scrip nor wearing apparel except what they stood up in, than he is by the modern missionary arriving as a first-class passenger in a magnificent steamer and during his residence in the country lacking none of the comforts or amenities of life. Or it may be that the Japanese mind has advanced and developed during the past three centuries, has now less hankering after metaphysical subtleties, and fails to comprehend or to sympathise with abstruse theological dogmas and doctrines. If Christianity appealed to him as in the days of Francis Xavier as the one faith professed by the Western world, it would probably impress him to a far greater extent than it does at present when, as I have before said, he views Christianity as a disorganised body composed of hundreds of sects each rejecting, and many of them anathematising, what the others teach. He considers there is no need for investigation until Christianity has itself determined what is the precise truth that non-Christian countries are to be asked to accept.

Regarding the influence of the Buddhist and Shinto religions during the many centuries they have existed in the country on the lives of the people, I propose to make a few remarks. Too often one hears or reads of speakers and writers describing Japan as a country steeped in paganism and addicted to pagan habits and customs with all (somewhat indefinite this!) that they involve. To describe Buddhism as paganism merely shows a lamentable amount of ignorance; nor should I be inclined to include Shintoism in a term which, whatever its precise meaning, is invariably intended to be opprobious! After all, any religion must be largely judged by its effects on the lives of its adherents, and judged by that standard I do not think, as regards the Japanese, either Buddhism or Shintoism ought to be sweepingly condemned. If many of the customs and practices of both religions seem silly or absurd; if either or both inculcate or lead to superstition, it can at least be said of both that they teach a high moral code, and that the average Japanese in his life, his family relations, his philosophy, his patriotism, his bodily cleanliness, and in many other respects, offers an example to other nations which deem themselves more highly civilised, which possess a purer religion and too often, with that lack of charity which is frequently the result of an excess of ignorance, unsparingly condemn the Japanese as "pagans" or "heathens."

A CHERRY BLOSSOM PARTY

FROM A PRINT BY HIROSHIGE

CHAPTER V

THE CONSTITUTION—THE CROWN AND THE HOUSES OF PARLIAMENT

A Constitution, if we are to accept the dogmatic assertions of those who have written with a show of learning on the subject, ought to be evolved rather than established by any parliamentary or despotic act. The history of the world certainly tends to prove that paper Constitutions have not been over-successful in the past. There assuredly has been no lack of them in the last century or so, and although some, if not all, of them have been practically tried, a very few have attained any considerable measure of success. The English Constitution has long been held up to the rest of the world by writers on Constitutional history as a model of what a Constitution ought to be, for the somewhat paradoxical reason that it is nowhere clearly, if indeed at all, defined. It is largely the outcome of custom and usage, and it is claimed for it that on the whole it has worked better than any cut-and-dried paper Constitution would have done.

Nevertheless there does not appear to be any good and valid reason why a Constitution should not be as clearly defined as an Act of Parliament. Undefined Constitutions have worked well at certain periods when there was a tacit general consent as to their meaning, but they have not always been able to withstand the strain of fierce controversy and the coming into existence of factors which were undreamt of when these Constitutions were originally evolved, and definitions or additions or amendments thereto have, accordingly, become necessary.

The promulgation of a Constitution for Japan in February, 1889, was an event of great interest to the civilised world. There were, of course, at the time a large number of persons who prophesied that this Constitution would go the way of many others that had preceded it—that it would, in fact, be found unworkable and, being so found, Constitutional Government in Japan would eventuate, as it had elsewhere, in the resumption of autocratic rule as the only alternative to anarchy. It is pleasing to be able to record that these prophecies have, after nearly eighteen years' experience, not been fulfilled, and that the Japanese Constitution, well thought out and devised as it was, seems not only likely to endure but is admirably adapted to all the circumstances and needs of the country.

In order to fully comprehend the events that gradually led up to the establishment of Constitutional government in Japan, and the precise place of the Crown and aristocracy in that government, it is, I think, essential to make a rapid review of past events in that country.

In ancient times the Mikado was both the civil ruler and the military leader of his people. Under him there were exercising authority throughout the land about 150 feudal lords. Feudalism of one kind or another prevailed in Japan until 1868. Towards the end of the sixteenth century the feudal principle was apparently on the decline. In the year 1600, however, Tokagawa Iyoyasu, with an army composed of the clans of the east and north defeated the combined forces of those of the west and south at the battle of Sakigahara and proclaimed himself Shogun. The feudal lords of the various clans throughout the country then became his vassals and paid homage to him. The Tokagawa family practically governed the country till the Revolution of 1868, when the present Emperor took the reins of government into his own hands and finally abolished feudalism and with it the authority of the Daimios. Many persons even now believe that the Shogun, or Tycoon as he was usually called in Europe, was a usurper. As a matter of fact he received investiture from the Mikado, and his authority was, nominally at any rate, a derived one. At the same time there is no doubt that the real power of the State was in his hands while the *de jure* ruler lived in the capital in complete seclusion surrounded by all the appanages and ceremonial of royalty.

Up to the year 1868 Japan was divided into numerous provinces governed by Daimios, or territorial lords, each of whom maintained large standing armies. They were all subject to the Shogun, while retaining the right to rule their particular provinces in ordinary matters. In 1868 the Shogun fell, and there can be little doubt his fall was to some extent brought about by the concessions which had been made to foreign Powers in regard to the opening of the country to foreign trade. In 1868 the Shogun repaired to Kyoto, the first time for 250 years, and paid homage to the Mikado. Feudalism was then, as I have said, abolished, the Emperor took the reins of authority into his own hands, formed a central Government at Tokio and reigned supreme as an absolute monarch.

"The sacred throne was established at the time when

the heavens and earth became separated." This has long been an axiom of Japanese belief, but it has been somewhat modified of late years, even the assertion of it by the Sovereign himself. A leading Japanese statesman who has written an article on the subject of the Emperor and his place in the Constitution has asserted that he is "Heaven descended, sacred and divine." I do not think that the modern Japanese entertains this transcendental opinion nor, indeed, do I find that the Emperor himself has of late years put forward any such pretensions. For example, in the Imperial proclamation on the Constitution of the Empire on February 11, 1889, the Emperor declared that he had "by virtue of the glories of our ancestors ascended the Throne of a lineal succession unbroken for *ages eternal.*" Whereas in the Imperial Rescript declaring war against China on August 1, 1894, he contented himself with asserting that he was "seated on a Throne occupied by the same dynasty from *time immemorial.*" The italics are mine, and the difference in the pretensions which I desire to emphasise is certainly remarkable.

When granting a Constitution the Emperor, as has been and probably will be the custom of all monarchs so acting, declared that the legislative power belonged to him but that he intended to exercise it with the consent of the Imperial Diet. The convocation of the Diet belongs exclusively to the Emperor. It has no power to meet without his authority, and if it did so meet its acts and its actions would be null and void. In this respect the Diet is on precisely the same basis as the English Parliament. According to the Constitution the Emperor, when the Diet is not sitting, can issue Imperial ordinances which shall have the effect of law so long as they do not contravene any existing law. The article authorising these ordinances defines that they shall only be promulgated in consequence of an urgent necessity to maintain public safety or to avert public calamities, and all such ordinances must be laid before the Diet at its next sitting, and in the event of the same not being approved they become null and void.

To my mind, one of the most interesting portions of the Constitution is that which lays down succinctly and tersely the rights and duties of Japanese subjects. In this section there are contained within about fifty lines the declaration of innumerable rights for which mankind in various parts of the world during many hundreds of years fought and bled and endured much suffering. Just let me mention a few of them. No Japanese subject shall be arrested, detained, tried or punished unless according to law. Except as provided by law the house of no Japanese subject shall be entered or searched without his consent. Except in the cases provided by law, the secrecy of the letters of every Japanese subject shall remain inviolate. The right of property of every Japanese subject shall remain inviolate. Japanese subjects shall enjoy freedom of religious belief. Japanese subjects shall enjoy liberty of speech, writing, publication, public meetings and associations. Japanese subjects may present petitions. We have in these few brief provisoes the sum total of everything that, in effect, constitutes the liberty of the subject.

The Diet of Japan, like the Parliament of Great Britain, consists of two Houses—a House of Peers and a House of Representatives. The House of Peers is composed of (1) the members of the Imperial family, (2) Princes and Marquises, (3) Counts, Viscounts and Barons who are elected thereto by the members of their respective orders, (4) persons who have been specially nominated by the Emperor on account of meritorious service or by reason of their erudition, (5) persons who have been elected, one member for each city and prefecture of the Empire, by and from among the taxpayers of the highest amount of direct national taxes on land, industry, or trade, and who had subsequently received the approval of the Emperor. It will be seen that the members of the Imperial family, the Princes and Marquises, have an inalienable right to sit in the House of Peers, the latter rank on attaining the age of 25 years. In regard to Counts, Viscounts, and Barons there is no such right. Those ranks, like the Peers of Scotland and Ireland, meet together and select one-fifth of their number to represent them in the House of Peers for a term of seven years. Any subject over thirty years of age nominated by the Emperor for meritorious service or erudition remains a life member. Those returned by the cities and prefectures remain members for a period of seven years. It is provided by the Constitution that the number of members of the House of Peers who are not nobles shall not exceed the number of the members bearing a title of nobility.

The question of the necessity for the existence of a second chamber and the composition thereof has been keenly debated in this and other countries of recent years. It seems to me that in this matter Japan has hit upon the happy mean. She has combined in her House of Peers the aristocratic or hereditary element in a modified degree with the principle of life membership by which she secures the services and counsel of the great intellects of the land, and such as have done the State good service in any capacity. At the same time she has not excluded the representative element from her second chamber—a fact which must largely obviate any possibility of the House of Peers becoming a purely class body. A second chamber so constituted must obviously serve an extremely useful purpose in preserving an equilibrium between political parties, in preventing the rushing through and passing into law of hastily considered measures. For the composition of her second chamber, Japan has taken all human means possible to obtain whatever is representative of the stability, the intellect, the enterprise and the patriotism of the country.

The composition of the House of Representatives, which answers to our House of Commons, is as interesting as that of the Upper Chamber. When the Constitution was first promulgated the principle of small electoral districts obtained, one member being elected for each district. This system was found or believed to be faulty, and hence, after some years' experience, large electoral districts combined with a single vote have been instituted. It may be interesting to relate that both systems, the large and the small districts, were drafted by an Englishman, Mr. Thomas Hair. Cities whose population exceeds 30,000 are formed into separate electoral districts while a city with less than 30,000 inhabitants is, with its suburbs, constituted a district. The number of members allowed to each district depends on the population. For a population of 130,000 or under one member is allowed, and for every additional 65,000 persons above the former number an additional member is allotted. The number of members in the House of Representatives is 381, or little over half that of which our House of Commons consists. The population of the two countries is almost identical, and experience serves to show that the number of Members of Parliament in Japan is sufficiently numerous for all practical purposes and that any material addition thereto would be more likely to impede than to accelerate the wheels of legislative progress. Neither the Japanese Constitution nor the Electoral Law makes any provision for the representation of minorities, that aim of so many well-meaning persons in different countries. In Japan the majority rules as everywhere, and minorities must submit.

Manhood suffrage is not yet a *fait accompli* in Japan. Under the present law to qualify a Japanese subject to exercise the franchise he must pay 15 yen (about 30s.) or more, indirect taxation. Only a Japanese subject can vote at elections. No foreigner has any electoral rights, but if he becomes a naturalised Japanese subject he obtains all the privileges appertaining to that position.

Each House of Parliament in Japan possesses a president and vice-president, who are elected by the members. The president of each House receives an annual allowance of 4,000 yen (about £400) and the vice-president 2,000 yen (about £200). The payment of Members of Parliament is in vogue in Japan. The elected and nominated, but not the hereditary, members of the House of Peers, and each member of the House of Representatives, receives an annual allowance of 800 yen (about £80). They are also paid travelling expenses in accordance with the regulations on the subject. It may be interesting to state that there is a clause in the Constitution which enacts that the president, vice-president, and members of the two Houses who are entitled to annual allowances shall not be permitted to decline the same! It says much for the estimate of patriotism entertained in Japan when the Constitution was promulgated that such a clause as this should have been considered necessary.

Debate in both the Japanese Houses of Parliament is free and the proceedings public. There will be no occasion for the uprising of a Wilkes in Japan to obtain permission to publish Parliamentary Debates. The Constitution, however, contains a proviso for the sitting of either House with closed doors upon the wish of the president or of not less than ten members, the same being agreed to by the House, or upon the demand of the Government with or without the consent of the House. When in the former event a motion for a secret sitting is made, strangers have to withdraw from the House and the motion is voted on without debate. The proceedings of a secret meeting of either Chamber are not allowed to be published.

The Japanese Constitution, which is certainly a document containing not only provisions of an epoch-making nature but most elaborate details in regard to even minor matters, includes in seven or eight lines one or two excellent rules in regard to what is termed "The Passing of the Budget." Under these rules, when the Budget is introduced into the House of Representatives the Committee thereon must finish the examination of it within fifteen days and report thereon to the House, while no motion for any amendment in the Budget can be made the subject of debate unless it is supported by at least thirty members.

The Constitution of Japan, as I have remarked, contains a vast amount of detail. The framers of that Constitution seem to have been endowed with an abnormal amount of prevision. In fact they foresaw the possibility of occurrences and made provision for those occurrences that nations which are, or which consider themselves to be, more highly civilised have not yet taken any adequate steps to deal with. For example, Article 92 of the Constitution enacts that in neither House of Parliament shall the use of coarse language or personalities be allowed, while Article 93 declares that when any member has been vilified or insulted either in the House or in a meeting of a Committee he shall appeal to the House and demand that proper measures shall be taken. There shall, it is decreed, be no retaliation among members. The Constitution also contains several salutary regulations in reference to the disciplinary punishment of members.

The establishment of a Parliament in Japan has produced parties and a party system. I suppose that was inevitable. In every country there is, and as human nature is constituted there always will be, two parties representative of two phases of the human mind: the party in a hurry to effect progress because it deems progress desirable, and the party that desires to cling as long as possible to the ancient ways because it knows them and has had experience of them and looks askance at experiments—experiments for which that somewhat hackneyed phrase a "leap in the dark" has long done service. I have no intention, as I said in the Preface, of dealing at all with Japanese politics. There is no doubt a good deal of heat, and the resultant friction, evoked in connection with politics in Japan as elsewhere. Perhaps this young nation—that is, young from a parliamentary point of view—takes politics too seriously. Time will remedy that defect, if it be a defect. At the same time, I may express the opinion that, however severe party strife may be in Japan, and though the knocks given and received in the course thereof are hard and some of the language not only vigorous but violent, the members of all parties have at heart and as their objective point the advancement of Japan and the good of the country generally.

The Japanese Constitution, though not a very lengthy, is such an all-embracing document that in a hurried survey of it, it is possible to overlook many important features. It provides for the establishment of a Privy Council to deliberate upon important matters of State, but only when consulted by the Emperor. It enforces the responsibility of the Ministers of State for all advice given to the Emperor and decrees that all laws, Imperial ordinances and Imperial rescripts of any kind relating to affairs of State, must be countersigned by a Minister of State. The Constitution also defines the position, authority, and independence of the judges. That Constitution contains a proviso all-important in reference to the upright administration of the law, a proviso which it took years of agitation to obtain in this country, that no judge shall be deprived of his position unless by way of criminal sentence or disciplinary punishment. All trials and judgments of the court of law are to be conducted publicly. Provision is made, when there exists any fear of a trial in open court being prejudicial to peace and order or to the maintenance of public morality, for the same to be held in camera. I may add, before I take leave of the Constitution, with a view of showing how all-embracing as I have said are the various matters dealt with therein, that it defines and declares that the style of address for the Emperor and Empress shall be His, Her, or Your Majesty, while that for the Imperial Princes and Princesses shall be His, Her, Their, or Your Highness or Highnesses.

In regard to no matter connected with Japan have I found so large an amount of misconception prevalent as in reference to the position of the Emperor of that country. The divine descent which is still sometimes claimed for the sovereigns of Japan and which has never, so far as I know, been officially repudiated, has caused some persons to regard the Emperor from a somewhat ludicrous standpoint. In this very prosaic and materialistic age, when very few persons have profound beliefs on any subject, the spectacle of one of the sovereigns of the earth still claiming a divine origin is one that appeals to the ludicrous susceptibilities of that vague entity "the man in the street." It is not well, however, that people should criticise statements in royal proclamations or in royal assertions too seriously. Even in this country there are documents issued from time to time bearing the royal sign manual which every one regards as interesting but meaningless formalities—interesting because they are a survival of mediæval documents which meant something some hundreds of years ago and still remain though their meanings have long since lapsed. And yet there are persons in this country who peruse such documents and know that they are simply words signifying practically nothing, who severely criticise the assertion of a long-used title by the Japanese Emperor upon issuing a royal proclamation. I am not aware whether his Imperial Majesty or his Ministers of State implicitly accept his divine descent, but this I do know—that those persons who regard the present Emperor of Japan as a State puppet, arrogating more or less divine attributes, are labouring under a profound delusion. There is no abler man in Japan at the present moment. There is no abler man among the sovereigns of the world. In fact, I should be inclined to place the Emperor of Japan at the head of the world's great statesmen. He is no monarch content to reign but not to govern, concerned simply about ceremonial and the fripperies and gew-gaws of royalty. He is a constitutional sovereign certainly. He has always shown the deepest respect for the Constitution ever since its promulgation, and never in the slightest degree attempted to infringe or override any portion of it. At the same time he is an effective force in the Government of Japan. There is nothing too great or too little in the Empire or in the relations of the Empire with foreign Powers for his ken. He, in a word, has the whole reins of government in his hands, and he exercises over every department and detail of it a minute and rigid supervision which is, in my opinion, largely responsible for the efficiency of the internal administration of the country as also for the place that Japan holds among the Great Powers of the world.

I cannot leave a consideration of this subject without referring to the assistance rendered to the Emperor by, as also to the debt Japan owes to, some six or seven great men in that country whose names I shall not inscribe here because to do so would be to some extent invidious, several of whom do not, as a matter of fact, hold any formal position in the Government of the country. The wisdom of these men has been a great boon for such a country as Japan, and if she is not now as sensible of it as she ought to be future ages will, I feel sure, recognise the debt that Japan owes to them. Some persons with an intimate knowledge of Japan have told me that it is not, after all, a constitutional State but in effect, though not in name, an oligarchy. This word has in the past often had unpleasant associations, and one does not like to apply it in reference to the Government of a progressive and enlightened country. Still the word strictly means government by a small body of men, and if in those men is included the larger part of the wisdom of the country, and they exercise their power solely and exclusively for the benefit of the country, I am not certain that such a form of government is not the best that could be devised. Of course, humanity being as it is, an oligarchy, has its dangers and its temptations. I will say, however, of the wise men of Japan, the men to whom I have been referring and who whether in office or out of office have exercised, and must continue to exercise, a marked and predominant influence on the government of the country, that their patriotism has never been called in question, and no one has at any time suggested that they were influenced by self-seeking or other unworthy motives, or had any aspirations save the material and moral advancement of Japan and her elevation to a prominent position among the Great Powers of the world.

CHAPTER VI

THE PEOPLE—THEIR LIFE AND HABITS

AFTER all, the life of the people is the most interesting, as I think it is the most instructive, matter connected with any country. It is assuredly impossible to form a clear or indeed any correct idea in regard to a nation unless we know something of the manners and customs, the daily life, the amusements, the vices of its people. Unless we can, as it were, take a bird's-eye view of the people at work and at play, at their daily avocations in their homes, see them as they come into the world, as they go through life's pilgrimage, and, finally, as they pay the debt of nature and are carried to their last resting-place in accordance with the national customs, with the respect or the indifference the nation shows for its dead.

If one is to arrive at a correct idea regarding the life and habits of the Japanese people it is, I think, essential to get away from the ports and large towns where they have been influenced by or brought much into contact with Europeans, and see them as they really are, free from conventionalities, artificialities, and the effects of Western habits and customs which have undoubtedly been pronounced in those centres where Europeans congregate.

The house in Japan does not play the important part it

does in this country. When a man in England, whatever his station in life may be, contemplates taking a wife and settling down, as the phrase goes, the home and the contents thereof become an all-important matter and one needing much thought and discussion. In Japan there is no such necessity. A Japanese house is easily run up—and taken down. The "walls" are constructed of paper and slide in grooves between the beams of the floor which is raised slightly above the ground. The partitions between the rooms can easily be taken down and an additional room as easily run up. The house is, as a rule, only one storey high. The carpets consist of matting only, and practically no furniture is necessary. A witty writer on Japan has aptly and wittily remarked that "an Englishman's house may be his castle, a Japanese's house is his bedroom and his bedroom is a passage." The occupant of this house sits on the floor, sleeps on the floor, and has his meals on the floor. The floor is kept clean by the simple process of the inhabitants removing their boots, or what do duty for boots, and leaving them at the entrance, so as to avoid soiling the matting with which the floor of each room is covered. This is a habit which has much to commend it, and is, I suggest, worthy of imitation by other countries. After all, the Japanese mode of life has a great deal to be said in its favour. It seems strange at first, but after the visitor to the country has got over his initial fit of surprise at the difference between the Japanese domestic economy and his own, he will, if he be a man of unprejudiced mind, admit that it certainly has its "points."

The bulk of the population is poor, very poor, but that poverty is not emphasised in their homes to the same extent as in European countries. The house—a doll's house some irreverent people term it—with paper partitions doing duty for walls, white matting, a few cooking utensils costs only a few shillings. It can, as I have said, be taken down and run up easily, and enlarged almost indefinitely. The inhabitants sleep on the floor, and the bedding consists not as with us of mattresses, palliasses, and other more or less insanitary articles, but of a number, great or small, and elaborate or otherwise, in accordance with the means of the owner, of what I will term quilts. The Japanese pillow is a fearful and wonderful article. I can never imagine how it was evolved and why it has remained so long unimproved. It is made of wood and there is a receptacle for the head. The European who uses it finds that it effectually banishes sleep, while the ordinary Japanese is apparently unable to sleep without it. In most houses, however poor, a kakemono, or wall picture, is to be seen. It is usually the only decoration save an occasional vase containing flowers, and of course flowers themselves, which are in evidence everywhere. Light is, or used to be, given by a " lamp," a kind of Chinese lantern on a lacquer stand, the light being given by a rush candle. I am sorry, however, to say that these in some respects artistic lanterns are being generally replaced by hideous petroleum or kerosene lamps, not only ugly but a constant source of danger in these flimsy houses.

The most important accessory of nearly all Japanese houses is the bath-room, or wash-house, to use a more appropriate term. The hot bath is a universal institution in the country, and nearly every Japanese man and woman, whatever his or her station in life, washes the body thoroughly in extremely hot water more than once daily. The Japanese, as regards the washing of their persons, are the cleanest race in the world, but many hygienic laws are set at defiance possibly because they are not understood.

A gradual improvement is, however, taking place in these matters, and the cleanliness as regards the body and their houses, which is such a pleasing feature of the people, will no doubt extend in other directions also.

Japanese houses are habitable enough in warm weather, but in winter-time they are, as might be expected, exceedingly cold, especially as the arrangements for warming them are of an extremely primitive nature. Those complaints which are induced or produced by cold are prevalent in the country.

The food of the people is as simple as their houses, and as inexpensive. A Japanese family it has been calculated can live on about £10 a year. A little fish, rice, and vegetables, with incessant tea, is the national dietary. The people living on this meagre fare are, on the whole, a strong and sturdy race, but it is questionable if the national physique would not be vastly improved were the national diet also. I have touched on this matter elsewhere, so I need not refer to it further here. Tobacco is the constant consoler of the Japanese in all his troubles. Why he smokes such diminutive pipes I have never been able to understand. They only hold sufficient tobacco for a few whiffs, and when staying in a Japanese house the constant tap, tap, tap of the owner's pipe as he empties the ashes out prior to refilling it reminds one of the woodpecker.

There are doubtless some persons, especially those persons who consider that to enjoy life a superabundance or even a plethora of material comforts are necessary, who, after reading a description of the home and fare of the Japanese peasant, will assume that his life is a burden and that he derives no enjoyment whatever from it. Nothing could be more erroneous. There is probably not a more joyous being on the face of the globe than the Japanese. His wants are few, and in that fact probably lies his happiness. He does not find his enjoyment in material things, but he has his enjoyment all the same, and I think on the whole that he probably gets more out of life and has more fitting ideas regarding it than the Englishman who considers an abundance of beef and beer its objective point.

To me one of the most pleasing features of Japan is the fondness and tenderness of the Japanese of all ranks and classes for children. The Japanese infant is the tyrant of Japan, and nothing is good enough for it. The women, as most people know, carry their babies on their backs instead of in their arms. A baby is, however, not so for very long in Japan. Very young Japanese girls may be seen carrying their little baby brothers and sisters behind their backs, and thus learning their maternal duties in advance. The position of women in Japan, married women, is not so satisfactory as it ought to be. The laws in regard to divorce are, I think, too easy, and a Japanese possesses facilities for getting rid of his wife which does not tend to the conservation of home-life. The custom, which was at one time universal, of women blackening their teeth, has largely diminished, and will no doubt in due course become obsolete. The idea which underlay it was that the woman should render herself unattractive to other men. There was no object in having such an adventitious attraction as pearly teeth for her husband, who might be presumed to know what her attractions really were. The Japanese woman in her education has inculcated three obediences, viz., obedience to parents, obedience to husband, and after the death of the latter obedience to son. Although the Japanese girl comes of age at 14 she cannot marry without her father's consent until she is 25.

The dress of the Japanese people is so well known that it is not necessary for me to describe it. The kimono is, I think, a graceful costume, and I am very sorry that so many women in the upper classes have discarded the national dress for European garments. Japanese women who wear the national costume do not don gloves. If their hands are cold they place them in their sleeves, which are long and have receptacles containing many and various things, including a pocket-handkerchief, which is usually made of paper, and sometimes a pot of lip-salve to colour the lips to the orthodox tint. The poorer classes, of course, do not go in for such frivolities. Talking of paper handkerchiefs reminds me of the innumerable uses to which paper is put in Japan; it serves for umbrellas and even for coats, and is altogether a necessity of existence almost for the great mass of the people.

I have referred to the lack of what may be deemed material comforts in Japan, as also to the fact that the Japanese are a joyous race but that their enjoyment is not of a material nature. They are, in fact, easily amused, and their enjoyment takes forms which would hardly appeal to a less emotional people. In the large towns the theatre is a perennial source of amusement. I have referred to the theatre in the chapter dealing with the drama, and remarked therein that the excess of by-play, irrelevant by-play, in a Japanese drama was rather wearisome to the European spectator. Not so to the Japanese. He positively revels in it. The theatre is for him something real and moving. He has, whatever his age, all the zest of a youth for plays and spectacles. How far the Europeanising of the country, which is having, and is bound still further to have, an effect on dramatic art, will affect the amusements of the people and their proneness for the theatre remains to be seen. There is so far nothing approaching the English music-hall in Japan. Let me express a hope that there never will be. It is a long cry from the graceful Geisha to the inanities and banalities which appear to be the stock-in-trade of music-hall performances in this country. These appear to meet a home want, but I sincerely trust they will be reserved for home delectation and not be inflicted in any guise upon Japan. The matter of music-halls suggests some reference to the ideas of the Japanese in respect of music. The educated classes appear to have an appreciation of European music, but Japanese music requires, I should say, an educational process. Some superficial European writers declare that the Japanese have not the least conception of either harmony or melody, and that what passes for music in the country is simply discord. It might have struck these writers that criticism of this kind in reference to a most artistic people could hardly be correct. Any one who has listened to the Geisha or heard the singing of trained Japanese would certainly not agree in such statements as I have referred to. Japanese music is like Japanese art—it has its own characteristics and will, I am sure, repay being carefully studied.

Festivals and feasts, religious and otherwise, which are many and varied, afford some relaxation for the people. There are, according to a list compiled, some 28 religious festivals, 16 national holidays, and 14 popular feast-days. New Year's Day is termed Shihohai, and on it the Emperor prays to all his ancestors for a peaceful reign. Two days subsequently, on Genjisai, he makes offerings to him and all his Imperial ancestors, while two days later still all Government officers make official calls. These are legal holidays. The 11th of February (Kigen Setsu) and the 3rd of April (Jimmu-Tenno-sai) are observed as the anniversaries respectively of the accession to the throne and the death of Jimmu-Tenno, the first Emperor. The 17th of October (Shinsho-sai) is the national harvest festival. On this day the Emperor offers the first crop of the year to his divine ancestor, Tenshoko Daijin. It may be interesting to record that the 25th of December (Christmas Day), is observed as a holiday by the Custom-house department "for the accommodation of foreign employees."

The popular festivals are equally interesting and curious. The 3rd of March (Oshinasama), is the girls' or dolls' festival, while the 5th of May (Osekku), is the boys' festival, or Feast of Flags. A three days' festival, 13th–15th of July (Bon Matsuri), is the All Souls' Day of Japan in honour of the sacred dead. The 9th of September (Kikku No Sekku), is the festival of chrysanthemums, the national flower, and the 20th of November, appropriately near the Lord Mayor of London's day, is the festival held by the merchants in honour of Ebisuko, the God of Wealth. The Feast of Flags—the boys' festival—is one much esteemed by the Japanese people. On the occasion of it every house the owner of which has been blessed with sons displays a paper carp floating from a flagstaff. If a male child has come to the establishment during the year the carp is extra large. It is considered a reproach to any married woman not to have this symbol flying outside the house on the occasion of this feast. Why the carp has been selected as a symbol is a matter upon which there is much difference of opinion. The carp, it is said, is emblematic of the youth who overcomes all the difficulties that lie in his path during life, but I confess I rather fail to see what connection there is between this fish and such an energetic youth. On this day the boys have dolls representative of

Japanese heroes and personages of the past as well as toy swords and toy armour. On the girls' festival—the Feast of Dolls—there is no outward and visible display. The fact of a girl having been born in the family is not considered a matter to be boasted of. On this feast there is a great display indoors of dolls. As a matter of fact dolls form a very important part of the heirlooms of every Japanese family of any importance. When a girl is born a pair of dolls are procured for her. Dolls are much more seriously treated than they are in European countries, where they are bought with the full knowledge that they will quickly be destroyed. In Japan the dolls are packed away for nearly the whole of the year in the go-down, and are only produced at this particular festival. I may add that not only the dolls themselves but furniture for them are largely in request in Japan, and that this dolls' festival is really a very important function in the national life.

New Year's festival is the great day of the year in Japan. In this respect it approximates to our Christmas. Not only the houses but the streets are decorated, and every town in the land has at this particular season an unusually festive appearance. At this period visits are exchanged, and New Year's presents are the correct thing.

On the Bon Matsuri, or All Souls' Day, the Japanese have a custom somewhat similar to that which obtains in Roman Catholic countries on the 2nd of November. On the first night of the feast the tombs of the dead during the past year are adorned with Japanese lanterns. On the second night the remaining tombs are likewise decorated, while on the third night it is the custom, although it is now somewhat falling into desuetude, for the relatives of the dead to launch toy vessels made of straw laden with fruit and coins as well as a lantern. These toy ships have toy sails, and the dead are supposed to sail in them to oblivion until next year's festival. These toy ships, of course, catch fire from the lanterns. Not so very many years ago the spectacle of these little vessels catching fire on some large bay was a very pretty one. I am afraid this feast has a tendency to die out—a fact which is greatly to be regretted, as there is behind it much that is poetical and beautiful.

Wrestling, as most people know, is a favourite amusement of the Japanese, and wrestling matches excite quite as much interest as boxing used to do in this country. Of late years English people have taken much interest in Ju Jitsu. The Japanese style of wrestling is certainly peculiar, and training does not apparently enter so much into it as is considered essential in reference to displays of strength or skill in this country. One sometimes sees very expert Japanese wrestlers who are not only fat but bloated.

The Japanese have long been celebrated archers, and archery, though it is largely on the wane, is much more in evidence than is the case in this country. It is an art in which a great many of the people excel, and archery grounds still exist in many of the towns.

Marriages and christenings have important parts in the social life of the people. These ceremonies, however, are not quite so obtrusive as they are in Western lands. As regards christenings, if I may use such a term in reference to a non-Christian people, the first, or almost the first, ceremony in reference to the infant in Japan is, or used to be, the shaving of its head thirty days after birth, after which it was taken to the temple to make its first offering, a pecuniary one, to the gods. This shaving of babies is no doubt diminishing, at any rate in the large towns.

STREET SCENE ON NEW YEAR'S DAY

FROM A PRINT BY HIROSHIGE

Indeed, everything in regard to the dressing of and dealing with the hair in Japan is, if I may use the term, in a state of transition.

Some writers on Japan have been impressed by the fact that the Japanese appear to be more concerned about the dead than the living. Ancestor worship plays an important part in the religious economy of Japanese life, and, as I have shown, the All Souls' Day in Japan is an important national festival. But the respect that these people have for their dead is not shown only on one or two or three days of the year; it may be deduced from a visit to any of their cemeteries. These are nearly always picturesquely situated, adorned with beautiful trees, and exquisitely kept in order. Indeed, the cemeteries are in striking contrast to those of European countries. The hideous and inartistic tombstones and monuments, the urns and angels, and the stereotyped conventionalities of graveyards in this country are all absent. There is usually only a simple tablet over each grave bearing the name of the deceased and the date of his death, and occasionally some simple word or two summing up succinctly those qualities he had, or was supposed to have, possessed. Near each grave is usually a flower-vase, and it is nearly always filled with fresh flowers. As I have remarked, flowers play an important part in the lives of the Japanese people, and with them no part is more important than the decoration of the graves of their dead. In England flowers also play an important part in connection with the dead—on the day of the funeral. It is then considered the correct thing for every one who knew the deceased to send a wreath to be placed upon his coffin. These wreaths, frequently exceedingly numerous, are conveyed to the cemetery, where they are allowed to rot on top of the grave. To me there is no more mournful sight than a visit to a great London cemetery, where one sees these rotting emblems, which quite palpably meant nothing save the practice of a conventionality. The Japanese, however poor his worldly circumstances may be, is not content with flowers, costly flowers on the day of the funeral; he places his vase alongside the grave of the departed, and by keeping that vase filled with fresh and beautiful flowers he sets forth as far as he possibly can his feeling of respect for the dead and the fact that the dead one still lives in his memory.

One cannot study, however cursorily, the lives of the Japanese people on the whole without being convinced of the fact that there is among them not only a total absence of but no desire whatever for luxury. The whole conception of life among these people seems to me to be a healthy and a simple one. It is not in any way, or at any rate to any great extent, a material conception. The ordinary Japanese—the peasant, for example—does not hanker after a time when he will have more to eat and more to drink. He finds himself placed in a certain position in life, and he attempts to get the best out of life that he can. I do not suggest, of course, that the Japanese peasant has ever philosophically discussed this matter with himself or perhaps thought deeply, if at all, about it. I am merely recording what his view of life is judging by his actions. He, I feel confident, enjoys life. In some respects his life no doubt is a hard one, but it has its alleviations, and if I judge him aright the ordinary Japanese does not let his mind dwell overmuch on his hardships, but is content to get what pleasure he can out of his surrounding conditions.

One very pleasing characteristic of the Japanese men and women to which I have already referred is the habit of personal cleanliness. In every town in the country public baths are numerous, and every house of any pretensions has a bath-room. The Japanese use extremely hot water to wash in. The women do not enter the bath immediately upon undressing, but in the first instance, throwing some pailsful of water over the body, they sit on the floor and scrub themselves with bran prior to entering the bath, performing this operation two or three times. Men do not indulge in a similar practice, and I have never been able to understand why this different mode of bathing should obtain in reference to the two sexes. In houses possessing a bath-room the bath consists merely of a wooden tub with a stove to heat the water. The bath is used by the whole family in succession—father, mother, children, servants. Shampooing also forms an important part of the Japanese system of cleanliness. It is not, as in this country, confined to the head, but approximates to what we term massage, and consists in a rubbing of the muscles of the body—a fact which not only has a beneficial effect physically, but is also efficacious in the direction of cleanliness.

Nearly every house in Japan possesses a garden, and the garden is a source of perpetual delight to every Japanese. He is enabled to give full vent therein to his love of flowers. Some critics have found fault with Japanese gardens on account of their monotony. Miniature lakes, grass plots, dwarfed trees, and trees clipped and trained into representations of objects animate and inanimate are the prevailing characteristics. A similar remark might, however, be made in regard to the gardens of, say, London suburban houses, with this exception—that the Japanese gardens show infinitely more good taste on the part of the cultivators of them. These little gardens throw a brightness into the life of the people which it is impossible to estimate.

In the chapter which I have devoted to the religions of the Japanese people, I have remarked that religion appears to be losing its influence upon the educated classes of the country, who are quickly developing into agnostics. No such remark can, however, be made in reference to the great mass of the Japanese people. For them religion is an actuality. Take it out of their lives and you will take much that makes their lives not only enjoyable but endurable. As a writer on Japan has somewhat irreverently observed, the Japanese "is very chummy with heaven. He just as readily invokes the aid of his household gods in the pursuit of his amours as in less illegitimate aspirations. He regards them as kind friends who will help, rather than as severe censors who have to be propitiated." The spiritual aspect of the Deity has not, I think, entered at all into the conceptions of the ordinary Japanese. His ideas in regard to God or the gods—his pantheon is a large and a comprehensive one—are altogether anthropomorphic. Every action of his life, however small, is in some way or other connected with an unseen world. In this matter, Buddhism and Shintoism have got rather mixed, and, as I have elsewhere said, if the founder of Buddhism were re-incarnated in Japan to-day, he would find it difficult to recognise his religion in some of the developments of Buddhism as it exists in Japan. Nevertheless, this anthropomorphic idea of God, however it may fit the Japanese for the next world, undoubtedly comforts him in this. The religious festivals, which are numerous, are gala days in his life, and the services of religion bring him undoubtedly much consolation. But he does not of necessity go to a temple to conduct that uplifting of the heart which is, after all, the best service of man to the Creator. Every house has its little shrine, and although some superior persons may laugh at the act of burning a joss-stick, or some other trivial act of worship, as merely ignorant superstition, I think the unprejudiced man would look rather at the motive which inspired the act. If this poor ignorant native burns his joss-stick, makes his offering of a cake, lights a lamp in front of an image, or takes part in any other act which in effect means the lifting up of his soul to something higher and greater than himself that he can now only see through a glass darkly, surely he ought not to be condemned. At any rate I will pass no condemnation on him. Outside the accretions which have undoubtedly come upon Buddhism and Shintoism in the many centuries they have existed in Japan, I desire once more to emphasise the fact, to which I have previously made reference, that both these religions have had, and I believe still have, a beneficial effect, from a moral point of view, on the Japanese people. There is nothing in their ethical code to which the most censorious person can raise the slightest objection. They have inculcated on the Japanese people through all the ages, not only the necessity, but the advisability of doing good. Buddhism, in particular, has preached the doctrine of doing good, not only to one's fellow-creatures but to the whole of animate nature. These two religions have, in my opinion, placed the ethical conceptions of the Japanese people on a high plane.

In my remarks on the people of Japan I do not think I can more effectually sum up their salient characteristics than has been done by the writer of a guide to that country. " The courtly demeanour of the people," he says, "is a matter of remark with all who visit Japan, and so universal is the studied politeness of all classes that the casual observer would conclude that it was innate and born of the nature of the people; and probably the quality has become somewhat of a national characteristic, having been held in such high esteem, and so universally taught for so many centuries—at least, it seems to be as natural for them to be polite and formal as it is for them to breathe. Their religion teaches the fundamental tenets of true politeness, in that it inculcates the reverence to parents as one of the highest virtues. The family circle fosters the germs of the great national trait of ceremonious politeness. Deference to age is universal with the young. The respect paid to parents does not cease when the children are mature men and women. It is considered a privilege as well as an evidence of filial duty to study the wants and wishes of the parents, even before the necessities of the progeny of those who have households of their own."

I do not think that it is necessary for me to add much to these wise and pregnant remarks. The more one studies the Japanese people, the more I think one's admiration of them increases. They have, in my opinion, in many respects arrived, probably as the result of the accumulated experience of many ages, at a right perception and conception of the philosophy of life. Judged from the highest, and as I think only true, standpoint, that is the standpoint of happiness not in a merely material but in a spiritual form, they have reached a condition that but few nations have yet attained. They may provoke the pity of the man who believes in full diet and plenty of it, and who fails to comprehend how a people living on a meagre fare of fish and rice can be contented, much less happy, but the Japanese in his philosophy has realised a fact that happiness is something other than material, and that a man or woman can be largely independent of the accidentals of life and can attain a realisation of true happiness by keeping under the, too often, supremacy of matter over mind in the average human being.

CHAPTER VII

TRADE—COMMERCE—AND INDUSTRIES

NOTHING is perhaps so strongly indicative of the progress that Japan has made as the record of her trade and commerce. I have no intention of inflicting on my readers a mass of figures, but I shall have to give a few in order to convey some idea as to the country's material development of recent years. Japan, it must be recollected, is in her youth in respect of everything connected with commerce and industry. When the country was isolated it exported and imported practically nothing, and its productions were simply such as were necessary for the inhabitants, then far less numerous than at present. When the Revolution took place trade and commerce were still at a very low ebb, and the Japanese connected with trade was looked upon with more or less of contempt, the soldier's and the politician's being the only careers held much in esteem. For innumerable centuries the chief industry of Japan was agriculture, and even to-day more than half of the population is engaged thereon. Partly owing to religious influences, and partly from other causes, the mass of the people have been, and still are in effect, vegetarians.

The present trade of Japan is in startling contrast with

that of her near neighbour China, which, with an area about twenty-three times greater, and a population nearly nine times as large, has actually a smaller volume of exports. All the statistics available in reference to Japan's trade, commerce, and industries point to the enormous and annually increasing development of the country. Indeed, the trade has marvellously increased of recent years. Since 1890 the annual value of Japan's exports has risen from £5,000,000 to £35,000,000, the imports from £8,000,000 to £44,000,000. That the imports will continue in similar progression, or indeed to anything like the same amount, I do not believe. Japan of recent years has imported machinery, largely from Europe and America, and used it as patterns to be copied or improved upon by her own workmen. Out of 25 cotton-mills, for example, in Osaka, the machinery for one had been imported from the United States. The rest the Japanese have made themselves from the imported pattern. There were also in Osaka recently 30 flour-mills ready for shipment to the wheat regions of Manchuria. One of these mills had been imported from America, while the remaining 29 have been constructed in Osaka at a cost for each of not more than one-fifth that paid for the imported mill.

Shortly after peace had been declared between Russia and Japan, the Marquis Ito is reported to have said to Mr. McKinley: "You need not be afraid that we will allow Japanese labourers to come to the United States. We need them at home. In a couple of months we will bring home a million men from Manchuria. We are going to teach them all how to manufacture everything in the world with the best labour-saving machinery to be found. Instead of sending you cheap labour we will sell you American goods cheaper than you can manufacture them yourselves." The Japanese Government seems to some extent to be going in for a policy of State Socialism. The tobacco trade in the Empire is now entirely controlled by the Government. The Tobacco Law extinguished private tobacco dealers and makers, the Government took over whatever factories it deemed suitable for the purpose, built others, and now makes a profit of about £3,000,000 sterling annually, while the tobacco is said to be of a superior quality and the workmen better paid than was the case under private enterprise. How far Japan intends to go in the direction of State Socialism I am not in a position to say. Many modern Japanese statesmen are quite convinced of the fact that the private exploitation of industry is a great evil and one that ought to be put a stop to. On the other hand, there are Japanese statesmen who are firmly convinced that the State control of industries can only result in the destruction of individual initiative and genius, with the inevitable result of reducing everybody to a dead level of incompetence. In this matter Japan will have, as other nations have had, to work out her own salvation. In the process of experiment many mistakes will no doubt be made, but Japan starts with this advantage in respect of State Socialism, precisely as in regard to her Army and Navy—that her statesmen, her leading public men, her great thinkers, have no prejudices or preconceived ideas. All they desire is that the nation as a whole shall boldly advance on that path of progress by the lines which shall best serve to place the country in a commanding position among the Great Powers of the world, and at the same time to promote the happiness, comfort, and prosperity of the people.

The Japanese are great in imitation, but they are

greater perhaps in their powers of adaptation. They have so far shown a peculiar faculty for fitting to Japanese requirements and conditions the machinery, science, industry, &c., necessary to their proper development. Japan is without doubt now keenly alive, marshalling all her industrial forces in the direction of seeking to become supreme in the trade and commerce of the Far East. The aim of Japanese statesmen is to make their country self-productive and self-sustaining. We may, I think, accordingly look forward to the time, not very far distant, when Japan will cease to import machinery and other foreign products for which there has hitherto been a brisk demand, when she will build her own warships and merchant steamers, as she now partially does, and generally be largely independent of those Western Powers of which she has heretofore been such a good customer.

At the present time the chief manufactures of the country are silk, cotton, cotton yarn, paper, glass, porcelain, and Japan ware, matches and bronzes, while shipbuilding has greatly developed of recent years. The principal imports are raw cotton, metals, wool, drugs, rails and machinery generally, as well as sugar and, strange to say, rice. Japan exports silk, cotton, tea, coal, camphor and, let me add, matches and curios. The trade in the latter has assumed considerable proportions, and I fear I must add that much of what is exported is made exclusively for the European market. According to the latest figures, the country's annual exports amounted to about £35,000,000, and its imports to about £44,000,000. I venture to prophesy that these figures will ere long be largely inverted.

Silk is the most important item of Japan's foreign trade. The rearing of silkworms has been assiduously undertaken from time immemorial, or "the ages eternal" according to some Japanese historians. Like so many other arts and industries of the country, silkworms are believed to have been introduced from China. For some time prior to the opening of Japan to European trade and influences the silk industry had rather languished owing to the enforcement of certain sumptuary laws confining the wearing of silk garments to a select class of the community, but so soon as Japan discarded her policy of isolation from the rest of the world the production of and demand for silk rapidly increased, and the trade in it has now assumed considerable dimensions. Strange to say, silk is still in Japan what linen was at one time in the North of Ireland —a by-industry of the farmer, a room in his house being kept as a rearing chamber for the silkworms, which are carefully looked after by his family. According to official returns, there are rather more than two and a half million families so engaged, and nearly half a million silk manufacturers. The largest part of the silk exported goes to the United States of America. Closely allied with the production of silk is the mulberry-tree, the leaves of which form the staple food of the silkworm. This plant is cultivated with great care throughout the country, and indeed there are many mulberry farms entirely devoted to the culture of the tree and the conservation of its leaves.

Rice, as I have elsewhere stated, forms the principal article of food of the Japanese people. Japan at present does not produce quite sufficient rice for the consumption of her population, and a large quantity has, accordingly, to be imported. The danger of this for an island country has been quite as often emphasised by Japanese statesmen as the similar danger in respect of the wheat supply of Great Britain has been by English economists. Many practical steps have been taken on the initiative of the Japanese Government in the direction of improving the cultivation of rice, the irrigation of the fields, &c. As time goes on no doubt the food of the people will become more varied. Indeed, there has been a movement in that direction, especially in the large towns. A nation which largely lives on one article of diet, the production of which is subject to the vicissitudes of good and bad harvests, is, it must be admitted, not in a satisfactory position in reference to the food of its people.

If rice is the national food, tea is emphatically the national beverage, despite the large consumption of saké and the increasing consumption of the really excellent beer now brewed in Japan. Like most other things, the tea-shrub is said to have been imported into Japan from China. Almost since the opening of the country, the United States has been Japan's best customer in respect of tea, and she has from time to time fallen into line with the requirements of the United States Government in regard to the quality of tea permitted to be imported into that country. For instance, when, in 1897, the United States Legislature passed a law forbidding the importation of tea of inferior quality and providing for the inspection of all imported tea by a fixed standard sample, the Tea Traders Association of Japan established tea inspection offices in Yokohama and other ports, and all the tea exported from the country was and still is passed through these offices. The tea is rigidly tested, and if it comes up to the required standard is shipped in bond to the United States. The quality of the tea is thus amply guaranteed, and it, accordingly, commands a high price in the American Continent. The value of the tea exported to the United States amounts to something like £1,200,000, and there are no signs of any falling off in the demand for it. Canada is also a good customer of Japan for the same article, but Great Britain and the other European countries at present take no Japanese tea. I do not know why this is the case as the tea is really excellent, and it has, as regards what is exported, the decided advantage of being inspected by experts and the quality guaranteed. The tea industry is undoubtedly one of great national importance, the total annual production amounting to about 65,000,000 pounds, the greater portion of which is, of course, consumed in the country.

I have already referred to the importance of Japanese arboriculture, and to the steps taken by the Japanese Government in reference to the administration of forests and the planting with trees of various parts of the country not suitable for agriculture. The State at the present time owns about 54,000,000 acres of forests, which are palpably a very great national asset. I may mention that the petroleum industry is growing in Japan. The quantity of petroleum in the country is believed to be very great, and every year new fields are being developed. The consumption of oil by the people is considerable, and it is hoped that ere long Japan will be able to produce all that she requires. The petroleum is somewhat crude, providing about 50 per cent. of burning oil.

Tobacco, as I have elsewhere remarked, is now a State monopoly, and forms a considerable item in the State revenue. The quality has much improved since the manufacture of it has ceased to be a private industry. The Japanese are inveterate smokers, and the intervention of the State in this matter, although it has been criticised by political economists in the country and out of it, and is undoubtedly open to criticism from some points of view, has, I think, been justified by results. The making of sugar from beetroot has been attempted in Japan, but the results have not been over-successful. The efforts in this direction are, however, being persisted in, and it is hoped that, especially in Formosa, the beet-sugar industry may develop in importance.

The manufacture of paper in Japan has long been an important national industry. Paper has been and still is used there for many purposes for which it has never been utilised in European countries. Originally it was largely made from rice, and the mulberry shrub has also been used for paper manufacture. The rise and development of a newspaper press in Japan and the impetus given to printing has, of course, largely increased the demand for paper. This is being met by the adaptation of other vegetable products for the purpose of making paper, and it seems quite certain that Japan will be totally independent of any importation of foreign paper to meet the great and greatly increasing demand for that article in the country.

Salt is, I may remark, a Government monopoly in Japan. No one except the Government, or some person licensed by the Government, is allowed to import salt from abroad, while no one can manufacture salt without Government permission. Salt made by salt manufacturers is purchased by the Government, which sells it at a fixed price. This particular monopoly has only recently been established, and the reason put forward for it is a desire to improve and develop the salt industry and at the same time to add to the national revenue. Whether a monopoly in what is a necessary of life is economically defensible is a question, to my mind, hardly open to argument. That the revenue of the country will benefit by the salt monopoly is unquestionable.

As might have been expected, the opening up of Japan to Western influences has induced or produced, *inter alia*, some Western forms of political and social and, indeed, socialistic associations. The antagonism between capital and labour and the many vexed and intricate questions involved in the quarrel are already beginning to make themselves felt in Japan. It was, I suppose, inevitable. Labour is an important factor in an industrial nation like Japan, and there is already heard the cry—call it fact or fallacy as you choose—with which we are now so familiar in this country and on the Continent, that labour is the source of all wealth. Japan will no doubt, like other countries, sooner or later have to face a solution of the problems involved in these recurring disputes and this apparently deep-rooted antagonism between the possessors of wealth and the possessors of muscle. Already many associations have been established whose aim and object is to voice the sentiments of labour and assert its rights. Indeed, there is a newspaper, the *Labour World*, the champion of the rights of the Japanese workmen. So far the law in Japan does not regard with as tolerant an eye as is the case in this country labour demonstrations and the occasionally reckless oratory of labour champions. The police regulations forbid the working classes embarking in collective movements and demonstrating against their employers in the matter of wages and working hours. A suggestion of a strike of workmen is officially regarded with an unfriendly eye, and strikes themselves, picketing, and various other Western methods of coercing employers to come round to the views of the employed, would not at present be tolerated in Japan. No doubt these Western devices will assert themselves in time. The attempt to keep down the effective outcome of labour organisation in

RICE PLANTING, PROVINCE OF HOKI

FROM A PRINT BY HIROSHIGE

a country with an enormous labour population is not likely to be successful for long. Socialism is making great progress in Japan, and the State has, whether consciously or not, given it a certain amount of countenance by the steps it has taken in reference to the tobacco and salt industries, &c. The extent to which newspapers are now read in Japan—a matter I refer to more fully in another chapter—will undoubtedly tend to mould public opinion to such a degree that no Government could afford to resist it.

The trade, commerce, and industries of Japan appear to me to be, on the whole, in a healthy and flourishing condition. In them, and of course in her industrious population, Japan possesses a magnificent asset. The country is rich in undeveloped resources of various kinds, the people are patriotic to a degree, and I feel sure that the additional burdens which the recent war with Russia has for the time entailed will be cheerfully borne. I am confident, moreover, that under the wise guidance of the Emperor and her present statesmen Japan will make successful efforts to liquidate her public debt, to relieve herself of her foreign liabilities, and generally to proceed untrammelled and unshackled on that path of progress and material development that, I believe, lies before her, and which will, I am sure, at no far-distant date place her securely and permanently in the position of one of the Great World Powers.

CHAPTER VIII

JAPAN'S FINANCIAL BURDENS AND RESOURCES

THERE are a good many people, some so-called financial experts among the number, who are of opinion, and have expressed themselves to that effect, that the financial position of Japan is an unsound one. They depict that country as weighed down with a load of debt, mostly incurred for her warlike operations against Russia, and the revenue as largely mortgaged for the payment of the interest on that debt. Some of these experts have told us that the facility with which Japan was able to raise loans on comparatively moderate terms in the European money-markets, and the rush that was made by investors to subscribe to her loans, are matters which must have a baneful effect on the rulers of Japan. These latter, we are assured, found themselves in the position not only of being able to raise money easily, but of positively having to refuse money which was forced upon them by eager investors when the Japanese loans were put upon the market. The result was, so it has been said, to encourage extravagance in expenditure and to lead Japan to suppose that whenever she wanted money for any purpose she had only to come to Europe and ask for it. The financial experts who so argue, if such puerile assertions can be dignified by the name of argument, talk as if Japan were like a child with a new toy. The Japanese statesmen—in which term I of course include the Mikado, one of the world's greatest statesmen—are by no means so simple as some of these financial experts would have us believe. Indeed, I will go further, and venture to assert that the statesmen are far more astute than the experts. The former emphatically know what they are about, financially and otherwise, and they are assuredly in no need of any Occidental giving them a lead in the matter. If I desired to adduce any evidence on that head I need only point to the *Financial and Economical Annual of Japan*, published every year at the Government printing office in Tokio. This exhaustive work deals with the different departments of Government. The section I have before me, which is for the year 1905, treats of the Department of Finance and it certainly serves, and very effectively serves, to show that the Japanese are not, as they so often have been depicted, children in matters of this kind. This Government handbook is not only exhaustive but illuminative. Published in English, everything of which it treats is explained in simple and concise language. There is an entire absence of that official jargon which tends, even if it is not intended, to render Government publications in this country unintelligible to the ordinary reader. The plain man who peruses this Japanese year-book can at least understand it, and he will, among other things, grasp the fact that the Japanese have got the whole question of finance in all its ramifications at their fingers' ends.

The total National Debt of Japan in 1905 amounted to 994,437,340 yen, or, roughly, £100,000,000 sterling—a sum which the publication I have referred to works out to be at the rate of 19·548 yen, or about 39s. per head of the population. Of the debt some £43,000,000 was incurred to defray a part of the cost of the war with Russia. As an indication of the estimate of the credit of Japan within her own territory as well as abroad, I may record the fact that the Exchequer Bonds which were issued in the country in 1904 and 1905 for the purpose of defraying the extraordinary expenses of the war were largely over-subscribed, the first issue to the extent of 452 per cent., the second 322 per cent., the third 246 per cent., and the fourth 490 per cent.—a record surely! Abroad Japan's loans were no less successful. The three issues made in Europe during the war were literally rushed for by the investing public, with the result that whereas in May, 1904, Japan offered for subscription a loan of £10,000,000, the issue price being £93 10s. and the rate of interest 6 per cent., in March, 1905, despite the fact of two previous loans and the exhaustion of the country incidental to a long and expensive war, she was able to place on the market a loan of thirty millions at 4½ per cent. interest, the issue price being £90.

A National Debt which amounts to less than £2 per head of the population compares very favourably with that of Great Britain, which totals up to something like £19 per head, leaving out of account the immense and yearly growing indebtedness of our great cities and towns. Furthermore, almost the whole of the National Debt of this country, as of the European Powers generally, has been incurred not only for unproductive, but as a matter of fact for destructive purposes. The vast loans of Europe have been raised for the purpose of waging bloody wars, some at least of which history has pronounced to have been gigantic, not to say wicked, blunders. Much of the

National Debt of Japan, on the contrary, has been incurred for useful, productive, and even remunerative purposes—improving the means of transport, constructing railways, &c. The various loans outstanding up to the year 1887, on which Japan was paying very high rates of interest, as much as 9 per cent. on one foreign loan, were in that year converted and consolidated by the issue of a loan bearing interest at the rate of 5 per cent. per annum—a proceeding which materially improved Japan's financial position and demonstrated that her credit stood high.

The war with China in 1894–5 necessitated fresh borrowing to the amount of over £12,000,000. Subsequent loans were issued in order to extend the railway system of the country and so develop its trade, for such public works as the establishment of a steel foundry, the extension of the telephone system, the introduction of the leaf tobacco monopoly, for the development of Formosa and, another most important matter, the redemption of paper-money. In the early days of her expansion Japan suffered greatly from the evils of inconvertible paper-money and strenuous efforts had for a long time been made by the Government for the redemption of the paper-money and the improvement of the general financial condition. In 1890 it was found that the reserve fund kept in the Treasury for the exchange of paper-money of 1 yen and upwards was insufficient to meet the demand. To meet this emergency, the maximum amount of convertible bank-notes issued by the Bank of Japan against securities was increased from 70,000,000 yen (£7,169,927) to 85,000,000 yen (£8,706,340), of which sum 22,000,000 yen were advanced to the Government without interest. This sum added to the original reserve fund of 10,000,000 yen (£1,024,275) was employed for completing the redemption of paper-money of 1 yen and upward. Subsequent loans for the purposes of the war with Russia I have already referred to. Besides funded Japan has also, like this country, had experience of unfunded debt in the shape of Treasury Bills, temporary loans from the Bank of Japan, &c. Financial operations of this kind are, however, I imagine, necessary for all Governments to meet current expenses. To briefly recapitulate Japan's indebtedness and borrowings generally up to the end of March, 1905, these amounted to, in all, £140,045,030, of which sum £38,187,369 has from time to time been paid off, leaving a balance of £101,857,661 owing by the nation.

When we consider that for this large, but not unduly large, sum Japan has waged two considerable wars, and raised herself to the position of a great naval and military Power, that she has developed and organised a magnificent Army, provided herself with a strong, efficient, and thoroughly up-to-date Navy, has constructed railways and public works, and generally has placed herself in a capital position to work out her own destiny free from the fear of foreign interference, I altogether fail to see how she can be accused of financial extravagance. There is certainly no extravagance in the administration of her finances. London might, I suggest, learn much from Tokio in this matter. The system of financial check and thorough and rapid audit of public accounts is in Japan as near perfection as anything of the kind can be. Though the late war did produce, as I suppose all wars do, peculation, most of it was discovered and the punishment of the culprits was sharp and decisive. There was no opportunity for financial scandals in the campaign with Russia such as occurred during the South African War. Every country, of course, produces rogues, and war seems, *inter alia*, to breed roguery on a large scale, but in the Japanese methods of finance the checks are so effective that roguery in the public services has a bad time of it in war as well as in peace.

As I have already remarked, I am of opinion the debt of Japan is by no means excessive, especially in view of the fact that a large part of it has been devoted to purposes which are profitable. The debt works out, as I have shown, at something under £2 per head of the population, and that population is steadily increasing. That Japan is well able to pay the interest on her debt there can be no question whatever, and that when the present debt becomes due for redemption she will be able to raise the necessary funds for that purpose on terms even more favourable than those at which she has hitherto placed her loans I am confident. I must emphasise the fact, since so many persons seem to be oblivious of it, that this is no mushroom South American Republic borrowing money merely for the purpose of spending it on very unproductive and occasionally very doubtful objects, but a Great World Power sensible of its obligations, sensible likewise of the policy and necessity of maintaining the national credit, and confident that the national resources and the patriotism of its people will enable it not only to bear the present financial burdens but even greater, should these be found necessary for the defence of the country or for its development.

The ability of a nation as of an individual to discharge its debts depends of course upon its resources. No man possessing even a perfunctory knowledge of the resources of Japan would surely venture to express alarm at the increase in her debt and scepticism as to her being able to meet the annual interest on that debt as well as the constantly increasing expenses of administration. The resources of the country have, in my opinion, as yet scarcely been realised, and certainly have not been anything like fully developed. And when I use the word resources I do not employ it as it is so often employed in respect of minerals, although the mineral wealth of Japan is considerable. Her resources, as I estimate them, are to be found in her large and rapidly increasing population—a population perhaps the most industrious in the world, persevering, enterprising, methodical, and performing, whatever be its appointed task, that task with all its might as a labour of love, in fact, not as the irksome toil of the worker who is a worker simply because he can be nothing else. It is this great industrial hive which in the near future will supply China and other Eastern countries with all, or nearly all, those articles they now obtain elsewhere. What I may term the European industries of Japan have of recent years been largely developed or evolved. Take, for example, an item, insignificant in one way—that of matches. In 1904 matches to the value of 9,763,860 yen, or, roughly, one million sterling, were exported, and, strange to relate, European clothing to the value of 287,464 yen.

The glib people who talk about Japan biting off more than she can chew, and with a light heart borrowing money she will find a difficulty in repaying, have apparently not grasped the fact that Japan possesses many very eminent financiers who have quite as much, if not more, claim to be considered financial experts than some of those gentlemen who pose in that capacity here in England. The Japanese financiers have, moreover, the advantage of an intimate knowledge of their own country and its potentialities.

The Japanese Government h: always had the benefit of the advice of these singularly able men, and the result has been that its financial operations of recent years at any rate have invariably been well organised and skilfully and economically effected. I cannot speak too highly of the capacity shown by the Japanese in everything relating to banking. The Banks—of course I refer to the National Banks and not to the European Banks having branches in the country—have very quickly attained a high status in the International Banking world, and are undoubtedly on a very firm financial basis. And there are many great houses in Japan which, although not ostensibly bankers, cannot be left out of consideration in any remarks on this head. They occupy a position somewhat analogous to that of the Rothschilds in this country. Let me take for example the house of Mitsui, the name of which constantly crops up in Japanese finance.

The history of this ancient house has much that is picturesque about it, reminding one of the old merchant princes of Venice. The family originally belonged to the Jujiwara clan, and its origin is traced back to a certain Mitsui who lived as a feudal lord in the fifteenth century. At the time of the fall of the Ashikaja Shogun he lived in a state of perpetual war, and the god of war was not propitious to him. He retired to a neighbouring village and became the overlord of the district. He was succeeded by his son, who removed to Matsusuzaka, where he settled down as a private citizen and man of business, and laid the foundations of the present Mitsui house. In the middle of the sixteenth century his descendant became a merchant. His son moved to Kyoto, where he started a large goods store, which is represented in Tokio to-day by the Mitsui Hofukuten. Subsequently, at the beginning of the seventeenth century, a member of the same house invented and introduced the system of retailing for cash, which was an absolute revolution of business methods at that time in Japan. In addition to that he organised an excellent system for the remittance of money from one part of the country to the other, as also a carrier's business—two very remarkable facts when one remembers in what a primitive and elementary condition of development the monetary business of Japan was at that period. In the year 1687 the Mitsuis were appointed by the Government purveyors and controllers of the public exchange, and in recognition of the excellent manner in which the duties were performed, they were given the grant of a large estate in Yeddo.

In 1723 the head of the family, carrying out the verbal wishes of his father, assembled his brothers and sisters and then and there drew up in writing a set of family rules which have ever since been practically the articles of association of the house of Mitsui. These rules embodied on business-like lines and in business-like language the principle that the family and not the individual forms the ultimate union in Eastern life. It was not one or the other of the six brothers of which the family consisted when these rules were drawn up that was to trade, but the whole family as one unit. There was to be unlimited liability as far as the property of each one was concerned, and the profits of all were to be divided. This agreement is the identical one under which the great house of Mitsui is run to-day. Under it the family prospered exceedingly, so that when Japan decided to take on some portion of Western civilisation, the Mitsuis acted as the principal financial agents of the Government, and it was mainly owing to the enormous financial resources of the house placed by them at the disposal of the Government that the country was enabled at the period of the revolution to pass successfully through what might have been a most disastrous crisis. As some reward for the great services rendered at the time, the present head of the house was created a peer. Since the opening of Japan to Western influence the business of the Mitsuis has enormously increased, and has been extended in various directions. In 1876 their money exchange business was converted into a Bank on the joint stock system, but with unlimited liability as far as the Mitsui family was concerned. In the same year, for the purpose of engaging in general foreign trade, the Mitsui Bussan Kwiasha was formed, better known in Europe and America as Mitsui & Co. In 1899 the family acquired from the Government the concession of the Meike coal-mines, and there was then formed the Mitsui Kaishan, or Mining Department, which has the management of this mining concession together with many others which have since been acquired.

To-day the house of Mitsui consists of eleven families under a system of joint liability bound together by the old rules drawn up close upon two centuries back. The wealth of the collective families is unquestionably great, and the confidence of the people of Japan in this great financial firm is shown by the immense amount of money it holds on deposit. In one or other branches of their varied businesses they give employment to a very large number of persons. They have initiated an exceedingly interesting system of insurance for their employees. Each is allowed 10 per cent. interest on his wages up to three years on condition of its being deposited in the Mitsui Bank, with the proviso that the sum shall be forfeited in case of the embezzlement of any of the Company's money.

During the late war, as well as in that with China, the Mitsui house had immense transactions with the Government in providing war material, steamers for transport, supplies, &c., and their magnificent organisation enabled them to carry out their various undertakings without the slightest hitch. I may also add that the name of Mitsui headed the various charitable funds which were started in the country in connection with the war. I am sure that this necessarily imperfect sketch of this famous Japanese house will convince my readers of the fact that in finance, as in other respects, Japan has already shown a capacity for holding her own with Western nations.

I have headed this chapter "Japan's Financial Burdens and Resources," but I am not quite sure that the word "burdens" is not a misnomer. Japan appears to me—and I may claim to have studied the matter with some little attention—to have no financial burdens, if burdens be taken to mean something that is inconveniently felt, that is difficult to carry. There is here no people weighed down under the crushing incubus of debt. There is a springiness and alertness, a go-ahead energy about the nation—symptoms not usually connected with the carrying of burdens. Japan seems to me to be in somewhat the same position in regard to finance as France was after the close of the war with Germany when the former nation found itself saddled with a tremendous debt incurred for war expenditure and the indemnity which had to be paid to the conquering nation. The fact, however, as we all know, instead of depressing the French people seems to have put the whole country on its mettle, with the result that the heavy interest of the enormous debt was easily met and effective steps taken to reduce the principal. The borrowings of Japan in

Europe in the future are likely to be small, because she will be able to obtain what she needs at home, and provided she is not drawn into any war she will find her expanding revenue sufficient not only for the current expenses of administration as well as for the interest on her debt, but over and above all this enabling her year by year to provide a sinking fund which will in due course materially reduce even if it does not entirely extinguish the national indebtedness. In my opinion Japan can look forward to its financial future with equanimity. In regard to its financial past it has the satisfaction of thinking that heavy in one sense though its financial obligations be they have not at any rate been squandered for unworthy purposes.

CHAPTER IX

EDUCATION

IN England a vast amount was last year heard respecting education. Speakers on platforms and writers in newspapers and other periodical literature day by day and week by week for many months kept pouring forth words, words, words on this matter. It is not my intention to refer at all beyond what I have said to the somewhat lively education controversy in England which even as I write is by no means ended. Any such reference would be out of place in a book of this kind, and even were it not I confess I have no inclination whatever to rush into this particular fray. But it seems to me a curious fact that other countries, Japan amongst the number, have long since settled, and apparently settled satisfactorily, a problem which here in England is still under discussion, acrid discussion, and is yet quite evidently far from being permanently solved. The provisions and arrangements a nation has made for the education of its youth are, to my mind, an excellent test of the precise standard to which its civilisation has attained; because the future of a nation is with its youth, and that future must largely depend on the extent to and the manner in which its youth have been taught not only all those subjects which are commonly classified as knowledge but their duties and responsibilities as citizens. Judged by this test, Japan has every right to rank high among the nations of the world. And it can also be said of her in this matter that the education of her people is no new thing. It is not one among the many things she has learned from the West. Education was in vogue in Japan when that country was isolated from the rest of the world. Certainly Japan's contact with Europe and America has vastly improved her educational system, enabling her, as it has done, to utilise to the full the great advance there has been in scientific knowledge of every description during the last half-century or so. But, as far back as the seventh century, if history or tradition be correct, an educational code was promulgated in Japan. Certainly this code was limited in its application to certain classes, but education was gradually extended throughout the country, and even in days somewhat remote from the present time every member of the Samurai class was expected to include the three R's, or the Japanese equivalent of them, in his curriculum. The ordinary Samurai was, in fact, as regards reading and writing an educated man at a time when British Generals and even British Sovereigns were somewhat hazy in regard to their orthography and caligraphy.

Soon after the Revolution of 1868 a Board of Education was instituted in Japan, and the whole educational system of the country—because one had existed under the rule of a Tycoon—was taken in hand and reorganised. Three years later a separate Department of Education was formed at a time almost synonymous with the setting up of School Boards in England. As soon as it got itself into working order the Education Department despatched a number of specially selected Japanese to various European countries as well as to the United States of America to inquire into and report upon the system of education in existence and its suitability for adaptation or adoption in Japan. When these representatives returned from their mission and sent in their reports a code was compiled and the Mikado, in promulgating it, declared the aims of his Government to be that education should be so diffused throughout the country that eventually there might not be a village with an ignorant family nor a family with an ignorant member. It was a noble ideal, and I may remark that, though of course it has not been realised in all its fulness and probably will not be for very many years to come, it has been to a larger extent attained than a somewhat similar ideal which the late Mr. Forster is supposed to have entertained in reference to the effect of the Education Act which established a system of compulsory education for England and Wales.

In succeeding years various changes were made in the system of national education, and in 1883 that which now exists was brought into force. This is in effect compulsory education. Since education was first organised on any plan in Japan the number under instruction has steadily risen, and at present more than 90 per cent. of the children regularly attend school. In 1873 the number was 1,180,000; it is now over 5,000,000. There are about 29,000 primary schools, of which about 6,500 are higher primary schools with a million pupils. The total cost of the primary schools is somewhere about £3,000,000.

The question will no doubt be asked, What kind of education do these 5,000,000 pupils receive, and to what extent is it adapted to make them good citizens of a great Empire? The subjects taught in the ordinary primary schools embrace morals, the Japanese language, arithmetic and gymnastics. One or more subjects, such as drawing, singing, or manual work may be added, and, in schools for females, sewing. In the higher primary schools the subjects of instruction include morals, the Japanese language, arithmetic, Japanese history, geography, science, drawing, singing, and gymnastics, and, in schools for females, sewing. Besides these agriculture, commerce, and manual work, as well as the English language, are optional subjects. The moral lessons taught in these schools, I may remark, are not based upon any particular religious doctrines or dogmas, but are entirely and absolutely secular.

Children have to be 6 years of age before commencing their scholastic education, and have to remain at school until they have attained 14 years. The parents or guardians of children are compelled to send them to school to complete, as a minimum of education, the ordinary primary school course. Education in the higher primary schools is not compulsory, and it is, accordingly, a pleasing fact that 60 per cent. of those children who have passed through the ordinary schools voluntarily go to the higher primary schools.

Every municipal or rural community is compelled to maintain one or more primary schools sufficient, as regards size and the number of the staff, to educate all the children in the district. The establishment of higher primary schools is voluntary, and that so many of them are in existence is ample proof that the benefit of higher education is fully appreciated in Japan. Instruction in all the schools is practically free. No fee may be charged save with the consent of the local governor, and when one is imposed it must not exceed the equivalent of 5d. per month in a town school and half that sum in a rural school.

As regards secondary education, it is compulsory for one school to be established in each of the forty-seven prefectures into which Japan is divided. The course of study at the secondary schools extends over five years, with an optional supplementary course limited to twelve months. The curriculum of the secondary school embraces morals, the Japanese and Chinese languages, one foreign language, history and geography, mathematics, natural history, physics and chemistry, the elements of law and political economy, drawing, singing, gymnastics, and drills. The course of study is uniform in all Japanese schools. Candidates for admission to the secondary schools must be over 12 years of age, and have completed the second year's course of the higher primary school. There are about three hundred of the secondary schools in existence—a number, as will be seen, six times as large as that obliged to be established by law. The pupils number over a hundred thousand and the cost approximates £500,000.

There are also 170 high schools for girls besides normal schools in each prefecture designed to train teachers for the primary and secondary schools. The course of study in these schools is for men four years, for women three years. The whole of the pupils' expenses, including the cost of their board and lodging, is paid out of local funds. There are also higher normal schools designed to train teachers for the ordinary normal schools. It will thus be seen that there is a systematic course of education for what I may term the common people in Japan, extending from the higher normal to the ordinary primary school.

There are besides in Japan higher schools, the object of which is to prepare young men for a University education. The expense of these schools is entirely borne by the State. Japan prides herself, and justly, in being unique in the possession of such schools. The course of study in them extends over three years and is split up into three departments. The pupils select the particular department into which they desire to enter, and their selection, of course, depends on the precise course of study they intend to take up on entering the University. The first department is for those who propose to study law or literature, the second for those who mean to go in for engineering, science, or agriculture, and the third for aspirants as medical men. Candidates for admission to these schools must be over 17 years of age and have completed the secondary school course.

A reference to these higher schools naturally leads up to the Imperial University of Tokio, as well as the kindred University at Kyoto. There are six colleges in the former, viz., law, medicine, engineering, literature, science, and agriculture, while Kyoto University possesses four colleges, viz., law, medicine, literature and science, and engineering. When the Imperial University was established almost all the Professors therein were Europeans or Americans, but there has been a material alteration in this respect, and now the foreign Professors are few. Most of the Japanese instructors have, however, been educated abroad. The course of study extends over four years in the case of students of law and medicine, and three years in the case of students of other subjects. There is not the same freedom in regard to study as exists at Oxford, Cambridge, and some other more or less leisurely seats of learning. In the Japanese Universities the students have to enter upon a regular prescribed course of study with some few optional subjects. The Universities confer degrees in law, medicine, engineering, literature, science, and agriculture. The examinations leading up to and for the degrees are much more severe than those in any University in this country, with the possible exception of that of London. It may interest my readers to learn that the largest number of degrees are taken in law, the smallest in science. We have heard a great deal of recent years respecting technical education in Great Britain, which many persons suggest is at a very low ebb. For what is in one sense a new country, Japan seems to have taken steps to provide an excellent system of technical education. There are a small number of State higher technical schools, agricultural, commercial, and industrious. Technical schools of lower grades are maintained by prefectures and urban bodies, and they receive grants in aid from national funds. There are in all about four hundred technical schools in the country. The few facts respecting education in Japan which I have put as tersely as possible before my readers, should, I think, convince them of the fact that in regard to this all-important question Japan has made and is making vigorous efforts—and efforts all of which are in the right direction. It must be remembered that in the education of her youth she has to face difficulties which are altogether unknown in this as in other European countries. One of these difficulties is the fact that Japanese literature is more or less mixed up with Chinese literature, and, accordingly, it is necessary for the Japanese to learn Chinese as well as Japanese characters, and also to study the Chinese classics. Another difficulty is the one I touched on in my remarks on the Japanese language, viz., the difference between the written and spoken languages of Japan. In old times the written and spoken languages were no doubt identical, but Chinese literature influenced the country to so great an extent that the written language in time became more and more Chinese, while the spoken dialect remained Japanese. The consequence is that the written language is more or less a hotch-potch of Chinese characters and the Japanese alphabet. Whether it will be possible to overcome these obvious difficulties remains to be seen. Several remedies have been proposed but none has so far been adopted. One remedy was the use of the Japanese alphabet alone for the written language, another the introduction and adoption of the European alphabet. Manifestly the difficulty of effecting such a change as the adoption of either of these plans would involve would be enormous. Still the retention of the present complicated system is without doubt the great obstacle in the way of educational progress in Japan, and it speaks eloquently for the patience and pertinacity of the youth of that country that they have effected so much in so short a time in view of the difficulties that have had to be encountered.

The strong points of the youth of Japan in the matter of education are, in my opinion, their great powers of concentration and their indomitable application to study and perseverance in whatever they undertake. Of their powers of absorption of any subject there can be no question. It has been urged, as against this, that the Japanese possess the defect not uncommon among people of any race, viz., that the capacity for rapidly assimilating knowledge is to some extent counteracted or rendered abortive by an incapacity to practically apply that knowledge. I may say for myself that though I have often heard this objection urged I have not seen any indications of this lack of ability to practically apply knowledge on the part of the Japanese. I should have thought that the Russo-Japanese war would have afforded ample demonstration of the ability of the Japanese to put to good account the knowledge they had acquired and assimilated in their seminaries.

I certainly think that the system of education, as it exists in Japan to-day, is one not only admirably adapted for the people of that country, but one from which some Western nations might learn a few things. Japan has, in her education system, settled the religious question simply by ignoring it. Her morality as inculcated in every school in the country, is a purely secular morality. I know that there are some persons who will deem secular morality a contradiction in terms. Indeed there are many eminent Japanese who do not approve of the present system. Count Okúma, for example, one of the ablest men in the country, bewails the lack of a moral standard. The upper classes have, he remarks, Chinese philosophy, the great mass of the people have nothing. In the Western world, he points out, Christianity supplies the moral standard, while in Japan some desire to return to old forms, others prefer Christianity ; some lean on Kant, others on other philosophers. Christianity may supply the moral standard in the Western world, as Count Okuma asserts, but if he has studied recent politics in a particular part of the Western world, he must have seen that Christianity in that part is by no means in accord as to the teaching of religion in its schools, or what moral code, if any, should be substituted for dogmatic instruction. Perhaps, after all, Japan has not decided amiss in for the present at any rate deciding that secular morality shall

AMATEUR CONCHOLOGISTS

FROM A PRINT BY HIROSHIGE

be the only ethical instruction given in her schools. That code which she teaches, so far as I have had an opportunity of studying it, is one which contains nothing that could be in the slightest degree objected to by the votaries of any religious system either in the East or in the West.

Although it has no direct connection with morality, secular or otherwise, it may be of interest if I give here a synopsis of the teaching given in Japanese schools in reference to the behaviour of the pupils towards foreigners. These rules have been collected by an English newspaper in Japan, and they certainly serve to show that the youth of Japan are in this matter receiving instruction which, whether regarded from an ethical standpoint or merely that of good manners, cannot be too highly commended.

" Never call after foreigners passing along the streets or roads.

" When foreigners make inquiries, answer them politely. If unable to make them understand, inform the police of the fact.

" Never accept a present from a foreigner when there is no reason for his giving it, and never charge him anything above what is proper.

" Do not crowd around a shop when a foreigner is making purchases, thereby causing him much annoyance. The continuance of this practice disgraces us as a nation.

" Since all human beings are brothers and sisters, there is no reason for fearing foreigners. Treat them as equals and act uprightly in all your dealings with them. Be neither servile nor arrogant.

" Beware of combining against the foreigner and disliking him because he is a foreigner ; men are to be judged by their conduct and not by their nationality.

" As intercourse with foreigners becomes closer and

extends over a series of years, there is danger that many Japanese may become enamoured of their ways and customs and forsake the good old customs of their forefathers. Against this danger you must be on your guard.

"Taking off your hat is the proper way to salute a foreigner. The bending of the body low is not to be commended.

"When you see a foreigner be sure and cover up naked parts of the body.

"Hold in high regard the worship of ancestors and treat your relations with warm cordiality, but do not regard a person as your enemy because he or she is a Christian.

"In going through the world you will often find a knowledge of a foreign tongue absolutely essential.

"Beware of selling your souls to foreigners and becoming their slaves. Sell them no houses or lands.

"Aim at not being beaten in your competition with foreigners. Remember that loyalty and filial piety are our most precious national treasures and do nothing to violate them."

It seems to me a pity that education on somewhat similar lines to that embodied in these interesting rules cannot be imparted to the youth of this and other European countries. It would certainly tend, I think, in the direction of good manners which are, I fear, sadly lacking in many of the pupils who have undergone a course of School Board instruction in England.

A question that may arise in regard to the details of Japanese education is how far and in what degree do the pertinacity and zeal of the youth of Japan for knowledge affect their physique. We know that *mens sana in corpore sano* is the ideal at which every one concerned with the education of young people of both sexes ought to strive,

There is no doubt whatever that too close an attention to study of any kind, too constant an exercise of the mental faculties, unless it is accompanied by a corresponding exercise of the body, very often has an injurious effect upon the human frame. Count Okuma, in referring to this matter, has pointed out that the great difficulty of the difference between the written and spoken languages is a very serious tax upon the pupils in all the schools, necessitating, as it does, the duplicating of their work. So much time, he considers, has to be spent by them in study on account of this duplicating that it is quite impossible for students to have sufficient physical exercise, while if it were decided to devote more time to exercise, the years allotted to education would have to be lengthened—a fact which must involve a serious loss in regard to the work of the nation. I do not take quite such a pessimistic view of the lack of physical education of the youth of Japan. In the first place, gymnastics form part, an important part, of the course of instruction in all schools throughout the country, and in the next place the young people of Japan, so far as I have been able to arrive at an opinion in the matter, are almost if not quite as enthusiastic in regard to various forms of outdoor sport as are those of this country. The buoyancy and enthusiasm of youth are, indeed, very much the same all over the world. It is only when youth comes to what are very often erroneously described as years of discretion that artificiality begins to assert itself. Base-ball, lawn-tennis, bicycling, and rowing are all extensively patronised by the young men of Japan, and cricket has of recent years come considerably into vogue. The students of the Imperial University have not only shown no disinclination, but, on the contrary, an avidity to combine athletics with their studies, and in base-ball especially they have more than held their own against the foreigner. I confess I have no desire to see the craze for outdoor sports which is so much in evidence in this country extending to Japan. Some of the public schools in England are much more famous for their cricket, football, and other teams than for the education imparted in them. Many a young man leaves those schools an excellent cricketer or football player, but, from an educational point of view, very badly equipped for the battle of life. The happy mean is surely the best in this as in other matters, and I venture to think that the youth of Japan in regarding education as the essential matter and outdoor sport as merely a subsidiary one have shown sound judgment.

In my remarks on education in Japan I have dealt principally with the schools for boys. I may, however, remark that in the arrangements she has made for the education of the other sex she has shown the same thoroughness. In the primary schools the boys and girls are taken in without any distinction, though separate classes are usually formed. There are subsequently higher schools for girls. The percentage of the female sex attending these schools is less than that of the other. There are in all about seventy-five of these schools in Japan with some twenty thousand pupils. The course of instruction in them is moral precepts, Japanese language, a foreign language, history, geography, mathematics, science, drawing, training for domestic affairs, cutting-out and sewing, music and gymnastics. I think in regard to these schools the Japanese authorities have shown sound judgment in decreeing that music shall not necessarily form part of the education of every young girl, but may be omitted for those pupils for whom the art may be deemed difficult.

Were a similar rule to be adopted in this country quite a number of people would be saved a large amount of unnecessary torture. There is also a higher normal school for women at Tokio, as likewise an Academy of Music. The Tokio Jiogakkwan is an institution established by some foreign philanthropists for the purpose of educating Japanese girls of a respectable class in Anglo-Saxon attainments. This institution has between two and three hundred pupils, but I am not in a position to state what measure of success, if any, it has achieved, nor indeed do I know what "Anglo-Saxon attainments" are supposed to be. Many of them I should have thought were quite unsuitable for the ordinary Japanese girl, tending, as they must, to destroy her national individuality. There is also a girls' college in Tokio called the Women's University. It does not confer degrees, but it gives a very high education, and it is largely patronised.

I stated at the commencement of this chapter that I was of opinion the provisions and arrangements a nation had made for the education of its youth were an excellent test of the standard to which its civilisation has attained. I hope the slight sketch I have given my readers of the system of education in existence in Japan will enable them to form an estimate as to the place Japan should occupy if judged by the standard referred to. In my opinion, seeing that it is less than forty years since the country passed through a drastic revolution—a revolution which destroyed all these social forces which had been in existence and had exercised a tremendous influence on the life of the people for many centuries—it is, I think, not only extraordinary but highly creditable to her rulers that Japan should have in that short interval organised and perfected such a system of education as exists in the country to-day. Under that system every boy and girl in the land receives an admirable course of instruction, and is afforded facilities for still further extending and enlarging that course, and, if his or her abilities, ambitions, and opportunities incline them that way, to proceed steadily onward in the acquisition of knowledge, until they obtain as a coping stone, that final course, in the capital either at the Imperial University or the Women's University where the sum of all the knowledge of the world is at the disposal of those who have the capacity and the aspiration to acquire it.

CHAPTER X

THE JAPANESE ARMY AND NAVY

A WORK on Japan which did not include some reference to the Army and Navy would manifestly be incomplete. It is hardly any exaggeration to assert that nothing in regard to the metamorphosis of Japan has so impressed the Western mind as the extraordinary progress of its naval and military forces. Both in this country and on the Continent it was, of course, known that Japan had been for years evolving both an Army and Navy, but I imagine most persons thought that this action on her part was merely a piece of childish extravagance, and that her land and sea forces would, if they were ever pitted against Europeans, prove as impotent as Orientals nearly always have proved. I am quite aware that naval and military experts of various nationalities who had studied matters on the spot were of a different opinion. They witnessed the high state of efficiency of both the Japanese Army and Navy, the patriotic spirit of the officers and men, their enthusiasm for their work, and that universal feeling of bravery, if it be bravery, which consists in an absolute contempt of life. Still I think, even to the experts, the splendid organisation and overwhelming superiority of Japan in her encounter with China came as somewhat of a surprise. The complete victory of the Island Nation in that struggle was, I know, to a certain extent discounted in some quarters by the stories that were published as to the wretched condition of both the Chinese Army and Navy, their utter unfitness and unpreparedness for war, the incompetence and corruption of the officers, and so on. There were many otherwise well informed persons who felt confident that though Japan had experienced little or no difficulty in mastering China, the case would be different when, if ever, she was involved in war with a European power. I do not think these doubts were prevalent or indeed present at all, in the minds of the naval and military authorities. No responsible statesman or official in Japan desired war. The Japanese are not in any sense a bellicose people. Still, the statesmen of the country were fully alive to the fact that it might be necessary to fight for the national existence. They had had experience in the past of the ambition of Russia to aggrandise herself at the expense of Japan. They saw, or thought they saw, that Russia had designs on Korea, and they were determined to frustrate those designs, and so perhaps obviate in the best manner possible future attempts on the independence of Japan itself. And hence it came about that serious efforts were directed to create an Army and Navy strong and efficient.

The creation, or perhaps it would be more correct to say the reorganisation, of the Army was entrusted, soon after the Revolution of 1868, to a few European officers, and it has proceeded throughout on European lines. The task was not so difficult as might have been expected. In old Japan the terms "soldier" and "Samurai" were synonymous, and the security of the territory of each of the great feudal princes depended on the strength of his army. The Continental system of conscription was adopted and still obtains. All Japanese males between the ages of 17 and 40 are liable to military service. The Service is divided into Active, Landwehr, Depôt, and Landsturn services. The Active service is divided into service with the colours and service with the first reserve. The former is obligatory for all who have reached the full age of 20 years, and such service is for a period of three years. Service in the first reserve is compulsory for all who have finished service with the colours, and lasts for a period of four years and four months. The Landwehr reserve is comprised of those who have finished the first reserve term, and it continues for a period of five years. The Depôt service is divided into two sections. The first, which lasts seven years and four months, is made up of those who have not been enlisted for Active service, while the second, extending over one year and four months, consists of those who have not been enlisted for first Depôt service. The Landsturn is in two divisions—one for those who have completed the term of Landwehr service and the first Depôt service, and the second for all who are not on the other services. This system of conscription, of course, lends itself to criticism, and it has been criticised by the military experts of great military nations, but on the whole it has been proved by the experience of the two wars in which Japan has been involved during the last twelve years to have worked well, and it probably answers as well as any system that could be devised, the needs of the country, and the characteristics of the people thereof. The Japanese are, as these recent wars amply demonstrated, patriotic to a degree. They not only have great powers of perseverance, but great capacities for assimilation and adaptation, and are considered by many military authorities probably the very best raw material in the world out of which to make soldiers. Conscription may not be an ideal system for any country. It is, of course, better from one point of view that the armed forces of a nation should voluntarily enlist rather than be pressed men. But conscription in Japan has never been, and is not likely to be, such a burden as is the case among some European nations. The Japanese idea of patriotism is something totally different to that which obtains in the West. The late war afforded ample evidence of that, were any needed.

The war with Russia has been so recently concluded that it is not necessary to enter at any length into a consideration of the Japanese Army. The history of that war gave ocular demonstration to the European nations, however incredulous they may previously have been on the subject, that Japan was in fact a great military Power. In the course of that war she put in the field somewhere about 700,000 men, conveyed them across the sea to a foreign country, and showed throughout the struggle a capacity for the most wonderful military organisation. The smallest details were most carefully attended to; there was an entire absence of that muddle so much in evidence when European nations are engaged in hostilities. Respecting the fighting qualities of the Japanese soldier it is hardly necessary to say anything. On the field of battle or during the long, arduous and monotonous work of a siege he has shown himself alike a model soldier. Perhaps he has shone most in the hour of victory by his moderation. Every foreign officer who saw the work done by the Japanese Army throughout the various incidents of the Russian War was lost in admiration. To me the most pleasing feature of that war was the ease with which the soldier, on coming back to Japan, returned to the peaceful pursuits of civil life. The bumptious braggadocio that European military nations have developed has no counterpart in Japan. The war was, in the estimation of the people, a sacred duty. The burdens which it entailed were cheerfully borne. The Japanese soldier bore his hardships or gave up his life equally cheerfully. At the same time the conclusion of the war came as a relief, and the mass of the soldiery gladly went through the Japanese equivalent of turning their swords into ploughshares. Japan has demonstrated that she is a great military nation, and the organisation of her Army is one that might well be studied by the military authorities of other countries.

The weak point of the Japanese Army is its cavalry. Whether cavalry in the warfare of the future will play the important part that it has played in that of the past is a matter upon which I do not care to dogmatically pronounce, especially as military authorities are by no means in agreement in regard thereto, or indeed as to the precise functions of cavalry in military warfare. The difficulties of Japan in regard to organising an efficient cavalry have been largely, if not altogether, owing to the lack of good horses in the country. The Japanese horses have not been conspicuous for quality, while the number available has not been anything like sufficient to enable the cavalry to be brought up to a proper condition of strength and efficiency. The Japanese military authorities have long been sensible of this fact, and the late war amply demonstrated it. With its usual thoroughness, the Government has, as soon as possible after the close of the war, taken steps to remedy this weak point in its military system, and quite recently two delegates of the Ministry of Agriculture have been despatched to Europe on a horse-purchase mission. Ten million yen have, I understand, been apportioned for the purpose of improving the national breed of horses, and the delegates have been instructed to purchase suitable animals for breeding. The Japanese Government has almost invariably been successful in anything it has undertaken, and I venture to predict—it is scarcely a hazardous prophesy—that the horse supply of the country will ere long be put on a satisfactory footing and the cavalry be rendered as efficient as every other branch of the Japanese Army.

There is no fear of a military autocracy in Japan. The recent war proved not only the bravery of the rank and file of the Army, but the high military talent of the officers. The art of war had evidently been studied from every point of view, and was diligently applied. The Japanese talent, in my opinion, consists not in a mere mechanical copying, but in a practical adaptation of all that is best in Western civilisation. The tactics and strategy displayed during the war with Russia showed originality in conception, brilliancy and daring. If that war did not discover a Napoleon among the Japanese generals, it can at least be said that Japan has no need of a Napoleon. As I have said, there is no fear of the development of a military autocracy in that country or the uprising of a general with Napoleonic ideas and ambition. The generals who justly earned distinction during the recent war are singularly modest men, with no capacity for self-advertising and no desire whatever for self-aggrandisement. They are not only content but anxious, now that the war is over, to sink into obscurity. History will, however, not permit of that. Their achievements in the recent campaign will long afford subject-matter for study and the instruction of the military students of the future. In this book I have as far as possible avoided mentioning names, otherwise I would gladly inscribe on its pages the names of those many generals who earned fame in the Russo-Japanese War. I feel perfectly certain that every endeavour will be made to maintain the Japanese Army in the high state of efficiency it has reached. At the same time I would emphasise the fact that that Army is intended solely for defence. Japan has, in a word, no military ambitions outside her own territory.

And as of the Army, so of the Navy. Perhaps the prowess of Japan's Fleet impressed the English people even more than the victories of her soldiers. Because the Navy, as it is to-day, is largely the outcome of English training and the application of English ideas. In the first instance Japan borrowed from the British Government the services of some of its best naval officers to develop the Japanese Navy. A naval college was established in the capital, modelled on the English system of training. A dockyard was also constructed at Yokosko under French guidance. It is, however, a mistake to suppose that Japan had no Navy or no ambitions in the direction of creating one prior to English naval officers being lent to the Japanese Government to assist in the reorganisation of the Navy. The determination to create a fleet on European lines was entertained by Japanese statesmen as far back as the 'fifties, when the European Powers and the United States of America were bringing pressure to bear on Japan with a view of obtaining trading facilities and the opening up of the country generally. The Japanese statesmen of those days were wise enough to see that unless Japan was to be permanently under the tutelage of the European Powers, it was necessary for her to construct a fleet and army on European lines. Soon afterwards a naval school, under Dutch instructors, was established at Nagasaki, and a certain number of selected officers and men were sent to Europe to undergo a course of instruction, and several war-vessels were ordered from Holland. In 1854 a two-masted ship was built in Japan from an English model, and subsequently two others. During the war between Russia and Great Britain a Russian sloop was wrecked on the Japanese coast, and permission was obtained for Japanese workmen to be employed in the repairs of the vessel, with a view of giving them an opportunity of gaining some practical knowledge of naval architecture. In 1855 the King of Holland presented a steam corvette to the Tycoon. In this year the now familiar Japanese ensign—a red ball on a white ground—was introduced, and has since remained the national flag.

On the arrival of Lord Elgin in Japan on a mission in 1857 a sailing vessel at Nagasaki was flying the flag of an Admiral of the Japanese Navy. In the same year a steam yacht was presented to the Tycoon by the late Queen Victoria, and was formally handed over to the Japanese Government by Lord Elgin. His secretary relates that the yacht got under way, commanded by a Japanese captain and manned by Japanese sailors, while her machinery was worked by Japanese engineers. The secretary, in his account of the incident, relates that "notwithstanding the horizontal cylinders and other latest improvements with which her engines were fitted, the men had learnt their lesson well, and were confident in their powers, and the yacht steamed gallantly through and round the Fleet, returning to her anchorage without a hitch." This authoritative statement ought to dispose of the absurd story which has long been a chestnut among the English community in Japan and the English naval officers on the China station, that when the old Confederate Ram, the *Stonewall Jackson*, was purchased in America and brought to Yokohama a somewhat ludicrous incident occurred. According to the story, which, I may observe, is one of the *ben trovato* order, when steam was got up in the vessel for trial purposes it had to steam round and about Yokohama Harbour, to the great danger of the foreign warships and merchant steamers there, until the steam was in due course exhausted and the machinery automatically stopped through the lack of any motive power to drive it, as the Japanese engineer in charge did not know how to shut off steam. The *Stonewall Jackson*, I may observe, did not take part in the now almost forgotten battle of Hakodate, which took place at the time of the Revolution, and may be regarded as the expiring effort of old Japan to stay the march of events in that country. In the battle of Hakodate the rebel fleet was totally destroyed, and the various clans in the country who possessed war-vessels of one kind or other presented them to the central Government. These vessels, it must be confessed, were not of much, if any, utility in the direction of forming a Navy, and I am not aware how many of them, or indeed whether any of them, were utilised for the purpose of inaugurating that Navy which has now become world-famous.

In 1858 the naval school, which, as I have already stated, had been established at Nagasaki, was transferred to Yeddo, and a few years later the Japanese Government determined to obtain the assistance of some English naval officers with a view of giving instruction in the school.

Application was accordingly made to the British Government through the Minister in Yeddo, and the sanction of the Admiralty having been obtained, a number of English naval officers were selected, and despatched to Japan as instructors in the Yeddo Naval College. Amongst these officers, it may be interesting to state, was Admiral Sir A. K. Wilson, V.C., G.C.B., the late Commander-in-Chief of the Channel Fleet. In the year 1873 a number of other naval officers were sent out from England, the previous staff having been withdrawn on the outbreak of the Civil War. This staff was in charge of Admiral Sir A. L. Douglas, till recently Commander-in-Chief at Portsmouth, and for some years subsequently an English naval officer was at the head of the instructing staff of the college. Japan was fortunate in one respect — in the Englishmen she entrusted with the evolution of her Navy. She was fortunate in attracting the men best fitted for the work, and also in inspiring them with a high conception of their task. Some Englishmen are of opinion that Japan has somewhat forgotten her obligations in this matter. Young Japan, they suggest, desires to forget the influences to which the country mainly owes its present magnificent fleet. That fleet is undoubtedly, for the most part, the outcome of English conceptions and English training. There is one man whose name, I think, deserves to be recorded in connection therewith. I refer to the late Lieutenant A. G. S. Hawes, of the Royal Marine Light Infantry, who left the English Service and worked strenuously, enthusiastically, and earnestly to build up the *personnel* of the Japanese Navy in the early 'seventies. There were others whose efforts in the same direction assisted in that consummation, but Hawes's services were unique and splendid. He believed in Japan, and he threw himself into his work with a zeal and ardour which were beyond praise. His services were dispensed with, as were those of the other English officers and men, when it was felt that Japan had learnt sufficient to work out her own destiny as a naval Power. The labours of these men may not have been adequately recognised at the time, but their work remains, and is in evidence to-day. Hawes received a decoration from the Mikado, and the British Government gave him a consular appointment in some obscure quarter of the globe, where he died a disappointed man, fully sensible of the value of the work he had performed and inspired, a firm believer in the future of Japan as a great naval Power, but disgusted with the non-recognition of his labours.

The Navy of Japan as it is to-day is a triumph of organisation. Discussing a short time ago the question with an ex-officer of the Mercantile Marine who had, by a curious chance, served as a Naval Reserve officer in both the English and Japanese Navies, he explained to me the wonderful progress of the latter by pointing out that it had been, as it were, called instantaneously into existence. The Japanese Navy, he observed, had no past and no traditions to hamper its development; its officers and administrators had only one desire—to get the best of everything in modern naval science from anywhere. There was no cult of seamanship, no dead wall of prejudice to trammel modern naval developments. There was no prejudice at the Japanese Admiralty against anything—save stagnation. Progress was the keynote and watchword of the Japanese Navy. My friend assured me that it was, as regards equipment, organisation, and general efficiency, the finest fighting force the world has ever seen. So far as my own knowledge of the matter goes, and so far as I am competent to express an opinion on the subject, I fully endorse these observations. A visit to a Japanese vessel-of-war, however perfunctory the knowledge of the visitor may be on matters naval, very soon convinces him of the fact that the Japanese naval officers and men are filled not only with ardour but enthusiasm for their profession, that efficiency and proficiency are the watchwords, and that the desire of every one connected with the Navy, from the Admiral downwards, is to maintain the *personnel* and *materiel* of the Fleet in the highest possible condition of efficiency.

If, as some Englishmen imagine is the case, there is a tendency on the part of young Japan to be oblivious of the fact that the Navy of the country is greatly indebted for its present state of efficiency to the zeal and efforts of English naval officers in its early days, there is no question that the feeling of the officers and men of the Japanese Navy to their English comrades is of a very hearty nature. The formal alliance with Great Britain was highly popular in the Japanese Fleet, and I have never heard any officer connected therewith speak in any but the highest and most cordial terms of their English *confréres*.

It is not, I think, necessary for me to refer to the deeds of and the work done by the Japanese Navy in the course of the war with Russia ; very much the same remarks that I have made in regard to the Army apply here. Nothing was lost sight of or omitted that could in the slightest degree tend to ensure or secure success. Everything seems to have been foreseen. Nothing was left to chance. The results were precisely what might have been expected, and what indeed were expected, by those who had an intimate knowledge of the manner in which the

Japanese Navy was organised for war. I regard it especially in alliance with the English Fleet, as one of the greatest safeguards for the peace of the world. I trust the alliance between this country and Japan may be of a permanent nature. I may remark in respect of the Fleet, as I have of the Army, that Japan has no unworthy ambitions. Her desire is to conserve what she possesses and to render her Island Empire secure from invasion or molestation.

Closely connected with the development of Japan's Navy is that of her Mercantile Marine. A few words in regard to it may therefore not be out of place here. The insular position and the mountainous condition of the country, as well as its extent of seaboard, early impressed on the makers of new Japan the necessity for creating not only a great mercantile fleet but also for developing the shipbuilding industry. Both these ambitions have been largely realised. At first their consummation was attended with many difficulties. The Japanese, as I have already remarked in this book, were many centuries ago enterprising sailors, but when the country was closed voyages of discovery or trade automatically came to an end. With the awakening of Japan a change immediately took place, and steps were taken to create and develop the Mercantile Marine. A Japanese gentleman, Mr. Iwasaki, in 1872 started a line of steamers, subsidised by the Government, the well-known Mitsu Bishi Company. Shortly afterwards another company was formed to compete against it. This line was also subsidised by the Government, but as the rivalry did not prove profitable to either the two lines were amalgamated in 1885 under the title of Nippon Yusen Kaisha. Since then a number of other shipping companies have been formed in Japan, and the Nippon Yusen Kaisha has largely extended its operations, opening up communication with Bombay, England, and the Continent, Melbourne, &c. In fact, the Japanese flag is now seen in many parts of the world, while the Japanese Mercantile Marine has advanced by leaps and bounds, and is still annually increasing. At the end of 1904 there were about 240 steamers flying the Japanese flag, with a gross tonnage of over 790,000. Japan now ranks high among the maritime nations of the world, and her position therein, unless I am very much mistaken, will still further advance in the years to come.

There are, I know, a great number of worthy people, both in this country and Japan, who regard the expenditure on an Army and Navy as entirely unproductive, and look forward to the halcyon days when all such expenditure shall cease and the taxation now devoted to these purposes shall be diverted to more worthy objects. I am afraid, as the world is at present constituted, there is no prospect of such a, in some respects, desirable consummation being effected. Nowadays the most effective means a nation can possess in the direction of the maintenance and enjoyment of peace is to be well prepared for war. That is a fact of which I am sure the men responsible for the government of Japan are firmly convinced; and I believe they are right. I am certain, as I have said before, that the world has nothing to fear from the armed strength of Japan by land or sea.

CHAPTER XI

JAPANESE ART—INTRODUCTORY—LACQUER WARE, POTTERY AND PORCELAIN

JAPANESE art is a subject which invites exhaustive treatment. To deal with it adequately in two or three chapters of a general work on Japan is obviously impossible. Still it is, I think, possible, within the limits at my disposal, to give my readers some conception of that art to which Japan is so greatly indebted for the extraordinary way in which she has impressed the world. The art of Japan is in a sense unique, and it may be that to some extent the Japanese atmosphere, so to speak, is essential in order to fully appreciate it. Mr. Chamberlain, in his "Things Japanese," has observed that "To show a really fine piece of lacquer to one of the uncultivated natives of Europe or America is, as the Japanese proverb says, like giving guineas to a cat." Much the same remark might, however, be made in reference to the art products of any country. Be that as it may, the Japanese people are now largely dependent on the foreigner for art patronage. It may be that this has resulted in art-artisans abandoning their old standard and devoting themselves to the manufacture of whatever pays best, prostituting the spirit of art to the promptings of gain, and compelling the native to cater for foreign taste rather than to adhere to Japanese canons of art. I am afraid that the commercial spirit is fatal to art of any kind. The true artist, like the poet, in an ideal state of existence would only work under inspiration, but, unfortunately, the artist, like the poet, is daily faced by that necessity which knows no law and demands the subsistence of the body as an essential for work of any kind.

Perhaps some of my readers might desire a definition of art. There are, I know, people in this world who can never approach the consideration of or deal with any subject unless the subject itself and every term in connection therewith is precisely defined. In reference to Japanese art I am inclined to employ the words of Mr. Walter Crane in opening, many years ago, the annual exhibition of the Arts and Crafts Society. He remarked: "The true root and basis of all art lies in the handicrafts. If there is no room or chance of recognition for really artistic power and feeling in design and craftsmanship—if art is not recognised in the humblest object and material, and felt to be as valuable, in its own way, as the more highly rewarded pictorial skill—the art cannot be in a sound condition. And if artists cease to be found among the crafts, there is great danger that they will vanish from the arts also, and become manufacturers and salesmen instead."

Japanese art is unquestionably of that kind which requires a certain educational process. It does not, for instance, at once appeal to that vague entity the "man in the street." There is a grotesqueness about some of it, a lack of perspective in much of it, which is caviare to a large number of persons. This much, however, can be said about Japanese art—that it is original. It is almost altogether the outcome of the artistic instincts of the people. Undoubtedly it has been to a large extent influenced by Buddhism, and, as we have seen, Buddhism is a foreign religion; but at the same time I think it may fairly be asserted that, though the Buddhist religion may have influenced and utilised Japanese art, it has never killed, or indeed affected to any degree, what I may term the individualistic artistic instincts of the nation. Japanese art requires to be closely studied. It is something that grows upon one, and the closer it is studied the greater its influence. To me one of its most pleasing features is what I have termed in the Preface its catholicity. It is not, as art is in so many European countries, the cult of a few, a sort of Eleusynian mystery into which a select number of persons have been initiated. It has, on the contrary, permeated, and exercised an influence upon, the whole nation, and been employed for even the most humble purposes. It is for this reason that, as I have previously observed, I am of opinion the Japanese may be considered and described as the most artistic people in the world.

I have referred to the grotesqueness and lack of perspective incidental to some descriptions of Japanese art. It certainly neglects chiaroscuro and linear perspective, and it displays an entire lack of form knowledge. The human figure and face have apparently never been studied at all. The colouring is frequently splendid, while the figures are for the most part anatomically incorrect. One would think that Japanese artists had never seen their own or any other human bodies. A rigid adherence to conventionality is, in my opinion, a defect of all Japanese art. By conventionality I do not, of course, mean what I may term the individuality of the art itself, but the fact that Japanese artists have felt themselves largely bound by the traditions of their art to treat the human and other figures not in accordance with nature, but altogether in accordance with the conventions of that art, and to entirely ignore perspective. I am quite aware that some enthusiastic lovers of things Japanese admire, or affect to admire, these defects. They have been described as a protest against the too rigid rules exacted in Western art. I suggest, however, that art in its highest form should seek to be true to nature, and in so far as Japanese art fails in this respect it is, I think, defective. At the same time I cordially admit that its defects are more than compensated by its splendid workmanship, its gorgeous colouring, and its striking originality.

It was only about forty or fifty years ago that Japanese art became known to any extent in Europe. Certainly the Portuguese missionaries introduced by Francis Xavier and the traders in the Dutch factory at Nagasaki were in the habit of exporting a few articles to Europe, chiefly porcelain ware made to order. I fear both missionaries and merchants regarded Japanese art, as we now know it, as barbaric, and never in the slightest degree realised either its beauties or its originality. Neither they nor the many millions of art-lovers in Europe dreamt that Japan was a country where art was universal, not esoteric—an art with schools, traditions, masters, and masterpieces. Probably the Paris Exhibition of 1867, to which the Prince of Satsuma sent a collection of Japanese artistic treasures, was the occasion when the true inwardness of Japanese art burst upon the Western world as a whole. It was a veritable revelation. It at once aroused enthusiasm and curiosity, and I fear cupidity, among European artists and art collectors.

Europe was awakened to the possibilities of Japan as an art nation, and Japan, failing to realise or properly appreciate the artistic accumulated wealth it possessed, commenced to part with it in a truly reckless manner. The depletion of the art treasures of the country commenced about this time, and though that depletion has been largely arrested, it is nevertheless still, to some extent, going on.

Japanese art, as it has come under the cognisance of a foreigner, may be considered in connection with four or five purposes to which it has been employed or adapted. First amongst these I place lacquer, next pottery and porcelain, then carving in wood and iron, metal-work and painting. The lacquer industry has been in existence in Japan so long as we have any authoritative history of the country. If any credence is to be given to tradition, long before the Christian era there was an official whose sole duty it was to superintend the production of lacquer for the Imperial Court, and specimens over a thousand years old, though rare, still exist. The process of lacquering is a somewhat intricate one, and varies, of course, in accordance with the time and labour spent on the article to be lacquered, and the cost of the same. After the article has been carefully made from specially selected wood—in the case of the choicest specimens of lacquer work this is usually a pine-wood of fine grain—it is first coated with a preparation composed of clay and varnish, which, after being permitted to dry, is smoothed down with a whetstone. When this operation has been concluded, the article proposed to be lacquered is covered with some substance, either silk, cloth, or paper. It is then given from one to five coats of the foregoing mixture, each coat being permitted to dry before the next is applied. After this has been effected, the whetstone is again employed with a view of obtaining a perfectly smooth surface when the lacquering proper commences. This may be a perfunctory or it may be a very complicated operation, according to the value of the article, layer after layer of the varnish—from one to fifty coats—being laid upon the material at intervals. After the final coat has been applied, the smoothing process commences. The whole of these operations are, however, only the preliminaries to the scheme of decoration, which is often very elaborate. The dusts of powders used for this purpose are of various kinds and of varying cost. When the ornamentation which often consists in colouring the groundwork with particles of gold dust has been completed, sometimes as many as a dozen coatings of transparent lacquer are imposed upon the same.

The art of lacquering in Japan dates back at least 1,200 or 1,300 years, and tradition assigns it a period more ancient still. There are, however, few if any articles of lacquer ware now in the country, whose origin can be traced back so many years. At any rate, there is no satisfactory evidence in regard to the antiquity of any specimens of lacquer ware dating back more than seven or eight centuries. In old Japan the manufacturer of lacquer work was intimately associated with the domestic life of the upper classes. Griffis tells us that nearly every Daimio had his Court lacquerer, and that a set of household furniture and toilet utensils was part of the dowry of a noble lady. On the birth of a daughter, he relates, it was common for the lacquer artist to begin the making of a mirror case, a washing bowl, a cabinet, a clothes rack, or a chest of drawers, often occupying from one to five whole years on a single article. An inro, or pill-box, might require several years for perfection, though small enough to go into a fob. By the time the young lady was marriageable, her outfit of lacquer was superb.

The names of many of the great lacquer artists of Japan are still venerated. The masterpieces of Hoyami Koyetsu who flourished in the sixteenth century, are still, though rare, procurable. Japan numbers on her roll of fame twenty-eight great lacquer artists. There have, of course, been many hundreds, and indeed thousands, in the past centuries whose work was superb, but the twenty-eight are deemed to be the immortals of this particular art. One of these great men, Ogawa Ritsuo, is famous for the number and variety of the materials—mother-of-pearl, coral, tortoise-shell, &c. &c., he used in his work. A profuse richness is its chief characteristic. One of his pupils imitated in his work various materials—pottery and wood-carving, and bronzes. The last famous artist in lacquer, Watanobe Tosu, died about thirty years ago. Whether he is destined to have a successor or successors remains to be seen. These lacquer artists, as I have indicated, worked not for lucre, but for love. Attached to some Daimios household, they devoted their lives, their energies, their imagination, their artistic instincts to the devising of splendid work and the making of beautiful, ingenious, absolutely artistic and, at the same time, entirely useful articles.

It is impossible within the space at my disposal to deal in detail with the large variety of lacquer work produced in Japan with the various kinds of lacquer, or with what I may term the artistic idiosyncrasies of Japanese lacquer work. One can now hardly believe that until the opening up of Japan half a century or so ago, few specimens of lacquer found their way to Europe, although Japanese porcelain had been largely imported and was highly prized. Even at the present time I do not think that the artistic beauties of Japanese lacquer work have been appreciated in this country to anything like the extent they deserve to be. I have heard people remark, for example, that they failed to understand the perpetual reproduction of the great snow-covered mountain Fusi-Yama in Japanese designs, while they could see nothing in these storks, bewildering landscapes, and grotesque figures. Perhaps the best explanation of the constant appearance of Fusi-Yama in all Japanese work is that which De Fonblanque gives. He says: "If there is one sentiment universal amongst all Japanese, it is a deep and earnest reverence for their sacred mountain. It is their ideal of the beautiful in nature, and they never tire of admiring, glorifying, and reproducing it. It is painted, embossed, carved, engraved, modelled in all their wares. The mass of the people regard it not only as the shrine of their dearest gods, but the certain panacea for their worst evils, from impending bankruptcy or cutaneous diseases to unrequited love or ill-luck at play. It is annually visited by thousands and thousands of pilgrims." The Japanese artist in constantly reproducing Fusi-Yama has merely voiced national sentiment and feeling.

The substance applied to wood to produce what is called lacquer, is not what is generally known in England as varnish. It is really the sap of the *rhus vernicifera* which contains, among other ingredients, about 3 per cent. of a gum soluble in water. It has to undergo various refining processes before being mixed with the colouring matter, while the greatest care is exercised throughout with a view of obviating the possibility of dust or any other foreign matter finding its way into the mixture.

VIEW OF FUSI-YAMA FROM A TEA HOUSE

FROM A PRINT BY HIROSHIGE

The fine polish usually seen on lacquer work is not actually the result of the composition applied, but is produced by incessant polishing. The lacquered articles in old Japan were used for various purposes—mirror cases, fans, letter-carriers, the inro, which was at one time a necessary part of every Japanese gentleman's attire; it was secured to the sash, and utilised to hold medicine powders, for perfumes, as a seal-box, &c., seals being at one time, as indeed they are to some extent still, in use in place of a signature. But the amount of ancient lacquer ware now in Japan, or, indeed, of artistic articles made solely for use and not merely to sell, is, as I have said, small. European collectors have denuded the country; the treasures of the Daimios, which were almost recklessly sold when they were disestablished, and to a large extent disendowed, have been distributed all over the globe, and a large quantity, perhaps the largest quantity, of the lacquer work now made in the country is manufactured solely for the purpose of being sold as curios either at home or abroad. That this fact has largely lowered the artistic ideals and debased the artistic taste in Japan appears to be the general opinion. Much of the present-day work of Japan in lacquer, as in other articles, is certainly to my mind artistic and beautiful in the extreme, but obviously, men working almost against time to turn out "curios," for which there is a persistent demand on the part of visitors who are not always by temperament or training fitted to appreciate the artistic or the beautiful, are unlikely to produce such fine or original work as the artisan of old leisurely employed at his craft and pluming himself, not on the amount of his earnings or the extent of his output, but on the quality and artistic merits of his work.

Next to lacquer in importance amongst the Japanese arts, I think, comes ceramic ware, which has long had a great vogue in Europe, and indeed was highly prized here many years before the artistic skill of the Japanese in lacquer was generally known. That decorative art, as expressed in the pottery and porcelain of Japan, has been largely influenced by China and Korea seems to be unquestionable. The Japanese have nevertheless imparted to it a peculiar charm of their own, the outcome of originality in ideas, while the art has, through many centuries, been fortunate enough to have been fostered and encouraged by the great and powerful of the land. As a people the Japanese are entirely free from anything that savours of ostentation, and this fact is emphasised in their art just as it is in their homes. The charm of the ceramic ware of Japan, in my opinion, consists in the beauty of its colouring rather than in its figuring. This ceramic ware, as my readers probably know, differs greatly in appearance, quality, and, I may add, in price according to the particular part of the country in which it is produced. It is not necessary to be an art connoisseur to grasp the fact that, say, the famous Satsuma ware is distinct in almost every respect from that of Imari, Kaga, Ise, Raku, Kyoto, &c. All these different wares have charms peculiar to each. It is really marvellous to think that a country with such a comparatively small area as Japan should have produced so many different kinds of ceramic ware, each possessing distinct and pronounced characteristics, and having indeed little affinity with each other save in regard to the general excellence of the workmanship and the artistic completeness of the whole.

As I have said, both Korea and China have had a marked influence on the manufacture of pottery and porcelain in Japan. Korean potters appear to have settled there prior to the Christian era, and to have imparted to the Japanese the first rudiments of knowledge in regard to working in clay, but the development of the process was greatly due to Chinese influences. During the thirteenth century, one Toshiro paid a visit to China, where he exhaustively studied everything relating to the potter's art. On his return to his own country he introduced great improvements, both in manufacture and decoration, and made, it is believed, for the first time, glazed pottery. Soon afterwards household utensils of lacquer began to go out of use, being replaced by those made of clay, and a great impetus was accordingly given to the trade of the potter. Tea, which is believed to have been introduced into Japan from China in the year 800 does not appear to have come into general use till the sixteenth century. The "tea ceremonies" known as the Cha-no-yu came into vogue about the same time, and undoubtedly had an immense influence on the ceramic art. The articles used in the "tea ceremonies" included an iron kettle resting on a stand; a table or stand of mulberry wood 2 feet high; two tea-jars containing the tea; a vessel containing fresh water; a tea-bowl. It is not my purpose to describe the many interesting details of these "tea ceremonies." Suffice it to observe that they gave a great impetus to the manufacture of costly and elaborate china. The leaders of society, as we should term them, who took part in these ceremonies exercised a judicious and enlightened patronage of the ceramic art. They encouraged rising talent, and welcomed new developments. There can, I think, be no doubt that Japan, in an artistic sense, owes much to the frequenters of these "tea ceremonies." Tea-jars and tea-bowls especially became, under the patronage and guidance of these men, choice works of art, and were bestowed by the great and powerful on their friends, by whom they were greatly cherished and handed down as heirlooms. Some of these treasures still remain in the country, a large number have been purchased by art connoisseurs and taken to various parts of the world, while many, of course, have from various causes perished. Under the conditions of life which obtained in old Japan the ceramic art reached a pitch of excellence, not to say glory, which it is never likely to attain either in Japan or elsewhere. It was emphatically a period of art for art's sake. The patronage, if I may use a word perhaps not strictly accurate, of the great artists of those days was exercised in such a manner as to enable them to employ all their talents, artistic ideals, and enthusiasm in the direction of producing masterpieces of their craft.

The secrets of porcelain manufacture are believed to have been brought to Japan from China about the beginning of the sixteenth century. In the year 1513, Gorodayu, Shonsui, of Ise, returned from China and settled in Arita, in the province of Hizen, which at once became and still remains the headquarters of the famous Imari ware. The porcelain produced here is chiefly, but not altogether, the blue and white combination, but Arita also makes porcelain ware decorated in various colours and exceedingly ornate in appearance. It is, however, stated that this ornate Imari ware was first made for exportation to China to supply the Portuguese market at Macao, and that it was afterwards fostered by the Dutch at Nagasaki, whose exportations of the ware to Europe were on a considerable scale. This peculiar style of decoration is believed to have been due to the demands of the Dutch, whose patrons in Europe would have none other. One remark I may make in this connection, viz., that those enormous vases and other similar articles of Japanese ware which have long been so greatly prized in Europe, and many of which are magnificent specimens of decorative art, are not, in one sense, characteristically Japanese. The Japanese has always, if I may so express it, used art as the handmaiden of utilitarianism. Every article intended for the Japanese home had to be not merely a thing of beauty but a thing for use. It never entered the minds of the Japanese to hang beautiful specimens of their porcelain ware on their walls, or what did duty for walls, to collect dust. They used vases certainly of a moderate size to hold flowers, tea-pots and tea-cups for the purpose of making and drinking tea, water-bottles and various other articles for domestic use ; everything in fact was, as I have said, designed not only from an artistic but a utilitarian standpoint, and hence it is, I think, that art, as I have already remarked, has permeated the whole people. Even in the poorest house in Japan it is possible to see, in the ordinary articles in domestic use, some attempt at art, and, I may add, some appreciation of it on the part of the users of those articles. In my opinion when art is not applied to articles of general utility but is confined to articles not intended for use, art becomes, as is largely the case in this country, either the cult of a class or the affectation of a class, and its beauties and inward meaning cease to have any effect upon, just because they are not understood by, the great mass of the people.

Satsuma ware is probably the most widely known, and the most esteemed among foreigners, of Japanese porcelain. Its soft, cream-like colour is now known in every part of the world, while the delicate colour decorations imposed upon the cream-like background, certainly give a most effective appearance. I question however whether, from a purely artistic standpoint, Satsuma is worthy of being compared with many of the other porcelains in Japan. Much of it as seen in Europe was specially made for Europe, and having been so is, I suggest, not in the true sense artistic. As a matter of fact Satsuma ware was introduced from Korea, and was made in the first instance solely for the use of the Prince of Satsuma and his friends. The kilns were originally built on Korean models, and the potters in Satsuma remained a class apart, not being allowed to marry with the outside world.

Kaga ware is well known to all art connoisseurs. This porcelain is rare. The masters of the art of Kaga ware, with its exquisite colouring and elaborate ornamentation in gold and silver, have left no successors, while their output was small. The ware is of course still made, and as the clay of the district is of a dark red colour, the ware has a uniform tint.

Bizen ware reached the apotheosis of its perfection just before the Revolution. It is made in the province of Bizen. The better kind is made of a white or light bluish clay, and well baked in order to receive the red-brown colour, whereas the commoner kind is of a red clay.

The various Kyoto wares are remarkable for their quaint forms, and some of them are highly prized.

It would, of course, be impossible for me to attempt in detail a description of the other very numerous ceramic wares of Japan. Undoubtedly, as I have said, Satsuma is the most popular with Europeans, but it is not, and I do not think it deserves to be, the most highly prized by art connoisseurs. The ceramic wares of Japan may be classified under three headings: (1) Pottery, ornamented by scoring and glazing ; (2) A cream-coloured faience with a glaze often crackled and delicately painted ; (3) Hard porcelain. Under the first of these classifications may be included Bizen, Seto, Raku, and some other wares. Under the second I place Satsuma and some less important similar products. Among the porcelains the most famous are those of Kutania, Hizen, and Kyoto. In regard to decorations, the Japanese have utilised the seven gods of good fortune, many landscapes, a few of the domestic animals—the dragon, phœnix, an animal with the body and hoofs of a deer, the tail of a bull, and with a horn on its forehead, a monster lion, and the sacred tortoise. Trees, plants, grasses, and flowers of various kinds, and some of the badges in Japanese heraldry are also largely made use of. However grotesque some of these objects may be, or however grotesque the representations of animals and even landscapes may be, no one who has closely studied it can deny the fact that the effect of Japanese decorative art as applied to the ceramic ware of the country is, on the whole, magnificent. The more one studies it the more impressed one is with its marvellous beauty and the originality which has been brought to bear upon it. I defy any man or woman, who possesses the artistic sensibilities, even in a latent degree, to visit a gallery containing the masterpieces of Japanese ceramic art, closely study them in all their details, and minutely examine the attention which the artist has given to even the smallest of those details without being impressed by its power. It is, I consider, a liberal education to any person who has the slightest prepossession for art to wander through such a gallery and admire the masterpieces of these wonderful art-workers of Japan.

The demand for the various art products of Japan in

both Europe and America has had its perhaps inevitable result in not only the manufacture of articles simply and solely for the foreign market, but in the what I may term faking of modern to represent ancient art productions. "Old" Satsuma, for example, is a case in point. The genuine old Satsuma ware, by constant use, obtained, like meerschaum, a delightful tint. Modern Satsuma is comparatively white, and so, in order to pander to the taste of the European collector of the ancient article, the modern is stained to the required shade. The article itself is genuine, and indeed beautiful, but this "faking" of it to meet European and American tastes is one of the results, I fear, of Western influences. What the precise effect of European influences may be on the old porcelain art of Japan it is impossible to say. So far as I am concerned, I have no hesitation in expressing my own opinion that it will not be a healthy influence. Art for art's sake is, I admit, difficult when the plutocrats of the West, with a craze or a fad for Eastern art, are pouring out their wealth in order to obtain specimens thereof. Demand usually induces supply, and the Japanese artisan of to-day would be more than human did he not respond to the demand of the West for "Old Satsuma" and other specimens of the artistic treasures in pottery and porcelain of Japan. The spirit of commercialism is, as I have said before, fatal to art. If the artist is forced to work quickly and cheaply he quite evidently cannot bring his individuality into play. He must transform his studio into a workshop, and ponder only, or chiefly, upon the possibility of his output. I have been much struck in this connection with the remarks of a writer in regard to orders for art work sent from New York to Japan. "I can remember," he said, "one of our great New York

KUTANI EARTHENWARE, DECORATED WITH POLYCHROME ENAMELS
EARLY EIGHTEENTH CENTURY

INCENSE-BURNER
AWATA FAYENCE. EIGHTEENTH CENTURY

dealers marking on his samples the colours that pleased most of his buyers, who themselves were to place the goods. All other colours or patterns were tabooed in his instructions to the makers in Japan. This was the rude mechanism of the change, the coming down to the worst public taste, which must be that of the greatest number at any time."

As regards the modern porcelain of Japan I need say but little. Originality is apparently dead, and the makers of to-day are content to copy the past. No doubt the purely mechanical processes of manufacture have been greatly improved, and much, if not most, of the modern ceramic ware of Japan is extremely beautiful. At the same time some of it, especially that which is made solely for the foreign market, is to my mind neither artistic nor beautiful. It is decorated, if I may use such a term, in most of the colours of the rainbow, and rendered more gaudy still by a plethora of very poor gilding.

There is in Japan a certain school of progressive ideas in reference to the art of the country. This school is of opinion that Japanese art should not, so to speak, remain stereotyped, but that it should assimilate and adapt and apply all that is good and beautiful in Western art. The objects that this school has in view are no doubt laudable, but I confess I hope with all my heart that those objects will fail of accomplishment. There has been already far too much Europeanising of Japanese art, and the result, so far as I have been able to judge, is not encouraging in respect of any further advance or development in that direction. Japanese art, and especially the ceramic art, possesses, as I have before said, an individuality which can only be spoiled, even if it be not destroyed, by adding on to or mixing up with it the totally distinct art and art methods of Western civilisation. Were this done it would become a bastard or a mongrel art, and, as history affords abundant evidence, would in due course lapse into a condition of utter decadence.

Quite a volume might be written on the subject of marks on Japanese pottery and porcelain. These have long interested and frequently misled the collector. They are of various kinds. Sometimes there is a mark signifying the reign or part of the reign of an emperor, or the name of a place at which the article was made, or, more frequently still, the name of the particular potter whose handicraft it was. Sometimes Chinese dates are found impressed on the article without any regard to chronological correctness. Indeed, Chinese dates are to be found on Japanese porcelain indicating a period long anterior to that in which the manufacture of porcelain was known in Japan. These spurious dates have proved pitfalls for collectors. The mark is sometimes impressed with a seal or painted; occasionally it is merely scratched. The investigation of these marks is a recondite study assuredly full of interest, but, as I have said, prolific in pitfalls for the unwary or the too-credulous.

CHAPTER XII

JAPANESE ART (*continued*)—SCULPTURE—METAL WORK—PAINTING

PROBABLY of all the Japanese arts there is none more interesting or instructive than that of sculpture in wood and ivory. The sculpture of Japan undoubtedly had its origin in the service of the Buddhist religion. That religion, as I have attempted to show, has always utilised art in the decoration of its temples and shrines as well as in the perpetuation of the image of Buddha himself. At the beginning of the seventeenth century an edict was promulgated directing that every house should contain a representation of Buddha, and, as the result of this, the sculpture trade received a considerable impetus. Tobacco was introduced into the country in the same century, and the smoking thereof soon came greatly into vogue among the Japanese people. Tobacco necessitated a pouch or bag to contain the same, and this in turn induced or produced the manufacture of something wherewith to attach the bag to the girdle. Hence the evolution of the netsuké, now as famous in Europe as in Japan. The carving of netsukés developed into a very high art ; indeed, there is perhaps no branch of Japanese art which has aroused more enthusiasm among foreign collectors and connoisseurs. Quite recently I attended a sale of netsukés in London at which the bidding was both fast and furious, while the prices realised were enormous. The netsuké, strictly speaking, was the toggle attached by a cord to the tobacco pouch, inro, or pipe of the Japanese man, with the object of preventing the article slipping through the girdle or sash, but the word has been more loosely employed by foreigners until, in popular parlance, it has come to embrace all small carvings. Netsukés were nearly always representations of the human figure, and various reasons have been advanced to account for this fact. I need not consider those reasons in these pages, as they, as well as the arguments by which they are attempted to be supported, are almost entirely speculative. The distinguishing characteristic of the true netsuké is two holes admitting of a string being run through them. These holes were often concealed behind the limbs of the figure. The material of which netsukés were made varied, and consisted of ivory, wood horns, fish-bones, and stones of various kinds. Those made of wood are undoubtedly the most ancient, ivory being of comparatively recent importation into Japan. Nevertheless, the netsukés made of ivory now command the highest price. The names of many of the great netsuké-makers are still famous, and much of their work is certainly artistic and beautiful to a degree. I am afraid that in the collecting of netsukés many European lovers of Japanese art have burnt their fingers. The genuine old artistic productions are now extremely rare, but a brisk trade has sprung up in reproductions which are skilfully coloured to give them the appearance of age. The netsuké, I must reiterate, was an almost indispensable adjunct to the costume of every Japanese man, and it was, accordingly, made for use and not for ornament alone. Of late years wood and ivory sculpture in Japan has largely degenerated and deteriorated owing to the output of articles not of utility, but made for the foreign market—"curios," in fact.

No one who has visited Japan can have failed of being impressed by those gigantic statues of Buddha which have been erected in different parts of the country. The largest and best known is the Dai Butsu, at Kamakura, a few miles from Yokohama. The height of this great statue is nearly 50 feet, in circumference it is 97 feet. The length of the face is 8 feet 5 inches, the width of mouth 3 feet 2 inches, and it has been asserted—though I do not guarantee the accuracy of the calculation—that there are 830 curls upon the head, each curl 9 inches long. The statue is composed of layers of bronze brazed together. It is hollow, and persons can ascend by a ladder into the interior. The Dai Butsu at Nara is taller than the one at Kamakura. It is dissimilar to most of the others in the country in having a black face of a somewhat African type. This image is stated to have been erected in the year 750 A.D., and the head has, I believe, been replaced several times. In the Kamakura Dai Butsu both hands rest upon the knees, while in the one at Nara the right arm is extended upward with the palm of the hand placed to the front. The statue at Nara is made of bronze which is stated to be composed of gold 500, mercury 1,950, tin 16,827, and copper 986,080 lbs., the total weight of the statue being about 480 tons. Nearly all the Dai Butsus in the country are of ancient workmanship. There is a modern one constructed of wood erected in the year 1800 at Kyoto, 60 feet high. As a work of art it has, however, no pretensions, which rest entirely upon its size.

Criticisms in regard to the artistic merits of these immense images have been numerous and by no means unanimous. To my mind they are superb specimens of the work of the old metallurgists of Japan, and they are, moreover, deeply interesting as indicative of the ideas of their designers in regard to the expression of placid repose of Nirvana. Mr. Basil Chamberlain has appositely remarked in reference to the great statue at Kamakura: "No other gives such an impression of majesty or so truly symbolises the central idea of Buddhism, the intellectual calm which comes of perfected knowledge and the subjugation of all passion." And Lafcadio Hearn, that learned authority on everything Japanese, who has brought into all his writings a poetical feeling which breathes the very spirit of old Japan, has observed in regard to the same statue: "The gentleness, the dreamy passionlessness of those features—the immense repose of the whole figure—are full of beauty and charm. And, contrary to all expectations, the nearer you approach the giant Buddha the greater the charm becomes. You look up into the solemnly beautiful face—into the half-closed eyes, that seem to watch you through their eyelids of bronze as gently as those of a child; and you feel that the image typifies all that is tender and solemn in the soul of the East. Yet you feel also that only Japanese thought could have created it. Its beauty, its dignity, its perfect repose, reflect the higher life of the race that imagined it, and, though inspired doubtless by some Indian model, as the treatment of his hair and various symbolic marks reveal, the art is Japanese.

"So mighty and beautiful is the work that you will for

some time fail to notice the magnificent lotus plants of bronze, fully 15 feet high, planted before the figure on another side of the great tripod in which incense rods are burning."

Kaemfer, writing in the seventeenth century, remarked of the Japanese: "As to all sorts of handicraft, they are wanting neither proper materials nor industry and application, and so far is it that they should have any occasion to send for masters abroad, that they rather exceed all other nations in ingenuity and neatness of workmanship, particularly in brass, gold, silver, and copper." In metal work the Japanese have certainly cultivated art to a high degree. Much of that metal work was, of course, employed in connection with articles which modern conditions of life in Japan have rendered absolutely or almost entirely obsolete. The bronze workers of Japan were and indeed are still famous. Their work as displayed in braziers, incense-holders, flower-vases, lanterns, and various other articles evinces great skill, while the effects often produced by the artists in the inlaying and overlaying of metals with a view of producing a variegated picture has long been the wonder and admiration of the Western world. It is almost safe to assert that the finest specimens of work of this kind can never be reproduced. In casting, too, there was no lack of skill in old Japan. The big bell at Kyoto, which is 14 feet high by over 9 feet in diameter, is a sufficient object-lesson as to the proficiency attained in casting in bygone days. Much of the bronze work of Japan, especially in birds and insects, is to me incomparable. The modern bronze work of the country, though certainly beautiful, does not in any respect or any degree approach that of the masters of two or three hundred years ago. In the manipulation of metals and amalgams these men have reached a higher standard of perfection than had previously or has since been attained. The bronze work of Japan is not, in my opinion, as generally appreciated as it deserves to be. There is, I think, nothing of the same kind in the world to be compared with it when it was at its best. Like much of the other art of Japan modern conditions are, as I have said, not conducive either to its progress or development. Still, there is no lack of skill in this particular branch of art in Japan at the present time, and I have seen some very admirable, not to say magnificent, specimens of modern bronze work.

Armour is now nearly as effete in Japan as in this country, and yet in the decoration of armour the Japanese artist in metal was in the past not only skilful but beautiful. Fine specimens of armour are now extremely rare.) That particular kind of work has, of course, gone never to return. Next in importance to armour came the sword. Some of us can remember when the two-sworded men of Japan were still actualities, not, as they have now become, historical entities, the terror of the foreign community there. The sword was an important and, indeed, an essential weapon in the conditions of society that obtained in old Japan, not only for self-defence but for offensive purposes, either in respect of family feuds or individual quarrels, which were almost invariably settled by the arbitrament of the sword. That weapon was also used for those suicides known as hara-kiri, the outcome of wounded honour or self-respect, which were such prominent features in the Japanese life of the past. Some Western writers have attempted to poke a mild kind of fun at this proneness of the Japanese for the "happy despatch" on what seemed to the writers very flimsy or trivial grounds. To me, on the contrary, the practice

BRONZE INCENSE-BURNER AND SMALL FLOWER-VASE

EIGHTEENTH CENTURY

of hara-kiri, indefensible as it may be in some respects, indicates the existence of a high code of honour, the slightest infringement of which rendered life intolerable. The sword then had innumerable functions, and, like almost every article of utility in Japan, it became the subject of elaborate ornamentation. The blade itself was brought to a high state of perfection, and as regards the tempering of the steel has been the admiration of cutlers in every part of the globe. Indeed the sword-makers of Japan are famous from the tenth century downwards. Many of the sword-blades had mottoes inscribed on them, and most had designs ornate and often elaborate. The accessories of the blade and the ornamentation thereof lent full scope for that artistic adornment which has for ages past, as I have more than once remarked, been characteristic of almost every article used in Japan. The wearing of the sword was confined to persons of a certain rank, and different classes wore different kinds of swords. About the sixteenth century the custom of wearing two swords, one large, the other about the size of a dirk, came into fashion. The two-handed sword was essentially a war sword. The colour of the scabbard was almost invariably black with a tinge of red or green, and it was in most instances beautifully lacquered. The possessor of a sword gave full vent to his tastes in regard to the size and decoration of his weapon. According to Griffis: "Daimios often spent extravagant sums upon a single sword and small fortunes upon a collection. A Samurai, however poor, would have a blade of sure temper and rich mountings, deeming it honourable to suffer for food that he might have a worthy emblem of his rank." On January 1, 1877, the wearing of swords was abolished by an Imperial decree, and foreigners visiting or resident in Japan in that and the following years were able to pick up magnificent swords for a few dollars each.

I have not space to describe in detail the many accessories which went to form the complete sword for the strong man armed in old Japan, or the elaborate and artistic ornamentation of every detail. In many of the small pieces of metal work which adorned the swords gold, silver, platina, copper, iron, steel, zinc, besides numerous alloys were used. The abolition of sword-wearing gave a death-blow to the industry in connection with the making of swords except in so far as it has been continued for the purpose of turning them out for the European market. But during the many centuries the art of metal work, as exemplified in sword manufacture and the ornamentation of the sword and the various accessories of it, existed in Japan it reached a magnificent height of perfection. Dealing only with one period of it a French writer has remarked: "What a galaxy of masters illuminated the close of the eighteenth century! What a multitude of names and works would have to be cited in any attempt to write a monograph upon sword furniture! The humblest artisan, in this universal outburst of art, is superior in his mastery of metal to any one we could name in Europe. How many artists worthy of a place in the rank are only known to us by a single piece, but which is quite sufficient to evidence their power! From 1790 to 1840 art was at fever heat, the creative faculty produced marvels."

Besides the making and ornamentation of swords the metal workers in Japan attained great skill in the design and finish of many other articles which were in constant use by the people—pipes, cases to hold the Indian ink which formed the writing material, the clasps and buttons of tobacco pouches, besides vases, &c. In reference to the making of alloys these metal workers showed considerable ingenuity, the alloys used, amalgams of gold, silver, copper, and other metals in deft proportions, resulting in magnificent effects as regards ornamentation and permanency. Japan has undoubtedly been greatly aided in the height to which the art of the country of various kinds has attained by the plentifulness of minerals therein. Gold, silver, copper, iron, lead, tin, and many other minerals exist. Strange to say, gold at one time was considered no more valuable than silver—a fact which may account for the lavish manner in which it was used for decorative purposes in art of all descriptions.

I fear that an inevitable result of Western influences and the great, indeed drastic, changes which have been effected thereby in the ideas, manners, and customs of the Japanese people has been the decay, if not the destruction, of the art connected with metal work. Sword manufacture and everything relating thereto is, of course, gone; other metal industries are following suit. The result, as I have said, was inevitable, but it is none the less deplorable. Although it requires an expert to deal with and describe in all its infinite detail the metal work of Japan, it does not need an expert's knowledge to profoundly admire it and be lost in admiration at the skill displayed and the pains taken in respect of every part of it. The workers in this, as indeed in all the other art industries of Japan in the past, were quite evidently not men in a hurry or much exercised concerning their output, and scamping their work in order to establish a record. Their hearts must have been in everything they undertook, and their sole aim, whatever they did, to put into their work all their skill and knowledge and love of the beautiful. They, in fact, worked not for pelf but for sheer love of art, and so long as the work of these artists of various kinds endures the world will assuredly never cease to admire it.

Painting has, in Japan, long been greatly cultivated, and in some respects highly developed. There are various recognised schools of painting, but I shall not weary my readers with any attempt, necessarily imperfect as it would be, to describe them in detail. China and the Buddhist religion have profoundly influenced painting as the other arts of Japan. Indeed, the early painters of Japan devoted themselves almost entirely to religious subjects. Most of their work was executed on the walls, ceilings, and sliding screens of the Buddhist temples, but some of it still exists in kakemonos, or wall pictures, and makimonos, or scroll pictures. In the ninth century painting, as well as the arts of architecture and carving, flourished exceedingly. Kyoto appears to have been the great artistic centre. The construction of temples throughout the country proceeded apace, and it is related that no less than 13,000 images were carved and painted during the reign of one emperor. Kyoto was, in fact, the centre of religious art. We are told that the entire city was in a constant artistic ferment, that whole streets were converted into studios and workshops, and that the population of idols and images was as numerous as the human habitation. Nearly all the temples then constructed and adorned have vanished, but that at Shiba still remains to convey to us some idea of the artistic glories of this period of intense religious belief, which gave expression to its fervour and its faith in architecture, carving, and painting. About the thirteenth century flower and still-life painting came into vogue. Almost simultaneously religious fervour, as expressed in art, began to grow cold. The artist became the hanger-on of the Daimio, who was too often employed in burning temples and destroying their artistic treasures. The painter then painted as his fancy led him, and if he treated of religious subjects did not invariably do so in a reverential spirit. From time to time new schools of painting arose, culminating, in the eighteenth century, in the Shijo school, which made a feature of painting animals, birds, fishes, flowers, &c., from nature, instead of adhering to the conventional style which had previously prevailed. The colouring of some of the work of this school is superb and is greatly in request among art collectors.

Of late years painting in Japan seems, to some extent, to have come under Western influences. There is, indeed, a progressive party in painting which not only does not resist these Western influences but actually advocates the utilisation of Western materials and methods in painting and the discarding of all that had made Japanese painting essentially what it is. I confess to a hope that this progressive school will not make quite so much progress as its disciples desire. To introduce European pigments, canvas, brushes, &c., and discard the materials formerly in use, to get rid of the Japanese method of treating subjects, whether landscapes, country scenes, the life of the people, representations of animals, and so on, and replace that method by imitations of European schools of painting, must simply involve the destruction of all that is essentially and characteristically Japanese and the replacing of it by something that is not Japanese or indeed Oriental. The essence of art is originality. I admit that art may come under foreign influences and be improved, just as it may be degraded, by them. If the influences of foreign art are to be advantageous that art must, I suggest, be in some measure akin to the style of the art which is affected by it. For example, the influence in the past of China or Korea upon an analogous style of art in Japan. But for Japanese painters to remodel their peculiar style upon that of Europe must prove as fatal to Japanese painting as an art as any similar endeavour of European painters to remodel their style upon that of Japan would be fatal to the distinctive art of Europe. I make this statement with full knowledge of the fact that some art critics in this country declare that Mr. Whistler and other artists have been largely affected or influenced in their style by a study of Japanese art in painting and its methods.

I have referred to kakemonos, those wall pictures which are such a pleasing feature of the simple decoration of Japanese houses. Many of these are superb specimens of art, and the same remark may be made in reference to the makimonos, or scroll pictures. It may be that not every Western eye can appreciate these Japanese paintings fully at a first glance, but they certainly grow upon one, and I hope the time is far distant when kakemonos will be replaced in Japanese homes by those mural decorations, if I may so term them, to be seen in so many English houses, which are a positive eyesore to any person with even the faintest conception of art. The work of the old painters of Japan, as it appears on kakemonos and makimonos, is now rare. Much of it, as is the case with the other art treasures of the country, has gone abroad. I am, however, of opinion that painting has not deteriorated to anything like the same extent as some of the other Japanese arts. The subjects depicted by the artists have during the centuries from time to time changed, but the technique has altered but little. It does not, I know, appeal to everybody, but it is the kind of art, I reiterate, that grows upon one. No person who has interested himself in painting in modern Japan, especially on kake-

KAKEMONO ON PAPER

ATTRIBUTED TO MATAHEI

KAKEMONO ON PAPER

ATTRIBUTED TO SHIMMAN, UKIYO SCHOOL. EIGHTEENTH CENTURY

monos, can, I think, have failed to be impressed by the exquisite and beautiful work which the Japanese artists in colour to-day produce.

Silk and satin embroidery as an industry and an art at one time attained considerable importance in Japan, but of recent years has greatly declined. The craze among the upper classes for European dress has, of course, seriously affected the demand for elaborately embroidered silk and satin garments, and is bound to affect it to an even greater extent in the future as the custom of wearing European garb spreads among the people. No one with any artistic sensibilities can help regretting the fact that Japan is gradually but surely discarding the distinctive costume of her people. That costume was in every respect appropriate to their physique and facial characteristics. The same certainly cannot be said of European attire. However, it is now, I suppose, hopeless to arrest the movement in this direction, and in a comparatively few years, no doubt, the ancient and historic dress of the Japanese people will be as obsolete as the silks, satins, ruffles, &c., of our forefathers.

And what remark shall I make of Japanese curios, the trade in which has assumed such very large dimensions? Have they no claim, some of my readers may ask, to be included in a chapter on art? There is no doubt that many purchasers of them would be shocked were they to be told that there was nothing artistic in many, if not most, of these articles, that they were made simply and solely for the European market, and that the manufacture of curios for this purpose was now just as much a trade as is the making of screws in Birmingham. I am quite prepared to admit that some of the articles included in the generic term "curios," which can now be purchased in every large town in Great Britain, are pretty and effective, but as regards many of them there is certainly nothing artistic or indeed particularly or peculiarly Japanese. This making of curios for the foreign market has, as I have said, assumed considerable dimensions in Japan of recent years, and in connection therewith the Japanese has certainly assimilated many Western ideas in reference to pushing his wares. As an example in point of this I will quote here an anecdote told me by a friend who had a considerable knowledge of Japan in the 'seventies. During one of his journeyings inland, when staying at a Japanese tea-house, he was initiated into the use of Japanese tooth-powder, which is in pretty general use among the lower classes. On leaving Japan he purchased and brought to England a considerable quantity of this tooth-powder, and on settling down in London he discovered a Japanese shop where it was on sale. For some seventeen or eighteen years he purchased the tooth-powder at the shop, sold in the little boxes in which it was vended in Japan, not only using it himself but introducing it to a large number of his acquaintances. One day last year, on going into the shop referred to to make a further purchase, he was informed that they were run out of tooth-powder and did not quite know if they would have any more. My friend returned a month or two later to the same shop on the same errand bent, and asked if they had received a fresh supply. He was told that a further supply had come to hand of very much the same description, but at double the price. He purchased a box, the outside of which bore the following inscription in English: "Japanese Sanitary Dentifrice; Superior Quality. Apply the powder to the teeth by means of a brush, using moderate friction over the whole surface." On opening the box my friend found the powder was perfumed—perfumed for the European market! Now tooth-powder is, of course, not a curio, nor is the expression "moderate friction over the whole surface," I may remark, characteristically Japanese. The little anecdote is, I think, typical of the change that has come over and is still actively in progress in Japan—a change which, however inevitable, and beneficial though in many respects I believe it to be, is most assuredly not beneficial to the interests of art of any kind.

The fact of the matter is that the hurry-scurry of modern civilisation is not conducive to artistic work of any description. The man in a hurry is unlikely to accomplish anything of permanent value. Working against time is utterly subversive of the realisation of artistic ideals. The past, whether in the West or the East, when railways, telegraphs, telephones, newspapers, and all the adjuncts of modern progress were unknown, was the period when men did good and enduring work. They could then concentrate their minds upon their art free from those hundred-and-one discomposing and disconcerting influences which are the concomitants of modern civilisation. The true artist thinks only of his art; for him it is not merely a predominant, but his sole interest. He brings to it all his mind, his ideas and ideals, his energy, enthusiasm, pertinacity; in it is concentrated all his ambition. Extraneous matters can only distract his mind from his art, and accordingly are to be abjured. I fear this exclusiveness, this aloofness, is rare nowadays in the West; it is perhaps less rare in the East, but it is becoming rarer there as Western influences, Western ideas, and Western modes of life and method of regarding life make progress. The poet, the painter, the sculptor, the novelist, the dramatist, if their work is to be other than ephemeral, need an atmosphere of repose and quietude wherein the mind can work and fashion those ideas which are to be given material expression free from all distracting and disturbing influences. Where can the aspiring artist, under modern conditions of life, find such a haven of rest? And even if he find it I fear he too often has no desire to cast anchor there. The distractions of life are frequently alluring, and the embryonic artists of to-day assure us that they must, in modern jargon, keep "in touch" with modern thought with a view of, in modern slang, being "up-to-date." Ideas such as these—and they seem to me to be not only largely prevalent but almost universal—are in my opinion fatal, not only to the development but to the very existence of art. We see in this country the effect upon every department thereof. Poetry, painting, sculpture, literature, the drama, are by almost general consent in a state of utter decadence. The great poet or painter, the great artist in words, on canvas, in marble, or in wood—where is he? Are there any signs or portents of his advent? None. Modern conditions of life have killed the artist, and replaced him by artistic mediocrities or mechanicians who labour not for love but for lucre, and are more concerned about the amount of their output than the quality thereof. And as of England and Europe so I fear is it, and will it be to a greater extent, in the near future in Japan. The artist in lacquer, porcelain, metal, painting, embroidery, cannot exist under the conditions of modern progress. He may still produce good and beautiful work, but it will be no longer artistic in the higher sense of that word, just because those ideas and ideals which make the artist and connote art cannot exist in their fulness and purity amidst the hurry and bustle and turmoil and desire for wealth which are the essential characteristics of the civilisation of Europe and America to-day—a civilisation which Japan has imported, and to a large degree assimilated, and which she must accept with its defects as well as its advantages. We may, and must, regret the effect of this civilisation upon the art of old Japan, but there is no good shutting one's eyes to obvious facts or affecting to believe that in due course we shall witness a renaissance in Japan, a new birth of all that is great and grand and magnificent in her past history.

There has for some years been a movement to prevent, as far as possible, the passing out of Japan of its art treasures. The Government has diligently catalogued all that remain in the temples and public buildings to obviate their being sold, and museums have been built for the purpose of collecting and exhibiting all that is best and representative of Japanese art. There has also been a movement among the noblemen and the upper classes in the direction of forming private collections. It was time that steps such as these should be taken. It is a thousand pities they were not taken earlier. The drain of Japan's art treasures went on unchecked year after year, and it is probable that the private and public collections of Europe and America contain more Japanese art treasures than are now to be found in Japan itself. I am aware that in these collections are also to be found no little of the spurious, and many articles with no claim to be considered artistic in any sense of the word, but at the same time there is no doubt that, as I have said, for years, there was a constant export of artistic wealth from Japan. The Revolution of 1868, with its consequent cataclysms, caused the treasures of many of the great families to come on the market, with the result that they were bought up at prices often greatly below their intrinsic value and shipped from the country. They are of course gone for ever, and the only thing that now remains to Japan is to prevent as far as possible any of the treasures which she possesses meeting with a similar fate. I know perfectly well that art, like music, knows nothing of nationality, and that there is no reason why the resident of London or New York should not enjoy the beauties of Japanese art, and feast his eyes on the work of some great Japanese artist of three or four hundred years back just as much as the citizen of Tokio. This is in one sense true, but at the same time one cannot help sympathising with the patriotic desire of a people to retain in their midst specimens of the artistic conceptions and the artistic work of those famous men who are now ashes, but whose work remains as a symbol and an incentive to their countrymen to maintain a high standard, and to practise art simply and solely for the love of it.

CHAPTER XIII

JAPANESE ARCHITECTURE

THERE are, perhaps, some superior persons who may consider that Japanese architecture has no claim to be regarded as art. These persons have no conception of art in architecture unless it be Doric, Gothic, Byzantine, Early English, or something of the kind, and unless it be expressed in bricks and mortar. Now Japanese architecture is only wood, but though only wood, as regards its majestic beauty, seemliness, and adaptability to the purposes for which it is intended, it stands unique. Moreover, it is the only timber architecture in the world that has attained in any degree artistic importance. Almost every building in Japan is, or, to speak more accurately, was, constructed of wood—a fact possibly due to the interminable earthquakes to which the country was long, and is still occasionally, subjected. In Japanese architecture no brick or stone is used unless it be for foundations; nevertheless, this restriction to wood material has not prevented the Japanese architects of the past raising stupendous structures which in beauty of adornment and durability have long been the admiration of the Western world. The Temple of Nara, for example, was constructed three hundred years before the foundations of Westminster

Abbey were laid. As Dr. Dresser has pertinently remarked in this connection: "What buildings can we show in England which have existed since the eighth century and are yet almost as perfect as when first built? and yet our buildings rest on a solid foundation, and not on earth which is constantly rocked by natural convulsions." The porch of the temple of Todaji is erected upon pillars 100 feet high by 12 feet in circumference, and yet this porch is merely the entrance to another porch equally large, which again is itself the approach to the temple containing an image of Buddha 53 feet high with a halo 83 feet in diameter. The sanctuary of the ancient temple at Nara, already referred to, has columns quite 100 feet high consisting of a single stem. These ancient fanes are not bald architectural ruins. Their decoration, as ancient as the building itself, is quite as permanent. They are ablaze in every part with majestic decorations in gold and all the colours of the rainbow, as gorgeous and impressive now as they were when first applied by the hands of the decorators more than a thousand years ago. As a recent writer on this subject has appositely remarked: "It is in detail the Japanese architect most excels, for if he conceives like a giant he invariably finishes like a jeweller. Every detail to the very nails, which are not dull surfaces but rendered exquisite ornaments, is a work of art. Everywhere we encounter friezes and carvings in relief, representing in quaint colour harmonies flowers and birds, or heavenly spirits playing upon flutes and stringed instruments."

It must often strike the thinking man as a curious fact that these old religious edifices, whether in Europe or the Far East, seem to have a permanence about them such as is not characteristic of modern buildings of the same kind.

The reason, I think, must have been that the men who were employed in the designing and construction of these ancient buildings, whether in the East or West, were not mere mercenaries employed for a particular purpose, but men full of faith in their religion, a building in whose honour and for whose services they were employed to erect, and who threw into their work their whole souls, so to speak—gave, in fact, the best of what they had, and employed all their zeal, energy, and enthusiasm with a view of perpetuating, whether in stone, brick, or wood, the faith they so firmly held and so dearly loved.

Some of the problems that the Japanese builders of the past had to face in the erection of a few of the great temples which still adorn the country have proved insoluble to many European engineers and architects. The erection and support of the magnificent pagoda at Nikko is an example in point. Dr. Dresser has referred to this and pointed out what he deemed a great waste of material in connection therewith. He failed to understand for what reason an enormous log of wood ascended in the centre of a structure from its base to the apex—a log of wood about 2 feet in diameter—while near the lower end one equally large was bolted to each of the four sides of the central mass. When Dr. Dresser expressed surprise on the subject he was told that the walls must be strong enough to support the central block; and on his pointing out that the central block was not supported by the sides, he was taken up to the top of the building and the fact demonstrated to him that the huge central mass was suspended like the clapper of a bell. On descending again, while lying on the ground, he saw that there was quite an inch of space between the soil and the great pendulum—a safeguard against damage by earthquake. For many hundreds of years the centre of gravity of this building has, by its swinging, been kept within the base, and the fact shows, were evidence needed, that the Japanese architects who designed this great Nikko Pagoda and similar structures were men of scientific capacities who had thought out every problem connected with the safety and permanence of the building they were employed to design.

The domestic dwellings of the great mass of the Japanese people are of the simplest possible type. They are no doubt evolved from the hut of the Ainos, probably the aborigines of the islands, still to be found in the island of Yesso. There are no walls as we understand the term, the sides being composed, in winter, of amado, or sliding screens made of wood, and in summer of shoji, or oil-paper slides. This enables, in hot weather, the whole of the side of the house to be moved, and the air to be given free ingress and egress. Nor are these habitations divided off into permanent rooms, as in this and other European countries. Paper screens which slide into grooves divide the space according to requirements. The wood-work of these dwellings, which are largely composed of camphor-wood, is both within and without left unpainted, and they generally present a neat and alluring appearance. When one compares the dwelling-places of the poorest inhabitants of Japan with the hovels in this country, and more especially in Ireland, occupied by the peasants, one is really lost in wonder at the ignorance of those persons who call Japan, and no doubt still believe it to have been, an uncivilised country until it was brought intimately into association with Occidental nations.

As we ascend in the social scale in Japan we find, of course, a difference in architecture. The principle remains very much the same, but, as might be expected, the build-

TEA HOUSE, NEAR TOKIO

FROM A PRINT BY HIROSHIGE

ings are more elaborate and there is a wealth of ornamentation which is absent from those of the lower classes. I am inclined to think that what I may call ecclesiastical art has largely influenced the decoration of the houses of the nobles and upper classes in Japan. Many of the old feudal castles, which were gems of Japanese architecture, no longer exist, but some of those which still remain are exceedingly beautiful specimens of wooden architecture. The castle of Nagoya, built in the early part of the seventeenth century, is supposed to be the finest specimen of the kind in Japan.

But the Japanese never seems to have been overmuch concerned respecting his dwelling. To comprehend the beauty of Japanese architecture, to see it in its purity and to realise all the grandeur that can be crowded into it, it is necessary to study it in the religious edifices of the country. Plainness is the characteristic of the Shinto temple ; built as a rule of pine, it has a thatched roof. The fact of its being an edifice of the Shinto religion is self-evident from the torii which stand before every Shinto temple. There are no idols or exterior ornamentation of any kind. The walls are left untouched by either the painter or the lacquerer. In the Buddhist temples, on the contrary, the Japanese artist has had afforded him full scope for the exercise of his ornamental ingenuity. Numerous courtyards have to be traversed before reaching the temple itself. These courtyards contain many small buildings, bronze or stone lanterns, belfries, pavilions, pagodas, &c., &c., all elaborately decorated. Amongst the supplementary buildings connected with, but occasionally independent of, Buddhist temples, none is more interesting than the pagoda so intimately associated with Buddhism in every part of the Far East and so typically Oriental in its architecture. What may have been the precise origin of these five- or seven-storied erections, for what purpose they were intended, or what symbolism, if any, they were the expression of, is now largely a matter of conjecture. No one who has visited the East can at any rate have failed to be impressed by them. In Japan where, save the lower storey, the whole is lacquered red, they are a striking feature of the country. The lower storey, by the way, is decorated with numerous painted carvings. Topping the whole building is the twisted spire of bronze.

Like most other things in Japan, the origin and development of the architecture of the country is lost in the twilight of obscurity. Korea appears to have influenced Japanese architecture, just as it has Japanese art of various kinds. It is an extraordinary fact that this portion of Asia contiguous to the Japanese islands, which has for so many hundreds of years past exercised such a subtle influence on the art and industries of Japan, should at the commencement of the twentieth century have passed under the suzerainty of that country. When one fully comprehends the connection in various ways of Korea with Japan in all the past centuries, one begins to understand the sentimental feeling which has influenced the whole nation in regard to the possibility of Korea passing under the domination of any other Power. At the beginning of the third century Korea was invaded by Japan and, although the country was then conquered, it, as has not infrequently under similar circumstances happened in history, exercised a potent effect on both the art and architecture of Japan. Korean architecture, of course, was not original ; it was based on that of China, which in its turn came from Burmah, and that again probably from India. In the course of the seventh century, however, the imported architecture more or less assumed the general style which has since remained distinctly Japanese and although it undoubtedly embodies everything that was best in the architecture of the countries from which it derived its essential features, appears to me to have an originality of its own. No man who has not visited the great temples at Shiba and Nikko can understand to what heights of sublimity wooden architecture can rise, what a gorgeous *tout ensemble* can be accomplished by harmonious colour schemes deftly blended by artists who had made a study of colour and all the details connected therewith, and knew how to render a picturesque effect which should be imposing without being either gaudy or glaring.

I am afraid that the results of Western civilisation have been, and will continue to be, fatal to Japanese architects. Judging by the buildings which have been erected in the country since Western influences have reigned supreme Japanese architecture is not only dead but buried. These edifices—hotels, Government buildings, railway stations and so on, are an attempt to combine Western and Japanese styles. The result is an incongruity, to express it mildly, sufficient to cause the artistic mind to shudder. The men who built the temples at Shiba, at Nikko, and in various other parts of the country, and the pagodas which dot the land, are dead, and have left no successors. There is nothing, in my opinion, that is more likely to be influenced, and more injuriously influenced, by Western ideas than the architecture of Japan. There is a tendency in the country to erect European buildings, and I suppose it is one that it is impossible to complain of. The Japanese houses, although they have advantages in the summer-time, are undoubtedly not well fitted to withstand the rigours of winter; and I have no doubt that, from the standpoint of material comfort, a replacement of them by buildings erected on European lines might be an advantage. But from the artistic point of view such a change is one impossible to contemplate without a feeling of regret.

There is, of course, no human possibility of temples such as those at Shiba and Nikko ever again being erected in Japan. As I have previously remarked, buildings such as these are something more than mere material constructions; they are the embodiment in material form of a living faith which the designers and builders attempted to set forth in their work. An age of disbelief, of indifference, of agnosticism, is not conducive to the construction of such edifices. We need not go to Japan for evidence of that obvious fact. The hideous monstrosities in the shape of cathedrals, churches, and chapels that have been built in this country during the past century or two are abundant proof, were any needed, that the faith and piety whose outward and visible manifestation is to be seen in Westminster Abbey, Canterbury Cathedral, York Minster, and various other noble architectural fanes is no longer with us; it has gone, and, apparently, inspiration with it. We can now only construct walls, and put roofs on them—admirable edifices, no doubt, to keep out the rain, but signifying nothing from an artistic or idealistic point of view. And so it is in regard to Japan. Architecture there, considered as an art, is dead. It may be imitated or reproduced, but the reproduction will impose on no person of artistic sensibilities or knowledge, any more than a Sheraton reproduction hailing from the Tottenham Court Road would impose on a connoisseur as the genuine work of that great artist in furniture.

The art of Japan has, especially since the opening up of the country, been closely studied and investigated, and many learned tomes have been written concerning it. I do not, however, think that the art of the country as expressed in its architecture has received anything like the attention it deserves. This may possibly arise from the fact, to which I have already referred, that many people have what I may term a restricted definition or conception of art. Others there are, again, who consider wooden architecture to be almost a contradiction in terms. Words or definitions in a matter of this kind seem to me to be childish. The lover of the beautiful, the admirer of the historic, the investigator of the ebb and flow of religious systems and of the sentiments and spirit that have influenced and moulded them at different periods of their existence, can in the ancient wooden temples of Japan find abundant material for enjoyment, instruction, reflection. I have no hesitation in including these buildings in that surely expansive and comprehensive term, Art.

CHAPTER XIV

POSTAL AND OTHER MEANS OF COMMUNICATION

THE advancement of a nation, may, I think, be accurately gauged by the facilities it possesses or has developed for the communication of its inhabitants, either by personal intercourse or those other means which science has of late years discovered or evolved for the transmission of thought, whether on business or otherwise—the letter post, the telegraph, and the telephone. I accordingly purpose briefly describing the extent to which, in these respects, Japan has assimilated and utilised Western ideas.

I have already touched on the matter of railway communication, so I will not again refer to it in any detail. I may, however, remark that although railways in Japan have done much to open up the country and provide for more frequent and rapid intercourse between man and man, they still lack much in the matter of European ideas of comfort. There are three classes of carriages, and the fares of each are extremely low. The gauge is narrow; the carriages are open, as in America, with one long seat running down each side and a shorter one at the end. In the first-class carriages tea is provided, a kettle and teapot wherein to make the beverage being placed on the floor between the seats for the use of passengers. No doubt ere long the Japanese will be more impressed than they appear to be at present as to the necessity for express trains, high speeds, Pullman and restaurant cars, as well as for other now indispensable characteristics of English and American railways. The initial railway line in Japan was that between Yokohama and the capital. It was popular and well patronised from the first, in contradistinction to the record of railways in China, where the initial line—that between Shanghai and Wusung—had to be bought up and pulled up by the Chinese authorities, in view of the number of Chinamen who persisted in committing suicide by placing themselves in front of the train as a protest—and a most effective protest, it must be admitted—against the introduction into their country of this contrivance of the "foreign devils." The contrast in the manner in which the introduction of railways was received in China and Japan respectively is, I think, characteristic of the difference in the disposition and mental attitude of the people of the two countries.

A postal service modelled on that of Europe was inaugurated in Japan in 1871 by the introduction of a Government letter post between Tokio, Kyoto, Osaka, and Yokohama. Arrangements had, of course, long previously existed for the transmission of official correspondence throughout the country, but private letters were conveyed by private carriers. The following year the official postal service was extended to the whole of Japan, but not till twelve months later were private carriers abolished and the post-office, with all its various ramifications, constituted a State monopoly. Postcards, embossed envelopes, newspaper wrappers, and all the paraphernalia—so far as they had then been developed—

of European post-offices were adopted by the Japanese postal authorities, and caught on with the people with surprising rapidity. In 1875 mail steamers were established between Japan and the Chinese ports, and the next year Japan, which at that time had, as I have elsewhere mentioned, to view post-offices established in the treaty ports, herself planted Japanese post-offices in both China and Korea. The Postal Union was joined in 1877, and from that time the Japanese post-office has developed, *pari passu* with the post-offices of European countries until at the present time it is in some respects ahead of them in the matter of enterprise and the facilities it affords. The Inland Parcel Post was established in 1892, and it has had a marked effect in the opening up of the country and the familiarising of the people with many commodities, principally European, of which they had previously no knowledge. At the present time there are considerably over 6,000 post-offices. About a thousand millions of letters and postcards—a favourite means of communication—are handled yearly. The number of parcels at present sent through the post amounts to about eleven millions annually.

Every description of post-office business as known in Europe is not only transacted in Japan, but, so far as results go to show, each new phase seems to fill a distinct want on the part of the people. Take the matter of postal orders for example, the introduction of which in this country was so vigorously opposed by the banking community, but a facility which has proved of incalculable utility and convenience to the mass of the public. Postal orders, when introduced into Japan, quickly came into favour. In the first year only a certain number of offices were authorised to issue and to pay these orders.

This number has now been largely increased, and many millions of postal orders are at present annually sold in Japan. The International Postal Order Service has also assumed considerable dimensions, and has largely aided, I think, in the industrial and commercial development of the country.

Post Office Savings Banks were established in Japan as far back as 1875. The object, as in this country, was to encourage thrift among the mass of the people. The maximum deposit in one year of any depositor is limited to 500 yen (about £50). The Post Office Savings Bank has been largely utilised, and both the number of depositors and the sums deposited continue to grow on a scale which shows that the utility and benefit of this institution are greatly appreciated by the Japanese people. At first the Savings Bank was worked at a loss; it took time to develop, while in its infancy banking methods were probably not as well understood by the Japanese authorities as they now are. At the present time the Post Office Savings Bank in Japan is so worked that it not only pays all its expenses but returns a profit to the national exchequer. In this respect it very favourably compares with the Post Office Savings Bank as administered in this country, which is not only worked at a loss, but, owing to various causes, has entailed a liability, nominal though it be, on the British taxpayer.

Telegraphs were first introduced into Japan in 1869, and, as was the custom at that time in almost all countries, the telegraph followed the railway. The first line was between the capital and Yokohama. As time progressed some steps were taken in the direction of developing the system, but it was not until 1878 that the telegraph service in Japan was placed on a proper footing. In 1879 the International Telegraph Union was entered. At the present time Japan is covered by a network of telegraph wires, and every important island is in communication with the capital. Telegrams may be sent either in the Japanese or European languages. Like every other means of communication, the telegraph has been rapidly adopted by the Japanese people, and it now forms such a part of the national life that it is almost impossible to imagine the country without a telegraph system. There are about 2,600 telegraph offices in Japan, and over twenty million messages are annually despatched therefrom. I think it will be admitted that—especially in view of the difficulties occasioned by the necessity of the operators in the telegraph offices being conversant to some extent with the characteristics of two absolutely different descriptions of languages—the progress made by Japan, and the development and extension of the telegraph service of the country, have been really remarkable.

When the question of introducing telephones into Japan came up for consideration it was treated somewhat more practically than was the case with reference to a similar matter in this country. There was there as here a difference of opinion as to whether telephonic communication should be left to private enterprise or be constituted a Government monopoly. After somewhat prolonged investigation it was decided that the telephone service should be set up and worked by the Government, and in the year 1890 the first telephone, that between Tokio and Yokohama, was opened. At first, strange to say, this new device of Western civilisation appears somewhat to have hung fire, and no general demand sprung up for the fitting of the telephone to private houses. It required, as indeed was the case in this country, some education of the people in regard to the paramount advantages of always having this means of communication at hand. The process of education in this respect was not prolonged. Before the telephone had been many years in the country the demand for its installation in houses and offices became so great that the Government had to obtain a special grant of money in order to carry out the necessary work. According to the latest returns there are somewhere about 350 telephone offices open to the public, while the approximate number of messages transmitted is about 150,000,000. The time is not far distant when, as I think will also be the case in this country, the telephone will be deemed to be an indispensable adjunct of almost every house in the towns of Japan.

In connection with the means of communication one or two remarks in reference to tramways may not be out of place. These are entirely, or almost entirely, electric, and have certainly, if we are to judge by the patronage accorded to them, been very favourably received by the Japanese people. According to the latest returns I have available there were twenty-two tramway companies in Japan, which between them, in the year 1904, carried the very respectable total of over 73,000,000 passengers. All of these lines save one are electric. The first electric tramway, that in Kyoto, was opened in 1895, so that the development of the country in this direction has proceeded rapidly. The Tokio Electric Tramway Company pays a dividend of 11 per cent., and although this is a record which some of the other lines have not yet attained, and may not possibly attain, nevertheless these matters must not be altogether looked at from the point of view of dividends. The shareholder very probably regards them from that standpoint, but I suggest that the facilities given to a town may be as great or even greater by a tramway paying 2, or 3, or 5 per cent. as by one paying double that figure. Indeed, large dividends are often earned by cutting down expenditure or abstaining from expenditure designed to increase the facilities of passengers. There is every prospect of electric tramways being extended to every town of any importance in Japan, and I am confident they will greatly aid in the industrial development of the land.

I cannot leave a consideration of the means of communication in Japan without making some reference to that somewhat peculiar vehicle which is by so many persons deemed to be essentially characteristic of the country, although, as a matter of fact, I believe it is of comparatively recent introduction, having been introduced either by a European or an American; I refer, of course, to the jinricksha. Before Japan became to so great an extent the objective point of the globe-trotter, and Europe, through the medium of numerous books, was rendered conversant with everything relating to the country, nothing more struck the imagination of the new arrival in Japan than the sight of this extraordinary vehicle—a kind of armchair on wheels with two shafts, pulled by a man scantily clad and with extremely muscular legs. Whoever was the individual responsible for the invention of the jinricksha, he certainly conferred a great boon on all foreigners resident in Japan before railways and tramways and other means of communication became as prevalent as they now are. The long distances traversed by the man between the shafts of a jinricksha and the speed he attained and maintained were

AERIAL TRANSPORT; BASKET SLUNG ON ROPES, PROVINCE OF HIDA

FROM A PRINT BY HIROSHIGE

almost a marvel to the foreign visitor. It was possible to get about the country in one of these vehicles quite as fast as any horse-drawn vehicle could convey one, and quite as comfortably. I have heard it stated that the men who pull these vehicles unduly develop their legs at the expense of other portions of their body, and that the speed at which they run and which they certainly keep up for extraordinarily long periods has extremely injurious effects on their constitution, so that they are, as a rule, not long-lived. I am not aware, nor have I been able to ascertain, whether such statements are mere theories or have any foundation in fact. This much I will say, that the Japanese jinricksha-runners are an extraordinary class in reference to the speed which they attain dragging a goodly weight for a very long distance. It does not seem likely that the jinricksha, acclimatised as it has been in Japan, will be ousted by other modern contrivances for getting about the country. It is still very much in evidence, and it is universally admitted by those who have had experience of it to be a most comfortable means of locomotion. Why it has never come into favour, at least to any extent, elsewhere than in Japan I have never been able to understand. Certainly jinrickshas can be hired at Shanghai, and they are to be seen at one or two other places in the Far East, but it may be regarded as a distinctly Japanese vehicle, although, as I have said, there is nothing Japanese about it excepting its adaptation in the country.

I remarked at the commencement of this chapter that we may properly gauge the progress of a nation by the facilities it possesses or has developed for inter-communication personally and otherwise. I hope the few remarks I have made on this head may enable my readers to form some idea as to the position of Japan in this matter. I have not wearied them with statistics, but I have, I think, said enough to show that in everything relating to communication, whether it be the locomotion of the individual or the facilities given to him to communicate his wishes, desires, aspirations, sentiments, Japan is now well in line with all the other great civilised Powers, and has reason to be proud of the progress she has made and the manner in which she has adapted to the requirements of her people the ideas and inventions she has obtained from Europe and America.

CHAPTER XV

LAW AND ORDER

IN every nation which aspires to be regarded as civilised the supremacy of the law and the maintenance of order are matters of supreme importance. The most perfect code of law ever devised is quite evidently of no importance unless adequate means exist for enforcing its provisions, and although justice may be lauded as a most admirable object of attainment, yet, unless the courts of the country are independent, hold the scales evenly and use the sword with impartiality, justice will remain merely a sentiment, and there will be no practical exemplification of it. I have considered in this book as tersely as possible most of the factors of civilisation in Japan. Let me briefly deal with this matter of law and order.

When the Revolution was effected in 1868 the whole legal procedure of the country was thrown more or less into a condition of disorganisation. Prior to 1868, as my readers will have seen, feudal principles prevailed in Japan. The feudal lords, or Daimios, administered justice, or what passed for it, within their own territories, and they were answerable to the central authority. In theory the feudal lords were commissioners of the ruling sovereign from whom they derived their authority; in practice they were very largely a law unto themselves, and their subjects had little or no practical chance of redress in the event of their suffering any injustice. It is very difficult to ascertain whether there was in reality a legal code of any kind in existence and under the ken of these feudal lords. The legal system then in vogue appears to have been based for the most part on custom and usage. A writer on the subject has remarked that the few written laws were of a thoroughly practical character. Unfortunately I have not had an opportunity of acquainting myself with the nature of these laws. They were probably, like everything else in the country, imported from China, and indeed the Chinese legal system has been supreme in Japan until recently, and even now I am not quite certain that much of its influence does not remain. I have read that the fundamental principle underlying the written laws referred to was that: "The people should obey the law, but should not know the law." The code was accordingly a secret one. I have not space, nor indeed have I any inclination, to deal with what is, after all, an academical question as to the law prevalent in Japan prior to the Revolution. It was probably for the most part, just as in other countries when feudalism existed, a kind of rough-and-ready justice, which perhaps served its purpose well at the time, and depended more as regards the matter of justice upon the administrator of it than upon the code itself. Though the Revolution took place in 1868, it was not until 1871 that the Daimios were deprived of all their administrative authority. The whole of the country was then divided into districts under the control of the central Government, and all relics of feudalism and class privileges, which had been numerous, were ruthlessly swept away. In due course a civil code, commercial code, code of civil procedure, and code of criminal procedure were issued. One or two of these codes were found not to work well in practice, and they have been submitted to and revised by committees specially appointed for that purpose.

As I stated in the chapter on the Constitution the independence of the judges is recognised and provided for. The legal system of Japan at the present time is eclectic. As I have said, the Chinese system of legal procedure long obtained, and its influences may perhaps to some extent still remain. Nevertheless Japan has gone to various countries and selected what she deemed good in each for her present legal system. The jurisprudence of both France and England have been largely drawn on. In reference to the civil law custom is, as might have been expected in view of the circumstances of the country, still strongly relied on. There has often been a difficulty in ascertaining custom owing to the changed and changing conditions of the nation, and in reference thereto very much the same procedure has followed as in this country where the question of custom is so frequently pleaded in the courts of law. Some of the German system of jurisprudence has also been included in the Japanese legal system. As I have elsewhere observed, the suggestion to abolish extra-territoriality, and with it the foreign courts in Japan, met with a considerable amount of opposition from the foreign community there who believed that they would not be able to obtain justice in the Japanese courts. These fears have been shown to be groundless, and it is now generally recognised that the foreigner in Japan need have no fear of going into a Japanese court where he is, whether it be a civil or criminal matter, certain to obtain a perfectly fair trial.

Closely connected with law is the matter of police. In Japan the police of the country are entirely under the control of the State, just as are the constabulary in Ireland. The police are under the orders of the Minister of the Interior, who has a special office for dealing with the matter. The cost of the force is, however, paid by each prefecture, the State granting a small subsidy. According to the latest statistics, the police force of Japan amounted to something under 35,000 officers and men. When we consider that this body of men is responsible for the enforcement of the law and the preservation of order among some 47,000,000 people, it will, I think, be admitted that the number is not excessive. The social condition of the Japanese police, if I may use such a term, is higher than that of the police in this and other countries. In Japan the police force had its genesis after the abolition of feudalism, and, as a matter of fact, a large proportion of the first members thereof belonged to the Samurai class. The social position and intellectual attainment of these young men gave what I may term a standing to the police force in Japan which it has not yet lost. Of course, nothing like the same class of men is now attracted to it, the salaries are comparatively small and the work is not over-congenial for people whose ideas are such as those of the Japanese.

I may mention, as an interesting feature in this connection, that the Government have established a police and prison college in Tokio, where both police and prison officials are effectively trained for the discharge of their duties. This college was established when extra-territoriality was abolished, with the view of ensuring a higher training in view of the additional responsibilities that would devolve upon the police and prison officials.

From police I naturally come to some consideration of prisons. There are a large number of people in this country who have the idea in their mind that prisons are a weak point in all foreign countries, and that it is only in England that these regrettable institutions are properly managed. In fact the idea now seems to be prevalent here that we have gone too far in the direction of making prisons comfortable, and that excellent alliteration "Coddled Criminals" has more than once done duty in print in this connection. I consider that the present prison system in Japan is regulated and administered on sounder principles than those that obtain in this country. There are in all about 140 prisons in Japan. All the old prisons in the country were constructed of wood and arranged on the associate system. A separate cell system is, however, specially provided for foreign criminals, who are given clothes, bedding, and other articles to which they are used. The Government, a few years ago, commenced the construction of a number of new prisons, for the most part built of brick, in which a mixed system of separation and association, according to the offences of the prisoners, will be employed. The windows of these prisons were directed to be made especially large, so that the prisoners might have plenty of light and air. This is a matter in which some foreign Governments, that of this country included, might well take a lesson from Japan.

It is pleasing to be able to state that since 1899 the inmates of the prisons have been decreasing in number. There is nothing quite analogous to the ticket-of-leave system in this country. Parole is suggested by a prison governor to the Minister of Justice in reference to any prisoner whom he may deem worthy of the privilege, provided that prisoner has completed three-fourths of the sentence imposed upon him and has shown a disposition to live more worthily. I do not quite know how this latter fact is made plain in gaol, but at any rate the prison governor has to be convinced of it. A prisoner thus released remains under police supervision during the remainder of his sentence.

In Japan the death penalty is not confined to murder. It may be inflicted for robbery with violence, homicide, wounds inflicted by children upon their fathers, mothers, and grand-parents, as well as for arson. This sounds a somewhat drastic blood code, but when I state that the average number of persons executed in Japan does not exceed thirty a year, it will be seen that either the crimes mentioned are infrequent or that the punishment of death is only inflicted in extreme cases.

One interesting feature of the Japanese prison system is the granting of medals to criminals who have shown an amendment of their lives by good conduct and diligence at their work. The privileges enjoyed by persons possessing these medals are so interesting that I will transcribe them here:—

1. All medallists are supplied with superior kinds of garments and other articles.

2. Each medallist is allowed to send out two letters per month.

3. Medallists enjoy the privilege of bathing prior to other prisoners, hot water being used in accordance with the general custom of the Japanese people.

4. The supply of accessories is increased in quantity every week for medallists, according to the number of medals granted, to the extent of an increased expense of two sen or less for one meal per person. This increase is granted once a week to the possessor of two medals,

and three times a week for each possessor of three medals.

5. The allotment of earnings is made in the following proportion, the remainder being applied to prison expenses :—

Three-tenths to each felon to whom one medal has been granted.

Four-tenths to each misdemeanant to whom one medal has been awarded.

Four-tenths to each felon having been granted two medals.

Five-tenths to each felon possessing three medals.

Six-tenths to each misdemeanant granted three medals.

There is no need for me to deal with the question of punishment of criminals in Japanese prisons. I may, however, remark that in respect of foreign criminals every effort is made to treat them in accordance with their conditions of national life in regard to bathing, food, &c. In reference to the question of prison labour, which has become somewhat of a vexed economic problem in this country, the Japanese authorities do not appear to experience much difficulty. The object of the prison system of labour is to give the prisoners a careful training, and to encourage diligence, so that on their return to the world they may not experience difficulty in obtaining employment. The labour is of two kinds—Government, and for private individuals. In the latter case the necessary labour is obtained from the prisons direct, the employers supplying the material. I think this part of the system is perhaps open to question, as it has been found in other countries productive of grave abuses.

The discharged prisoner in Japan, as in other countries, finds a difficulty in obtaining employment, and several societies similar to those in existence here have been established with a view of assisting discharged prisoners. I have not sufficient information to enable me to say what measure of success these societies have achieved. In a country like Japan, which is endeavouring to perfect all her institutions, I hope that the discharged prisoner problem will be solved otherwise than by philanthropic societies. The criminal who has completed his sentence ought to be deemed to have purged his offence, and has a right to return to the community and obtain work until, if ever, he again misconducts himself.

I hope my few remarks on the subject of the means taken in Japan to maintain law and order will tend to convince my readers that in every detail of her administration Japan has shown a capacity for adapting what is good in foreign nations and moulding it for her own purposes. The foreign community in Japan has long since got over its state of panic in regard to the danger of suing and being sued in Japanese courts, and the possibility of being an inmate of a Japanese gaol. The years that have elapsed since the treaties were revised have demonstrated clearly that, if anything, extra consideration is shown to the foreigner in all the details of the administration of the law in Japan. I remarked at the beginning of this chapter that the supremacy of the law and the maintenance of order are matters of supreme importance in every civilised country. Japan has recognised this fact, and she has acted upon the recognition thereof with most admirable results.

CHAPTER XVI

LITERATURE AND THE DRAMA

THE literature of Japan is a somewhat recondite subject, while the Japanese drama is at present, like many other things in the country, to a great extent in a state of transition. Still, some remarks on these two matters are, I consider, absolutely essential in order that my readers may form some idea of two important phases of Japanese life. The literature of Japan is indeed largely mixed up with the national life through many centuries—a reflection, in fact, of it. The late Sir Edwin Arnold, whose great authority on everything connected with Japan is generally admitted, has observed in reference to the literature of that country: "The time will come when Japan, safe, famous, and glad with the promise of peaceful years to follow and to reward this present period of life and death conflict, will engage once again the attraction of the Western nations on the side of her artistic and intellectual gifts. Already in this part of the globe persons of culture have become well aware how high and subtle is her artistic genius; and by and by it will be discovered that there are real treasures to be found in her literature. Moreover, England, beyond any other European country, is likely to be attracted to this branch, at present naturally neglected, of what may be called the spiritual side of Japanese life."

The drawback to the fulfilment of the somewhat optimistic forecast of Sir Edwin Arnold is the great difficulty experienced by the Western nations in acquiring a sufficient knowledge of the language in which the treasures of Japanese literature are embedded if not entombed. No man can ever grasp the beauties of a literature, and especially an Oriental literature, through the medium of a translation, however well done. A translation is like a diamond with the brilliancy removed, if we can imagine such a thing. It may be faultlessly correct in its rendering, and yet absolutely misleading in its interpretation of the original.

Japanese literature embraces poetry, history, fiction, books of ceremony and travel, as well as many works of an ethical nature. Poetry is supposed to have reached its most brilliant period in Japan a long way back—long even before Geoffrey Chaucer took up his pen to write those immortal lines which I fear but comparatively few Englishmen now read. In reference to this poetry of twelve hundred years ago, Mr. Aston—perhaps the greatest authority on the subject—remarks: "While the eighth century has left us little or no prose literature of importance, it was emphatically the golden age of poetry. Japan has now outgrown the artless effusions described in the preceding chapter, and during this period produced a body of verse of an excellence which has never since been surpassed. The reader who expects to find this poetry of a nation just emerging from the barbaric stage of culture characterised by rude, untutored vigour, will be surprised to learn that, on the contrary, it is distinguished by polish rather than power. It is delicate in sentiment and refined in language, and displays exquisite skill of phrase with a careful adherence to certain canons of composition of its own."

I confess my knowledge of the language is insufficient to enable me to read Japan's literary treasures in the original, and as I have remarked, no man through the medium of a translation can adequately form a correct opinion respecting any description of foreign literature. I fear, however, that modern Japan is as little concerned with its eighth-century poetry as the modern Englishman is with that of Chaucer, not to speak of those great poets, most of whom are now forgotten, who lived long before Chaucer and whose verses were not only read but sung throughout the length and breadth of the land.

In a much later period of the history of the country, literature was undoubtedly greatly in vogue. There was evolved what I may term a distinct literary class, the language and literature of China were diligently studied, and very much of the literature of this time is written in Chinese. That language, indeed, seems to have been at one period regarded in Japan very much as Latin was, and in some quarters is even still, regarded in Europe as the appropriate medium for expressing the most sublime thoughts of the brightest intellects. The fiction of this period, usually termed the Heian—and there is plenty of it still in existence—was for the most part written by women, so that it will be seen the female novelist is not, as some persons appear to imagine, a comparatively modern development. After the twelfth century—and most of the literature I have referred to is anterior to that—petty wars between the feudal princes appear to have been incessant, and the whole country was for a great number of years more concerned with fighting than with literature. History or historical romance seems to have been the favourite literary exercitation during this period. A good deal of the literature thereof is still, I understand, read in Japan, especially by its youth, for whom the stirring episodes embodied in the history and historical romances of these bellicose times seem to have an especial fascination.

The Tokugawa period, covering the 270 years during which the Government of the Tycoon was installed in Yeddo, was one during which literature made great progress in Japan. Those years were a time of profound peace; the country was cut off from the rest of the world, thrown in upon itself, and accordingly had ample leisure, and possibly much inclination, to develop its artistic side, especially in literature. The study of books was prevalent everywhere, and quite a band of teachers arose in the land whose mission it was to expound its ancient literature, and exhume for public edification and delectation many of the buried literary treasures of the past. These teachers were not content with mere oral description; they wrote what would now be termed treatises or commentaries, many of which show great depth of learning, by way of expounding and explaining the classics of Japan with a view of bringing them within the ken of the great mass of the people. This period (the Tokugawa) also had its works of fiction; it produced many dramas and, I believe, some, if not much, poetry. The romances of this time are, I am told, written principally for or down to the level of the common people. The classics of Japan were, and probably still are, like the classics of Greece and Rome in respect of the mass of the people of this country, not understood, and most likely were they, would not be appreciated. And hence in the Tokugawa period what I may term the popular writer was evolved, and he turned out, under a *nom-de-plume* for the most part, books for the lower orders. These works are now regarded as somewhat vulgar, but they are in many respects a mirror of the age in which they were written, and it is doubtful if they are much coarser in style than some of the novels published in England in the eighteenth century. Vulgarity, it must be remembered, is largely a matter of opinion, and because either the Japanese of to-day or the foreigner who has perused, perhaps in a translation, this fiction of a couple of centuries back, dubs it according to the opinion of to-day vulgar, it by no means follows that it was so considered in Japan two hundred years back.

Since the Revolution of 1868 it is doubtful if Japan has produced any distinctive literature. The whole country and all the national modes of thought have been in a state of transition, a condition of unrest—circumstances not conducive to the production of classical literature; moreover, literary ideas and conceptions have changed and are still changing—changing rapidly. The development of a powerful newspaper press must have a marked and far-reaching effect on Japanese literature. So also must the study of Western literature by the educated classes—a study which is both extensive and increasing. Japanese literature is now undoubtedly in the melting-pot, so to speak, and what will be the precise result it is impossible to determine. It must be confessed that the modern Japanese who has been educated according to Western methods, and is adequately acquainted with the languages and literature of Europe, is infrequently an admirer of the peculiar literature of his own country. Possibly it suffers by comparison. Japan has produced no Dante, or Shakespeare, or Milton. The moods of her people, and probably the limitations and peculiarities of the language, have prevented the possibility of the appearance of such divine geniuses. There is, its critics declare, an absence of sustained power and sublimity in Japanese literature generally, while the didactic and philosophical, if not altogether lacking, is extremely rare therein. But it seems to me the height of absurdity to compare the literature of a country like Japan with the literature of some other land where everything is, and always has been, essentially different. To properly comprehend, and probably to be able to appreciate Japanese literature, it would be necessary to get, so to speak, into the atmosphere in which it was produced. To judge it by twentieth-century standards and canons of criticism and from European standpoints is not only unfair but must create a totally false impression.

In every country which has attained any degree of civilisation, and even in some countries whose civilisation is still imperfect, the drama has played an important part, and Japan has been no exception to the rule. Its dramatic literature is, I believe, of considerable extent, and to understand, much less appreciate it properly would require very profound study. Many of the more or less ancient dramas are works not only containing the dialogue of the play but much descriptive matter. They were, as a matter of fact, written for theatres in which there were to be not actors but marionettes, singers being engaged to sing the lines out of sight while the puppets depicted the characters. Some of these dramas have, since they were written, been adapted for the ordinary stage and the characters portrayed by Japan's most famous actors. The theatre was long looked down upon and it is only of comparatively recent years that it has been looking up.

A LABOUR OF LOVE

FROM A PRINT BY TOSHIKATA

A large number of persons in this country still appear to be under the impression that there are no actresses on the Japanese stage. This is, of course, a mistake, caused no doubt by the fact that in Japanese theatres the female characters in a play are so often impersonated by men. Some two or three centuries back actors and actresses used, as in Europe, to play in the same piece, but this was for some reason or other interdicted, and ever since there have been companies composed of men and women respectively. In the male companies some of the female parts naturally fell to men and in the female companies the male parts were of necessity depicted by women. Of recent years the tendency is to revert to the ancient practice and to come into line with the custom of European countries in this matter, and ere long, no doubt in Japanese theatres the female characters will be taken by women and the male characters by men.

The theatre has always been a popular institution in Japan, and the pieces usually played have very much the same *motif* as the dramas formerly so popular in this country—the discomfiture of the villain and the triumph of virtue. The Japanese theatre does not appeal to the ordinary European visitor, or indeed to many Europeans living in the country. In the first place, the performance is too long for the European taste, and in the next, most Japanese plays are of one kind, and concerned with one period—the feudal. There is, moreover, a plethora of by-play—sword exercise and acrobatic performances—which have nothing whatever to do with the plot of the piece. In fact, irrelevancy appears to the European the chief characteristic of what he sees on the stage of a Japanese theatre. Nor does the play, as is usual in serious dramas in this country, revolve round one character, the hero or heroine. Indeed it is not always easy to earmark, so to speak, the leading character, and it is occasionally doubtful in many Japanese plays whether there is any hero or heroine. But the same remark may be made here as in reference to the literature of the country. It is probably essential to get into the Japanese atmosphere in order to properly appreciate a Japanese play. The drama in Japan at any rate serves, and so far as I have had an opportunity of forming an opinion in the matter, serves well, its purpose to interest and amuse the frequenters of the theatres, besides which the lessons it inculcates are for the most part of a moral nature.

The high art of the Japanese theatre is represented by the "Nô," which I suppose fills much the same position as does the Italian opera in this country. The "Nô" is, I believe, very ancient. The written text is sung; there is a principal and a secondary character and a chorus. The dialogue is as ancient, some critics say as archaic, as the time in which the play was written, and I understand it requires being educated up to it in order to fully appreciate the "Nô." The ordinary Japanese would probably just as much fail to comprehend or like it as would the Englishman from Mile End, were he taken to Covent Garden, and invited to go into raptures over one of Mozart's or Meyerbeer's masterpieces. A performance of the "Nô" would probably interest those who find excitement in a representation of "Œdipus Tyrannus," or some Greek play. Still, the "Nô" is appreciated by a large number of the intellectual classes in Japan, who find an interest in the representation of this Japanese opera, as I suppose it may be termed.

As I have already said, very much the same remarks

made in reference to the literature of Japan apply to its drama. That country is still in the transition stage, and both its drama and its literature will undoubtedly be profoundly modified in future years. Western literature and Western dramatic art have already exercised considerable influence, and there are movements on foot whose object is to replace the old ideas and methods, especially in the matter of the representation of dramatic works by those which obtain in Europe and America. Whether these movements will be successful or not remains to be seen. There is certainly a large body of public opinion not only opposed but antagonistic to them. In spite of the rapid development of Japan in recent years, there is a very strong conservative party in the country—a party which, though it recognises or acquiesces in the desirability of change in many directions, is not prepared to throw overboard everything because it is old. I sincerely hope that the distinctive literature and dramatic art of the country will not be allowed to die out. Japan cannot afford to forget the past with its influences on the national life and character, influences at work for many ages which have assuredly had a material effect in elevating her to the position she at present occupies.

CHAPTER XVII

NEWSPAPERS IN JAPAN

JAPAN having taken on most of the characteristics and some of the idiosyncracies of Western civilisation, has naturally developed a newspaper press of its own. Of course newspapers in Japan are no new thing. Mr. Zumoto, editor of the *Japan Times*, claims for Japanese journalism an origin as far back as the early part of the seventeenth century. "Long before," he remarks, "our doors of seclusion were forced open by the impatient nations of the West, our ancestors had found a device by which they kept themselves in touch with current events and news. The news-sheets of those days were roughly got up, being printed from wooden blocks hastily purchased for each issue. They were meagre in news, uncouth in form, and quite irregular in appearance, there being no fixed date for publication. Neither were they issued by any particular and fixed publisher. Anybody could issue them, and at any time they pleased. These sheets were called Yomuri, which, being translated, means 'sold by hawking.'" These ancient newspapers had, however, palpably nothing in common with modern journalism, and anything in the shape of criticism or comment, or any attempt to guide or mould public opinion was, of course, not to be found therein. He would have been a bold man at the beginning of the seventeenth century, or indeed very much later, who would have ventured to print and publish anything tending to influence public opinion, or having the appearance of being a criticism on those in authority.

We may take it that for all practical purposes the rise of the native newspaper press of Japan did not take place till some time after the Revolution of 1868. If its rise has been recent its progress has certainly been rapid. There can be no question that both the rise and development of the vernacular press has been largely influenced by English journalism. There have always, since the opening of the country, been English newspapers in Japan, and very admirable newspapers too. One or more Englishmen have started papers printed in Japanese, and although these ventures were not commercially successful, they, at any rate, showed the way for Japanese journalism. Mr. Kumoto in his very interesting remarks published in Stead's "Japan and the Japanese," gives an amusing illustration of the somewhat amateur business lines on which the native Japanese newspapers were at first produced. He quotes the following notice which appeared in one of them: "The editors note with satisfaction the growing prosperity of their venture, and notify their subscribers that in view of the increased labour and trouble entailed on them by their increasing circulation, the gracious subscribers will kindly spare them the trouble by sending for their copies instead of having them delivered to them as before." There has certainly been a remarkable development in the Japanese newspaper press since this somewhat jejune announcement was published. Tokio at the present time possesses about forty daily newspapers, and there is hardly a town in the country of any importance that has not one or two papers of its own. There are now more than a thousand magazines and newspapers of various kinds published in the country—a number which yearly increases, and is certain to increase in the near future to a very much greater extent.

But besides newspapers, Japan possesses news agencies on somewhat similar lines to those that exist in this country, whose function it is to supply the press with the latest news on every matter of public and, I am afraid, sometimes of merely private importance. Whether these news agencies perform useful functions either in this country or in Japan, is a matter upon which I shall express no opinion. News acquired in a hurry in competition with other agencies which exist for a similar purpose, and purveyed to journals printed in a hurry and read in a hurry, does not often allow of discrimination being exercised in regard to its circulation. The sensational element in the native press in Japan is quite as much in evidence as in that of this country. In regard to this kind of literary fare, the appetite increases with feeding, if I may vary an old French proverb, and the sensational journals of the Japanese capital are increasing in demand from every part of the country.

As to the part which the press of Japan exercises in moulding public opinion, I confess I have not formed any clear idea; indeed, it is one upon which it is difficult to come to any conclusion. How far the press there moulds, and how far it follows public opinion is somewhat problematical. Be that as it may, many of the native papers are vigorously and effectively written, and indeed many eminent men in Japan have been either directly or indirectly connected with the press. The newspapers of

Japan differ in this respect from those of this country—that there is a press law there, and newspapers are in theory, at any rate, somewhat more hampered in their criticisms and the publication of news than is the case here. This press law seems to have irritated the English more than the vernacular press of Japan, especially during the late war. Under the provisions of the law, a warning is always given to an offending newspaper before any official action is taken. The English journals in Japan have, perhaps not unnaturally, not so far been able to divest themselves of the idea that they have still extra-territorial rights, and are consequently justified in publishing any criticisms or news irrespective of the provisions of the press law.

Newspapers in Japan do not of course attain such large circulations as some of those in England. I do not think there is any paper in the country with a circulation exceeding 100,000, and there are only one or two which reach anything like that figure. Advertising in Japan in papers has not attained the same importance as in this country. Of course all the journals, whether daily or weekly, have a large number of advertisements, but the non-advertisement portion of the paper forms a greater portion of the whole than is the case here. It may interest some of my readers to know that poetry which has long been tabooed by the press of this country is still a feature in that of Japan, and that the novel "to be continued in our next," is also served up for the delectation of Japanese readers.

A free press in a free country is no doubt an admirable institution, but it has its disadvantages. I need not enumerate them, as my readers probably know them as well as I do myself. Indeed, both in England and

America of late years we have had plenty of object-lessons, were any needed, in regard to these disadvantages. "The yellow press" is a phrase which has now come into general use to denote the certain kind of journalism which lives and thrives by pandering to the desire that so many persons in this world have for morbid sensationalism and the publication of nauseating and shocking details. People who have appetites of this kind are in need of having them perennially gratified, and accordingly it naturally comes about that the conductors of journals such as I have referred to, if they cannot provide a sufficient quantity of sensationalism true or partly true, have either to invent it or exaggerate some perhaps innocent or innocuous incident. I am sorry to say that yellow journalism is not only not unknown in Japan, but is apparently in a very flourishing condition there. I regret the fact all the more because the people of Japan are not yet sufficiently educated or enlightened to receive what they read in the newspaper in a sceptical spirit. That educational and enlightening process is only effected by a long course of newspaper reading. Even in this country we can remember the time when any statement was implicitly believed because it was "in the papers." Now some other and better evidence of the truth of any report is needed than the publication thereof in a newspaper. Young Japan will no doubt ere long assimilate this fact, and when it does the yellow press of Japan will probably find its *clientéle* a diminishing quantity. I hope my readers will not deduce from these remarks that I entertain, on the whole, a poor opinion of the native press of Japan. Considering the difficulties it has had to contend with, I consider that the progress it has made during the comparatively few years it has been in existence is as wonderful as anything in the country. And I am furthermore of opinion that the influence it exercises is, on the whole, a healthy one. It has done a great work in the education of the mass of the Japanese people in the direction of taking a broader view of life and teaching them that there is a world outside their own particular locality and beyond their own country. And while referring to the newspaper press I may also give a meed of praise to the large number of journals and magazines of a literary, scientific, and religious nature. The effect of these ably conducted periodicals as an educational influence must be immense. The number of them is gradually growing, and the support rendered to them serves to show, were any proof needed, how profoundly interested the Japan of to-day is in all those questions, whether political, scientific, religious, or literary, which are not the possession of or the subject of discussion among any particular nation but are exercising the minds and consciences of the civilised world.

One pleasing feature of the native press of Japan I cannot help referring to, and that is the friendly sentiments which it almost invariably expresses in regard to Great Britain. As I have before remarked, it was this country which in some degree influenced at first the Japanese press. I am pleased that of late at any rate, since the somewhat heated agitation in reference to the revision of the treaties has come to an end, its tone has been almost universally friendly to this country, and its approval of the alliance between Japan and Great Britain was not only unanimous but enthusiastic.

The English newspapers in Japan are still, as they have always been, ably conducted journals. Captain Brinkley, the editor of one of them, is a great authority on everything connected with Japan, and the paper he edits is worthy of all that is best in English journalism. At the same time it is hardly necessary to remark that the English press in Japan exercises little or no influence outside the immediate circle it represents. It very naturally looks at everything, or almost everything, not from the point of view of the Japanese but from that of the foreigner in Japan. It may be truthfully averred of the foreign press that, considered as a whole, it has never done anything or attempted to do anything to break down the barriers caused by racial differences. The European press in Japan has in tone always been distinctly anti-Japanese, and the sentiments which it has expressed and the vigorous, not to say violent, language in which those sentiments have been expressed has undoubtedly in the past occasioned much bitterness of feeling among the Japanese people or that portion of it which either read or heard of those sentiments. The characteristics or idiosyncracies of the people of Japan were either exaggerated or misrepresented, and there were not unnaturally reprisals quite as vigorous in the native newspapers. During the war with China, for example, the attitude of the European press was exasperating to a degree—that is, exasperating to the Japanese people. There were journals which avowedly took the part of China and expressed a desire for China's success. The victories of Japan in the course of the war were sneered at and at first belittled. Subsequently, when the success of Japan was self-evident, it was suggested by some of these newspapers that she was suffering from swelled head and was in need of being put in her place and kept there. And, accordingly, when certain of the European Powers stepped in and deprived Japan of the fruits of her victories, the action of those Powers was applauded, and the undoubted sympathy of the English people in England with Japan in the matter was derided by English editors in Japan as mere maudlin sentimentality. Language of this kind occasioned deep resentment among the people of the country. The foreign press is now, I am glad to say, saner, inasmuch as it to some extent recognises facts and the trend of events, but I fear it even still is for the most part representative of a community which regards the Japanese from the standpoint that most Europeans in the Far East regard the Eastern races with whom they are brought in contact. The position of the English papers in Japan has, I should say, been considerably affected of recent years by the development of the vernacular press. Twenty-five years or so ago they were practically the only organs that voiced public opinion of any kind in the country. Now they only voice the opinion of a section of the foreign community. A reference to a quarter of a century ago brings up memories of a gentleman connected to some extent with the newspaper press in Japan of those days. I refer to the late Mr. Wergman, who owned and edited and filled—I am not quite certain he did not print—that somewhat extraordinary journal, the Yokohama *Punch.* It appeared at uncertain intervals, and it dealt both in print and illustration with various members of the foreign community in Yokohama and its neighbourhood with a vigour and freedom, not to say licence, which would now hardly be tolerated. Its proprietor is long since dead, and so I believe is the journal which he owned and whose fitful appearances used to create such a mild excitement among the foreign community in Yokohama.

The functions of the press as a mirror of the times, as a censor of men and things, and as a guide and a leader of public opinion are of considerable importance. As I have before remarked the press of Japan is at present if not in its infancy at any rate in its youth. It is accordingly ebullient, energetic, optimistic. Time will no doubt correct many of its failings. Be that as it may, I certainly am of opinion that, considering everything, it has attained a wonderful degree of development, that it has reached a position of great importance in the country as an educational and enlightening influence, and that all who wish well to Japan may look upon its future with hope. It will no doubt play an important part as the years roll by in the development of the country and in the holding up before the people of worthy ideals in reference to economic conditions, material progress, and the conservation of the prestige and security of the Japanese Empire.

CHAPTER XVIII

JAPANESE MORALITY

IN the Preface I remarked that Japanese morality was a thorny subject. I use the word morality in its now generally accepted rather than in its absolutely correct meaning. Morality, strictly speaking, is the practice of moral duties apart from religion or doctrine; it treats of actions as being right or wrong—is, in brief, ethics. The old "morality" play, for example, was not, as some people seem to suppose, especially concerned with the relations of the sexes; it was a drama in which allegorical representations of all the virtues and vices were introduced as *dramatis personæ*. However, words, like everything else in this world, change their meaning, and, though the dictionary interpretation of morality is, as I have stated it, colloquially at any rate, the word has now come for the most part to signify sexual conduct, and it is in that sense, as I have said, I use it.

The subject of the morality of the Japanese is one that has been much discussed for many years past, and accordingly is one in regard to which it may be urged that there is little or nothing more to be said. I am not of that opinion. In the first place, much of the discussion has been simply the mere assertions of men, or sometimes of women, who either did not have the opportunity, or else had not the inclination, to investigate matters for themselves, and were therefore largely dependent on the hearsay evidence of not always unprejudiced persons. Or they sometimes jumped to very pronounced and erroneous conclusions from extremely imperfect observation or information. Let me take as an example in point, a lady, now dead, who wrote many charming books of travel—the late Mrs. Bishop, better known as Miss Bird. In her journeyings through the country Miss Bird relates in "Unbeaten Tracks in Japan," that she passed through a wide street in which the houses were large and handsome and open in front. Their highly polished floors and passages, she remarks, looked like still water, the kakemonos, or wall pictures, on their side-walls were extremely beautiful, and their mats were very fine and white. There were large gardens at the back with fountains and flowers, and streams, crossed by light stone bridges, sometimes flowed through the houses. The lady, who was on the look-out for a resting-place, not unnaturally expressed a desire to put up at one of these delightful sylvan retreats, but her native attendant informed her that was impossible, as they were kashitsukeyas, or tea-houses of a disreputable character. Miss Bird, on the strength of this information, thought it incumbent upon herself to pronounce the somewhat sweeping judgment that "there is much even on the surface to indicate vices which degrade and enslave the manhood of Japan." Such a statement is, of course, the merest clap-trap, but even were it true, it might be permissible to remark that if vice exists it is surely better for it to be on than beneath the surface. Such vice as does exist in Japan is, in my opinion, distinctly on the surface, and I have no hesitation in describing the morals of the Japanese people to be, on the whole, greatly superior to those of Western nations.

There can, I think, be no question that a large number of European people have formed their estimate of Japanese women either from a visit to a comic opera such as "The Geisha," or from a perusal of a book like Pierre Loti's fascinating work, "Madame Chrysanthéme." This is in effect the story of a *liaison* between a man and a Japanese girl of the lower classes, with, of course, a large amount of local colouring, and rendered generally charming by the writer's brilliant literary style. Unfortunately, that large number of Europeans who have never visited Japan have taken the French academician's study of a girl of a certain class as a life picture of the typical Japanese woman who is, accordingly, deemed to be more or less, to use an accepted euphemism, a person of easy virtue. Nothing could, of course, be more erroneous, no conclusion further from the truth. The remarks of Mr. Arthur Diosy in his book, "The New Far East," on this head are so much to the point in reference to the utter misconception of even many visitors to Japan in the matter of the chastity of the average Japanese women that I venture to transcribe them: "Has it not been repeated to him (the globe-trotter) that these people have no conception of virtue or of modesty? So he frequently treats the maids at the inn, the charming human humming-birds who wait upon him at the tea-house, and the Geisha summoned to entertain him, with a cavalier familiarity that would infallibly lead to his summary expulsion from any well-regulated hotel or public-house, or other places of public entertainment at home, did he dare to show such want of respect to a chambermaid or to one of the haughty fair ones serving at a bar. He means no harm in nine cases out of ten ; he has been told that Japanese girls don't mind what you say to them, and as to the tea-house girls, well, they are no better than they should be . . . but they are good little women, as capable of guarding their virtue as any in the world, and it saddens one to think how often they endure, from a feeling of consideration for the foreigner who does not know any better, they pityingly think, cavalier treatment they would not submit to from a Japanese."

Having said so much I feel I am free to admit that a somewhat different standard of morality does obtain in Japan to that which exists, or is supposed to exist, among Occidental nations. After all, morality is to some extent a matter of convention, and a people must, I suggest, be judged rather by the way in which it lives up to its standard than by the standard itself, which among some Western nations is not always strictly observed. The whole subject of morality between the sexes is one upon which a portly volume might be written. The sexual relations have been affected by many circumstances, some of them entirely conventional and having little or nothing to do with morality as such, while poetry and romance and sentiment have been allowed to complicate, and still render difficult a dispassionate consideration of the whole matter. Macaulay in one of his essays has observed that "the moral principle of a woman is frequently more impaired by a single lapse from virtue than that of a man by twenty years of intrigue." He explains this seeming paradox by asserting that "a vice sanctioned by the general opinion is merely a vice, while a vice condemned by the general opinion produces a pernicious effect on the whole character." "One," says Macaulay, "is a local malady, the other is a constitutional taint." I have quoted the famous historian in this connection because his observations are, I think, illustrative of my contention, viz., that morality is largely a matter of convention, sanctioned or condemned by what Macaulay terms "the general opinion."

I frankly admit that prostitution has never been regarded in Japan as it is, or is affected to be, in this and other European countries. In ancient days the public women of the capital and the large towns were as famous as in Athens of old, and were regarded as amongst the best educated and best mannered of their sex. The Japanese have ever looked upon prostitution as what is termed a necessary evil, and they have always sought to regulate and supervise it with a view of obviating those evils, terrible in their consequences, which are frequently the result of permitting it to go unchecked. And accordingly the Yoshiwara has long been a recognised institution in every considerable town in the country, the Yoshiwara being that particular portion of the town in which prostitutes are alone permitted to reside. There is, so far as I know, no prostitution outside the Yoshiwara, and the inmates thereof are subject to a rigorous supervision and inspection, medical and otherwise, which has produced excellent results. The inmates of the Yoshiwara are not recruited as are the similar class in the West. Here the "unfortunate" usually plies her trade as a *dernier ressort*. In a moment of temptation she has "gone wrong," as the phrase goes, the fact becomes public, she is too often cold-shouldered and hustled even by her immediate relations, and her downward progress is swift and certain. Nor is there for her, except in rare cases, any chance of rehabilitation. She is too hopeless to exclaim "Resurgam!" and if in an optimistic frame of mind she did so purpose she would find the consummation difficult if not impossible. She is, in a word, on the way to irretrievable ruin and a shameful end, and she knows it.

Such is, as I have said, not the case in Japan. The lot of the prostitute there has never been regarded with the loathing which it excites in this country. Houses of ill-fame were, and are still, recruited not from those whose previous lapse from virtue has rendered no other mode of livelihood possible than that from immorality, but by those whom stern necessity has driven to the step as a means either of supporting themselves or of assisting parents or their near relatives. Such a sacrifice—a terrible sacrifice, I admit—has in Japan never been regarded with horror, but as in a sense laudable. The finger of scorn must not be pointed at a woman who has voluntarily sacrificed what women hold most dear, not from lust or from the desire of leading a gay life or pampering or adorning the body, but perhaps to save father or kin from ruin or starvation. The Yoshiwara has, of course, other recruits, but in the main its inmates are not the victims of lust but of self-sacrifice. There is too often a whole tragedy in the story of a Japanese girl of this kind, and it is deplorable when the self-righteous European comes along and points the finger of scorn at her. I am aware that though not despised, as in this country, the lot of the inmate of the Yoshiwara is often, if not always, a horrible one. She is, as a rule, sold, or sells herself, for a lump sum of money to which amount is added the cost of her outfit, usually as much as the price paid to the woman or her relatives. Until this amount was worked off—and the accounts were, of course, not over accurately kept—the woman was to all intents the chattel of her master. This has, undoubtedly, for many centuries been the custom of the country. I am glad, however, to be able to state that quite recently the highest court in Japan has decided that, whatever custom may have decreed, the law gives, and will give, no sanction to any such custom. A girl confined in the Yoshiwara was forcibly taken away therefrom. The owner of the house in which she resided, as her debt had not been liquidated, considered he had a lien upon her, and he invoked the aid of the law to assist him to assert what he considered to be his rights and retake possession of the girl. The case was strenuously fought and taken to several courts, with the result I have stated. This decision will probably have far-reaching effects and declaring, as it does, that the inmates of the Yoshiwara are not slaves or chattels, it is to be cordially welcomed.

The assertion of Miss Bird, already referred to, that the manhood of Japan is enslaved and degraded by vice is one which I have no hesitation in describing as gross exaggeration. Vice, of course, there is in Japan, vice of various kinds and degrees, but the ordinary Japanese man is not, in my opinion, nearly so immoral as the average European. The chastity of the Japanese woman I place still higher. The fact, already stated, that the inmates of the Yoshiwara are not generally recruited from those who have lapsed from virtue might be urged in proof of this. Nor is the fact that prostitution is not in Japan regarded with the same loathing as in this country, in my opinion, to be taken as any evidence of an immoral tone. The ideas that obtain on the matter, in Japan at any rate, hold out the possibility of moral redemption for the inmates of the Yoshiwara, and as a matter of fact many women in Japan who, through the force of compulsion, have entered this place, frequently marry, and marry well, and subsequently live absolutely chaste lives. The standard of morality among the married women of Japan is, I may remark, high, and is rarely lowered.

I hope I shall not shock my readers if I remark that I consider the stringent regulations that exist in Japan as to the supervision of the Yoshiwara in many respects admirable. It will probably surprise many persons to learn that the high state of organisation in regard to everything connected with the superintendence of these places, as also the development of lock hospitals, is largely due to the zeal and exertions of the late Dr. G. Birnie Hill, of the Royal Navy, who was for many years lent by the Admiralty to the Japanese Government for that purpose. Under his auspices a stringent system of medical supervision was organised, which has been attended with excellent results in the direction of stamping out and obviating diseases which, I may observe, are of foreign importation. I know that the existence of any system of medical inspection will, in the estimate of a large number of estimable men and women in this country, be regarded as proof positive of the immorality of the Japanese. "We mustn't recognise vice," is their contention. I am of opinion, on the contrary, that we should either recognise vice and restrict, restrain, and regulate it, or else make vice illegal, as the Puritans did, and fine or imprison both men and women addicted to it. I could understand either of these two courses, but I must confess that I altogether fail to fathom the state of mind of those persons who adopt neither opinion, but either assert or infer that in the name of religion, morality, modesty, and many other commendable things, we should permit our streets and thoroughfares to be infested by women plying their immoral trade with all the resultant consequences.

THE ETERNAL FEMININE

FROM A PRINT BY TOSHIKATA

As I stated at the commencement of this chapter, a nation should be judged not only by its standard of morality but by the degree in which it lives up to or falls short of that standard. Judged by this, surely the fairest, the only fair, rule, Japan has every reason to be considered a moral country. Those shocking crimes which appear to be the outcome of either the aberration or the inversion of the sexual instincts are almost unknown there. Nor do I consider that the public estimate of prostitution on the whole makes for immorality. If an evil exist, and prostitution is undoubtedly an evil, it is surely better to regulate it than to affect to be oblivious of it. The Japanese attitude towards prostitution at any rate leaves a door open for the woman who has, from whatever the reason, lapsed from the paths of virtue to return thereto. This appears to my mind to be a more satisfactory state of things than the continual harrying and worrying of prostitutes in the name of indignant virtue and the driving of them on the streets. The aspect of the great thoroughfares of London, especially by night, does not give the Oriental visitor thereto a high idea of English morality. It is, nevertheless, an extraordinary fact that the Englishman or the Englishwoman who has mayhap lived in London most of his or her life, when he or she visits Japan in the course of, perhaps, "a round the world trip" in ninety days, and learns that there is in each Japanese town a Yoshiwara, the inmates of which are subject to supervision and regulation, lifts up his or her hands in holy horror, returns home with a virtuous indignation, and has no hesitation in henceforth declaring, whether in speech or writing, that the Japanese are a grossly immoral people.

The average Japanese is, very rightly in my opinion,

indignant at the constant assertions of writers, well or ill-informed, that his country is essentially immoral. He is not only indignant but astounded. He has, if he has been to this country, seen here much that has not tended to impress him with the belief that the English people are themselves in a position to dogmatise on this vexed question of morality. He is, if he has visited the great cities and towns of Great Britain, by no means convinced that the action of Japan in establishing a Yoshiwara whose inmates are under proper supervision, medical and otherwise, is not better from every point of view, that of morality included, than turning loose women into the streets to accost every passer-by and place temptations in the way of youth. On the other hand, the Japanese who has not left his own country, but is of an observant nature and of a logical disposition, fails to comprehend why the European in Europe should dogmatise upon and affect to be disgusted with what he terms the immorality of the Japanese. The Japanese who has lived all his life in his own country has had ample opportunities for studying the Europeans resident there, and I fear he has not always been impressed by their high moral tone or their ultra-moral conduct. I might say much more upon that head, but I shall refrain.

I conclude this chapter by reiterating the expression of my belief that the Japanese are, when rightly considered, a moral people. They have their own code of morals, and they act up to it. There are few nations of whom as much could be said.

CHAPTER XIX

JAPAN AND CHINA

THE results of the war between Russia and Japan seem to have caused a large number of persons to work themselves into a state of incipient panic regarding what has been graphically, if not quite correctly, termed " the yellow peril." Japan, a nation of some 47,000,000 people, had thrown down the gauntlet and totally defeated, both by land and sea, one of the great military Powers of the world. Japan had done all this as a result of some quarter of a century spent in modelling and training her Army and Navy on European lines, and adopting European arms of destruction. Of course, so argued the panic-mongers, China must be impressed by such an object-lesson—China, which has for so many years past been, and is still being, squeezed by the European Powers. The result of Japan's triumph would inevitably be, so we were asked to believe, that China would invite the former to organise the Chinese Army and Navy on Japanese lines. As the outcome thereof, a nation, not of forty, but of four hundred millions, would be trained to arms, and, if the Chinese raw material proved as good as the Japanese, a nation so powerful, if it proceeded West on conquest bent, would carry everything before it, and, unlike the last

Eastern invaders of Europe, the Turks, would be unlikely to be stopped on its onward course at Vienna. The German Emperor was amongst those who have voiced the cry of "the yellow peril." He does not, however, appear to have cast himself for the part of John Sobieski, with Berlin instead of Vienna as the decisive battle-ground. The persons who have so argued and have attempted to raise this silly cry of "the yellow peril," with a view of alarming Europe were, I think, merely the victims of an exuberant imagination. Their facts have no existence save in the realms of fancy, and as they reasoned from faulty premises on imperfect or erroneous information, their conclusions were, as might have been expected, not only inaccurate, but absurdly ludicrous. There is no "yellow peril," no prospect whatever of it, either present or remote.

The attitude of China, that vast though heterogeneous nation, is, since the close of the Russo-Japanese War, I admit, one of the most intense interest. Some persons may consider that in a book about Japan any other than a passing reference to China is out of place, and that, moreover, for me to deal with the attitude of China is to wander into political regions—a peripatetic proceeding I deprecated in the Preface. I am of opinion, however, that it is impossible to thoroughly understand Japan and to appreciate the attitude of that country to the Western Powers without some remarks respecting the present and prospective relations of China and Japan. I also think that some consideration of this bogey of "the yellow peril" is not only out of place but indispensable in order to form a correct idea of the precise effect of recent events in the Far East and the possible outcome of them.

To any person who has closely studied Far Eastern problems the attitude of China since the close of the war between Japan and Russia is in no way surprising; the forces that have long been steadily at work in that ancient Empire are now only attaining any degree of development. There is nothing, in my opinion, in the history of the world more dramatic than the way in which China has waited. That country is now, I believe, about to show that the waiting policy has been a sound one, and I am confident it will eventually prove triumphant. In 1900 I expressed in print the opinion that not a single acre of Japanese soil would ever be permitted to be annexed by a foreign country; I spoke of the policy of China for the Chinese, and remarked that that principle and policy had been repeated throughout the length and breadth of that vast Empire, and had been absorbed, as it were, into the very marrow of its people. It is in many respects interesting and curious, indeed almost comical, the manner in which that lesson has been driven home upon the Chinese. Russia has always been to them a powerful, persistent, and aggressive neighbour, a more formidable aggressor, indeed, because perhaps nearer, than any of the other Powers of Europe, whom I am sorry to say China has always looked upon very much as the substantial householder regards the burglar. Now that Japan has tried conclusions with Russia and has soundly thrashed the latter, great, slumbering China, proud, conservative, but supremely conscious of its latent resources, has been waking up. The Chinese, as a matter of fact, have very little veneration, respect, or esteem, for their Japanese neighbours. The former plume themselves on being the aristocrats of the East, and they reason, with some show of plausibility, that if the upstart Japanese have been able to so thoroughly rout the Russian forces the potential possibilities of China on the warpath are enormous. Every thoughtful student of the East has looked forward to what I may term the Japanisation of China as one of the inevitable results of the recent conflict in the Far East. To a certain extent the Japanisation of China has commenced, but at the same time one cannot be oblivious of the fact that the Chinese, with their traditions and sense of self-importance, have not the slightest intention of slavishly following in the lead of those islanders whom they have always contemned, but mean to strike out a line for themselves. If what we believe to be civilisation is to be developed in China, it will be developed by the Chinese themselves. If they are going to possess railways, telegraphs, telephones, and all the machinery of that material advancement which we call progress, and sometimes civilisation, the Chinese themselves will be the importers and adapters and, in due course, the manufacturers thereof.

Now that the great fight in the Far East is over, it certainly looks as if the Chinese at last realised the fact that development is an inevitable necessity. The master-spirits in the country have assuredly come to the conclusion, possibly with regret, that China can no longer remain in that delightful state of isolation which permitted every man in the Empire to spend the arc of his life, from his cradle to his grave, in a state of restful security. China is, in spite of herself, and certainly against the inclinations of the mass of the populace, being swept into the maelstrom of struggle now that the people, or rather their leaders, realise the position. Their attitude seems to me to be magnificent. If railways have to be made they will be made by the Chinese; the concessions already granted must—this is the universal feeling—be bought back, even at a profit, from those who have acquired them, by the Chinese themselves. Not one new concession must, on any pretence whatever, ever again be granted to a foreigner. And if this Western civilisation is to be forced upon the Chinese, they intend to take it with all its attendant precautions. They are naturally a peaceful and unaggressive people, but they have grasped the fact that, as a strong man armed is in the best position to safeguard his house, however peaceful his individual proclivities may be, so too, if a nation is to defend its territory and its territorial wealth against spoliation, it must be armed for that purpose.

For many years past Great Britain and France and other countries have been sending missionaries to China to expound to the Chinese people those sublime doctrines enunciated in the Sermon on the Mount. The Chinese have diagnosed, from the acts of the European Powers generally as well as from the actions of individual Europeans resident in China, the precise value to be attached to Christianity. For purely defensive purposes China will have almost immediately an Army which has been effectively described by the *Times* correspondent as being able to relieve the European Powers of any anxiety respecting the integrity of the Chinese Empire. People who have not visited the Far East, and who entirely derive their opinions and information in regard thereto from the newspapers, cannot possibly realise what effect the policy of the European Powers has had upon nations like China and Japan. A professedly Christian country like Great Britain going to war to force the sale of opium on a people who did not want to be debauched; a power like Germany annexing Kiaochao as a golgotha for two murdered priests

—proceedings such as these, and there have been many such during the last forty or fifty years, have been taken seriously to heart by the Far Eastern races, whether in China or Japan. All the time the Occidental Powers, with a total lack of any sense of humour, have persisted in sending missionaries to these people to inculcate doctrines which are the very antitheses of the practices of European nations to these people whom it is sought to convert. It would be, in my opinion, nothing more than the outcome of eternal justice if this great big, old, sleepy China, which has been for so many years pricked and prodded and despoiled, were at length to take up arms for a great revenge. But China, if my prevision be correct, is going to do nothing of the kind. What she does mean to do is simply to keep China for the Chinese. She is not, as so many persons imagined and still imagine would be the case, going to be led as a powerful ox with a Japanese driver. Chinese students are in hundreds in Japan, learning from that country all that the Japanese have acquired from Europe. Young, alert, capable men I found them without exception, sucking the brains of all that is best in Japan precisely as the Japanese have sucked the brains of all that is best in Europe for their own objects and to their own advantage. The immediate danger in China seems, so far as I can judge, to be that the anti-foreign feeling, which is undoubtedly intense especially in the south of the Empire, may come to a head any day and prematurely explode. The nincompoops and quidnuncs and newspaper men ravenous for copy who prate about a "yellow peril" may, in this latter fact, find some slight excuse for their blatant lucubrations. There is no real "yellow peril." Poor old China, which has been so long slumbering, is just rousing herself and making arrangements for defence against the "white peril," materialistic civilisation, and misrepresented Christianity.

The only "yellow peril" that I have been able to diagnose is the peril to the trade of Europe and the United States of America with China—a peril that appears to me to be imminent. That Japan intends to capture a large, indeed the largest, proportion of that trade I am firmly convinced. That she will succeed in effecting her object I have not the slightest doubt. At the present moment only about 5 per cent. of the imports into China are from Japan, the remainder being either from India, Europe, or America. Situated in close contiguity to China, having assimilated everything of importance not only in regard to the employment but the manufacture of machinery from Europe and the United States, possessing an industrious and intelligent population, Japan is quite obviously in a magnificent position to supply China, and supply her on much better terms, with the greater number of those commodities which China now has to import either from Europe or America. Japan, as I have said, intends to lay herself out to capture the major portion of this trade; she is quite justified in doing so, and there is every reason to suppose that she will attain her object.

That the Chinese students who have come to Japan and are flocking there month by month in increasing numbers, with a thirst for knowledge and a desire to assimilate all those Western influences and ideas and aids that have placed Japan in her present prominent position among the nations, when they, in due course, return to their own country, will of a certainty exercise a considerable influence therein, there can be no doubt. I also feel sure that Japan will render considerable assistance to China in regard to the remodelling and reorganisation of the

Chinese Army and Navy. It is as certain as anything in this uncertain world that before very many years have elapsed the naval and military forces of China will undergo as great a transformation as those of Japan have undergone. I believe, and I may say that this belief is shared by a number of naval and military men who have had practical opportunities for forming an opinion in the matter, that the raw material existing in China for the making of an effective and efficient Army and Navy is as good as that in Japan. We know that the late General Gordon, who had excellent opportunities for arriving at a sound conclusion in the matter, expressed himself in glowing terms in regard to the capabilities of the Chinaman as a soldier were he properly trained, organised, and officered. But that China, any more than Japan, entertains ambitious military projects I utterly disbelieve. The only aspiration of China as regards Europe is—to be let alone. She fears, as she has every reason to fear, European aggression. She has had ample experience in the past that the flimsiest pretexts have been utilised for the purpose of filching her territory and exacting from her pecuniary fines under the name of indemnities. We know by a recent incident that the indemnity exacted from China by this country in respect of the Boxer rebellion was not really required for the ostensible purposes for which it was imposed. A large proportion of it lay at the Bank of England unappropriated, and eventually was attached by a rapacious Chancellor of the Exchequer for the purpose of alleviating the burdens of the British taxpayer. China is determined to have no more incidents such as this in the future, and the Russo-Japanese War has given her occasion for serious thought in the matter as well as pointed an obvious moral. As a result of her cogitations, she has concluded that the most effective means she can take in the direction of preserving the inviolability of her territory and preventing the exaction of periodical monetary tributes on the part of foreign Powers, is to establish a strong and efficient Army and Navy. As a matter of fact, I consider that in so determining China is acting not only in her own interests, but in the interests of the Great Powers of Europe.

Not very many years ago that excellent sailor, Lord Charles Beresford, wrote a book entitled, somewhat too previously, "The Break-up of China." In selecting a title for his work Lord Charles without doubt voiced the opinion prevalent, not only in this country but in Europe, at the time he wrote it. The statesmen of nearly all the foreign Powers then seemed to have arrived at the conclusion that the scramble for China was imminent and, utilising their experience from what took place when the scramble for Africa was effected twenty years ago, they began apportioning in advance the territory that ought to fall to their lot. In this matter, however, they were wofully mistaken; the diplomatic physicians of the world may have diagnosed the symptoms quite accurately, but the patient surprised them all in regard to the course of the disease and her recuperative powers. There will be no "break-up" of China, and consequently we are not likely to witness any scramble for China. There has undoubtedly been an awakening of China, an awakening to her danger, to a sense of the extent to which her interests were imperilled. She wants, as I have said, to be severely left alone, and she is determined as far as possible to effect that consummation. The men of light and leading in China know perfectly well that they cannot now, even if they would, shut their country against European trade, European residents, European visitors. They are prepared to accept all these, but they will not have European interference. China is determined to work out her own destiny or salvation, call it which you will, and Japan is both willing and anxious to give her all possible assistance in that direction. The "yellow peril" bogey is, in my opinion, the silliest and most absurd cry that has ever been put forward by responsible persons.

CHAPTER XX

EUROPEANS IN JAPAN

LIKE everything else in Japan, the status and position of the foreigner have been materially changed, in fact revolutionised, of recent years. When the country was, in the first instance, opened after its long period of isolation from the rest of the world, treaties were signed with Great Britain, the United States, France, and nearly all the other European Powers, whereby Japan agreed to open seven ports, subsequently known as "treaty ports," to foreign trade in which ports foreigners were to be permitted to reside and to carry on their business. Foreigners were at the same time—not by the wish of the Japanese Government, but as the outcome of the pressure put upon Japan by the various Powers—granted extra-territorial rights, that is to say they were exempt from the jurisdiction of the Japanese courts of law. This being the case foreign courts were constituted in Japan with jurisdiction over the subjects of the nation which set up the court. In these courts foreigners sued and were sued, and crimes committed by and against foreigners were tried. As regards Great Britain a Supreme Court for China and Japan was constituted whose headquarters were at Shanghai. There were Consular Courts and a very involved kind of legal procedure generally established, mostly by Order in Council, which I need not consider in detail as it is now effete. There was, moreover, as regards Great Britain at any rate, a Bar practising in these courts, one member of which, Mr. F. V. Dickins, is justly remembered not for his forensic but for his literary efforts in the direction of depicting the inner life of the Japanese people. Into these foreign courts all the jargon, the quips and quibbles of English law were imported. These courts were, not unnaturally, an eyesore to the Japanese people. I may observe in passing that these extra-territorial courts still exist in China, and though the Supreme Court of China and Japan has been shorn of that part of its title which refers to Japan it remains, and is likely for some time longer to remain, the supreme legal tribunal of the English residents in the Chinese Empire. But besides extra-territorial courts there were extra-territorial post-offices. The English, the American, and, I think, the French Governments had post-offices in Japan which transacted postal duties of all kinds just as if they had been in London, New York, and Paris instead of in a foreign country. There may have been some excuse for this in the early days; but these foreign post-offices remained until quite recently, depriving Japan of a portion of her revenue at a time when she had developed a magnificent postal service of her own. Over and above foreign courts and post-offices there were actually foreign municipal bodies. A certain amount of ground at the treaty ports was constituted a foreign settlement wherein the foreigners resided. Within these settlements a municipal council was formed, which regulated everything therein. In these settlements the Japanese Government had no more power or authority than they had in

Battersea. These settlements were in effect foreign territory on the Japanese soil, to use what seems to be a paradox.

In exchange for the privilege of extra-territoriality granted to foreign residents in Japan, they were placed under restrictions. These included not being able to travel in the country outside a radius of 25 miles from the treaty ports unless provided with passports, which, I may remark, there was never any difficulty in obtaining, and not being permitted to live beyond the same radius. Foreigners engaged in trade in Japan had a great advantage in regard to a very low scale of customs duties, not more than 5 per cent. *ad valorem*, but they were strictly prohibited from owning land. This system of extra-territoriality was extremely unpopular with the whole of the Japanese people, and a constant movement was in force in the country for the abrogation of what the Japanese considered an invidious distinction and in the direction of making every person who voluntarily took up residence in Japan answerable to the law of the land and under the jurisdiction of the Japanese courts. The revenue of the country was also, of course, injuriously effected by the post-office privileges already referred to as well as by the differential treatment of foreigners in regard to import duties. As was to be expected, any proposal for the abolition of extra-territorial rights and the revision of the regulations in regard to import duties met with a strenuous opposition from the foreign residents in Japan. On the other hand, it must be confessed that the Japanese people opposed any compromise in the direction of granting foreigners facilities in return for the privileges that were asked to be waived. The proposal to allow foreigners to own land was vigorously inveighed against.

So was a suggestion to establish mixed courts—the kind of compromise, by the way, which would probably have equally irritated foreigners and natives. It is, I think, satisfactory to be able to relate that in the end and after many years of agitation it was the British Government which took the initiative in the matter, and some ten or twelve years ago concluded a treaty with Japan wherein the privileges of English courts, European municipalities, and differential import duties were abandoned, while in return proprietary rights, except in regard to land, were granted to foreigners.

There are, mayhap, some persons at the present day who are not aware of the fact that for a good many years after Japan was to a limited extent opened to foreigners several of the Powers retained an armed force in that country for the protection of foreign residents. Great Britain, for instance, had a large number of marines at Yokohama. The presence of these troops was extremely unpalatable to the Japanese authorities, but of course pleasing to the foreign residents, who opposed their withdrawal just as they opposed the abrogation of extra-territoriality. I am afraid the reason for the removal of this armed force as far as Great Britain was concerned was economic rather than founded on any particular principle. Be that as it may, in 1873 Japan was successful in assuring the British Government that she was able and prepared to protect all foreigners residing in the country, and in that year the last foreign soldier was withdrawn from Japanese territory.

Those who remember the agitation—and a very fierce and noisy and provocative agitation it was—in opposition to the revision of Japan's treaties with the foreign Powers with a view of getting rid of extra-territoriality will have a lively recollection of the pessimistic forebodings of the speakers and writers in reference to the future of the foreign community in that country were the exclusive privileges they then enjoyed taken away from them. The gentlemen who uttered these sentiments were no doubt sincerely convinced of their truth, but I am glad to be able to relate that time has shown them to have been false prophets. There may be, and no doubt are, foreigners in Japan who bemoan the good old days, but I am confident that the great mass of the foreign community now recognises the fact that the revision of the treaties and the withdrawal of extra-territorial privileges were inevitable and that no evil results have ensued in consequence. The Japanese courts of law have neither terrorised nor oppressed foreigners. They have, on the contrary, sought to hold the scales of justice evenly, and I believe that these courts now enjoy, as I am sure they deserve, the fullest confidence in their integrity and justice of every foreigner residing in the country.

I have noticed a tendency on the part of writers on Japan to refer to the foreign community in that Empire as if it were a community bound together by some particular principle and working in unison for some definite object. Of course such a view is nonsensical. The foreign community in Japan, in which for the purpose of my remarks I do not include the Chinese, is one composed of a large number of nationalities which have very little in common, and amongst whom a good deal of rivalry prevails. It may have been that when the question of revising the treaties was being keenly agitated, self-interest, or what was deemed to be self-interest, occasioned a sort of fictitious unity among foreigners, but at the present time, so far as my observation has gone, there is very little real unity among the foreigners in Japan. The

English, of course, predominate in numbers, and they have also the major portion of the trade in their hands. Whether such a condition of things will much longer obtain is a moot question. I am of opinion, as I have elsewhere indicated, that the trade of Japan will very largely pass into the hands of the Japanese themselves, and that the foreign element in Japan is accordingly not only unlikely to increase in number but is almost certain to diminish.

In the early days when Japan was first opened to the Western world and English traders went there to push their commodities, we heard a good deal about the peculiar ethics of Japanese commercial morality. The European merchant either was, or affected to be, shocked at the loose commercial code of honour of those with whom he was brought into contact in Japan, and he expressed himself accordingly. However much or little ground there may have been for these accusations many years ago I am not in a position to judge. In forming any opinion in this matter, if that opinion is to be correct, it is, I think, essential to remember the conditions of society in Japan when it was first opened to European trade. In old Japan there were four recognised classes of society—the Samurai, the farmers, the artisans, and the merchants. The last two were somewhat looked down upon by the others. It is, accordingly, hardly to be wondered at that the condition of industry and commerce was the least satisfactory feature in the initial stages of national development. Despised alike by the gentry and the peasantry, the traders were in a somewhat sorry plight when Japan was thrown open. The low social status of the trading class in Japan was due to the feudal ideas which prevailed for so many centuries.

The people were impressed with the productive power of the soil, and jumped at the conclusion that the merchant class must necessarily be immoral, since it purchased the produce of the soil at a low price and sold it at a profit. Very similar ideas have prevailed in countries other than Japan. It is not so very many years ago that in England a man of good family, much less a member of the aristocracy, going into trade was looked upon with no very favourable eyes. We know that the ideas that not so very many years ago obtained in this country in reference to this matter have entirely altered. Trade is now considered to furnish most excellent scope and opportunities for the energy and capital of all classes of the community. And the same ideas have been working in Japan. The merchant there is no longer a member of a despised class. The scions of the most ancient families in Japan, as in England, have embarked in trade and brought to their business those high ideals which they have derived from their ancestors. The criticisms of commercial morality in Japan which were so prevalent not very many years ago are now entirely obsolete. I fear, however, that the effect of them still to some extent remains, and that there are a large number of people in this country who even now believe that the Japanese, from a commercial point of view, are what is termed "tricky." I hope my remarks on this head may serve to disabuse the minds of some of those persons who still entertain these extremely erroneous ideas.

I do not think that there is a very large amount of social intercourse between the Europeans in Japan and the Japanese themselves. The European in the East, or at any rate the Englishman in the East, so far as I have been able to judge, always appears to me to assume an air

—it may be an unconscious air—of superiority to the inhabitants of the country in which he resides. That this is frequently extremely galling to them there can be no question. Any one who has conversed with the intelligent native of India must be aware of that fact. Whether the greatness of the Anglo-Saxon race be in some degree or in a large measure due to the belief that the Anglo-Saxon has in himself is a question I need not consider But I think there can be no doubt of the fact that this sense of superiority, however much or little justification there may be for it, is a characteristic not likely to be appreciated by foreigners, and especially Orientals, and I think I am justified in remarking that the Japanese do not at all appreciate it.

The European may impress the Oriental in one of several ways; he has for the most part done so by his great military or naval prowess. That is the way in which Great Britain has impressed the natives of India. The English are in that country as a conquering race. They have practically never been defeated, and the respect which they have obtained is the respect that the weak have for the strong. In Japan such a state of things is no longer possible. The results of the Russian War have rendered it impossible for all time. An Oriental nation has met a European Power on the field and on the high seas, and soundly thrashed it. There is, however, another way in which the European might impress the Oriental. The former professes to have a purer religion and a higher code of morals. He has sought to impose his religion upon every race with which he has been brought into contact, and if he has not sought to impose his moral system, he has, at any rate, severely criticised that of the people with whom he has been brought into contact, and compared it with his own to their disadvantage. In Japan, where there is a large foreign community, the thinking, logical Japanese has had abundant opportunities for studying not only the principles of Western religions and Western morality, but also the practice of them by Western residents in his own land.

The result has been to give him much food for reflection. He reads the criticisms of Europe upon the Yoshiwara and the Japanese attitude generally towards prostitution, while he has ample evidence of the fact that many of the patrons of the Yoshiwara are to be found among the European community in Japan. And so of religion. The various Christian denominations of the Western world aspire to convert Japan, and send missionaries there for that purpose. The Japanese gives them a fair field, and he has shown no aversion to investigate their dogmas. At the same time he sees that a large proportion, I might perhaps say the majority, of the European residents in Japan do not trouble to attend the Christian places of worship, while many of them make no disguise of their contempt for Christianity in general and the missionaries in particular. What conclusion, may I ask, can the logical, reasoning Japanese come to in these matters?

There can be no doubt whatever that the foreign residents in Japan have accomplished a great work in regard to the development of the country. The settlements established by them at the various treaty ports and the administration of those settlements as municipalities reflected great credit upon all those concerned, and was a splendid object-lesson for the Japanese people. Great Britain, too, may, I think, be congratulated on the men she has selected to represent her at the Japanese Court. There is no man to whom both Great Britain and Japan are more indebted than the late Sir Harry Parkes. I cannot remember during how many years he was the British Minister at Tokio, but during the whole of his term of office he used his best endeavours in the direction of showing Japan the way she ought to go in the path of progress, and in rendering her all the assistance possible in that direction by procuring for her the very best assistance of every description. I strongly advise every person interested in Japan and its development to peruse the Life of Sir Harry Parkes, by Mr. F. V. Dickins and Mr. Stanley L. Poole. One interesting feature in Sir Harry Parkes's career I may record here, as I have had it on the authority of a gentleman conversant with the facts. Sir Harry was always a *persona gratissima* with the Japanese Government, and about the year 1877 he and the late Admiral Sir A. P. Ryder, then Commander-in-Chief on the China station, had a conversation respecting, in view of the aggressive policy of Russia in the Far East, obtaining a British coaling station much further north than Hong Kong. Admiral Ryder mentioned as an appropriate place the island of Tsu-shima, so famous in the recent war with Russia. Sir Harry Parkes promised to use his good offices with the Japanese Government to obtain permission to occupy this island with a view of its ultimate cession to Great Britain. The permission was duly obtained, and Admiral Ryder thereupon cabled home to the Admiralty for the necessary permission to take over the island. His request was promptly vetoed, and Great Britain, accordingly, lost for ever the opportunity of obtaining an admirable coaling station and a splendid strategical position in the Far East. It is quite certain that Japan does not now regret the refusal of Great Britain to accept her too generous offer.

Europeans have been in Japan, and very much in evidence, during the past half-century or so, but I do not think that the residents in the country have exercised much influence upon Japan. During that period there have been enormous changes ; the whole life of the nation has, in fact, been revolutionised. But these changes have not been wrought, or indeed greatly affected, by the European residents in the country. The changes have emanated from Europe and America—not that portion of Europe and America which went to Japan for its own objects. I make, of course, a particular exception in regard to those naval and military and scientific men to whose exertions Japan owes so much of her advancement. But I do say of the ordinary trader or merchant that he has come to Japan, and left it without producing much effect, if any, on the development of the nation, or leaving behind him any influences of a useful nature.

The European in Japan necessarily suggests some allusion to that large and annually increasing number of persons who visit the country. Their residence in Japan is usually of very limited duration, but, however short it may be, it is apparently quite long enough to enable them to form pronounced views upon many and varied matters connected with the country and the people. I have no hesitation in asserting that the erroneous opinions so prevalent in Europe in regard to Japan and the Japanese people are largely the outcome of the far too numerous books that have been written and published in reference to that country of recent years. "Ten Days in Japan" may be an alluring title for a book of travel, but quite evidently ten days are not sufficient to form an opinion and promulgate it upon every phase of Japanese life, nor for the solution of many vexed problems. And yet, so far as my perusal of these books has gone, the shorter the period a man or woman has spent in Japan the more pronounced his or her views in regard to the country. The matter is hardly worth referring to were it not that these opinions, hastily arrived at and apparently as hurriedly rushed into print, have been accepted by some people as incontrovertible facts. Another class of work that I think a reader should be warned against is the book of the man who has lived in Japan for a time and seen life only from a certain standpoint. The book of a bishop or a missionary may be and often is of undoubted value in reference to his work and matters connected with his work, but when the writer gets outside this particular province and deals with subjects his knowledge of which must be at the best second-hand he is almost certain to perpetrate some flagrant mistakes, and occasionally indite the most egregious nonsense. I shall not particularly apply these remarks, but I think it necessary to utter this word of warning as the literary effusions of some very estimable men and women in regard to Japan have given occasion for many false misconceptions being entertained in regard to that country.

The cry of "Japan for the Japanese" has undoubtedly been heard in that land, and during the agitation over the revision of the treaties the foreign community appeared to be under the impression that the policy emphasised in that cry was the one which Japan desired to attain. For myself I do not believe it. I am positive that Japan to-day has no desire to exclude foreigners, or to revert into her old position of isolation. I believe, on the contrary, that she desires to welcome foreigners and to give them every facility within proper limits for pursuing their enterprises. At the same time she has no desire for the foreign

A MINISTERING ANGEL

FROM A PRINT BY TOSHIKATA

adventurer, prospector, or embryo company promoter. She does not wish, in fact, that Japan shall be exploited either in respect of minerals or any other purpose with the object of directly or indirectly pouring wealth into London or any other city. The enterprising gentlemen from England and other countries who have sought to obtain concessions of various kinds in Japan have failed in their object. Their efforts would probably only have brought discredit on the country, and could hardly by any possibility have aided in its material advancement. There is only one word of advice that I should feel inclined to proffer the European in Japan, and that is to refrain less from exercising his caustic wit at the expense of the Japanese people. A nation which has passed through such drastic changes as have characterised Japan in the last two or three decades can no doubt furnish abundant opportunities for the jibes of the flippant, and the humour of those who consider they are endowed with a pretty wit. But the exercise of sardonic humour and an excessive sarcasm tends to promote ill-feeling and serves no useful purpose. The right spirit, in my opinion, for any man to regard Japan is as a nation struggling to obtain and assimilate all that is best in the world and aspiring to be in fact an eclectic power. It can at least be said of Japan that it is the only nation in the world's history which has entertained such aspirations and has sought to give effect to them.

CHAPTER XXI

A VISIT TO SOME BUDDHIST TEMPLES

I WAS lying awake in my room in the Myako Hotel, the window looking out across the town below towards the eastern hills and framed with clusters of red maple. It was the clear stillness of a frosty morning before dawn, not motion enough in the autumn air to stir a ripe red maple leaf, and as I lay in bed suddenly the air itself seemed to heave a sigh of music mellow, soft, and yet full, gradual in its coming as in its going, all-pervading, strange and wonderful. Stillness again, and then it came again, or rather not so much came as was there, and then was not there; for it seemed to come from no whither, and to leave not even the footprint of an echo in the air behind. There was sanctity in the very sound itself. Its music was like vocal incense arising before the "awful rose of dawn," beyond those purple eastern hills. How unlike, I thought, the jar and clangour of our church bells in London on a Sunday morning rattling like a fire alarm, whose only possible religious suggestion is to tumble out of bed to escape the flames of hell. The musical summons of this bell was sufficient, however, to induce me to go out for a stroll through the temples in the morning twilight.

All on the crest of the hill behind the hotel is a row of

temples crowning the height. One mounts a flight of steps and then comes on avenues with rows of ancient trees on either side that make the avenues look like great aisles of which the immense trees are the columns supporting the deep, blue roof. Nothing is more striking about these temples than the delightful harmony between their natural surroundings and the buildings themselves. They blend so perfectly that one loses sight of the meeting between nature and art. From the steps onward all seems a harmonious part of the sanctified whole. Trees, creepers, and natural flowers peep in and almost entwine themselves with the marvellously painted or carved foliage of the temple itself. The rich lichens and mosses of the tree-trunks vie in depth and beauty of colour with the inlaid traceries of the columns.

Early as the hour was I was not alone in the first temple I came to. With tinkling steps of wooden shoes a little woman pattered up the stone stairs to one of the shrines, pulled the heavy cord of the small bell above her head to awaken the attention of the Deity, and then with joined hands encircled with beads and with bowed head whisperered her morning prayer. I just caught in soft, supplicatory accents the opening words, "Namu Amida Butsu"—"Hear me, compassionate Lord Buddha"—words that soon become familiar as one visits these temples; the great refrain of these people's prayers when they pray before the image of "Him, honoured, wisest, best, most pitiful, whose lips comfort the world." And then, having finished her prayers, the little woman pattered back to her home in the town below, while others come and make their devotions likewise, all leaving the temple as if that placid, inscrutable image had whispered in the ear of each some word of comfort.

In the courtyard beyond the great Temple of Kiomidyu I came upon a wonderful bell. There was room for over a dozen men to stand inside the great bronze shell. It was hung just above the ground between plain timber uprights, and the mellow softness of tone was accounted for by the way in which it was struck. Instead of metal striking against metal a great tree-trunk is suspended horizontally outside; this is swung backwards and forwards and then allowed to strike against the metal. Even when standing close to it there is nothing one would call noise, but a great, full, rich sound fills the air in a manner impossible to describe. I passed on to the latticed shrine dedicated to Kamnoshut No Kami, the goddess of lovers. As I waited there three little Japanese girls came up the steps. Each had a small piece of paper in her hand, and winding them up they deftly placed the papers in the lattice with the thumb and little finger of their hands. On these were written their petitions. One of them held a bunch of brilliant maple leaves in her hand, and judging from their faces—plain little faces all of them—it was easy to understand they wanted divine assistance in their love affairs. It was difficult to understand the goddess retaining any reputation for compassion if their prayers were not answered. After they had gone next came a dainty little geisha, a pretty girl, whose lover must have been a sad worry to her, judging by the look on her anxious little face, as she placed her petition between the bars.

All through these temples it was obvious that the agnosticism, or indifference, or attitude of "politeness towards possibilities," which has apparently taken possession of the upper classes in Japan, possibly as the result of contact with the West, is in no way prevalent among the masses. In all the country parts that I visited and in the large temples in the great cities there was everywhere evidence of faith as sincere and devout as can be found in the churches of the most Christian country in Europe. Unlike China, there was nowhere any sign of the temples falling into decay. Every temple in China looks like a neglected mausoleum decaying over the corpse of a dead religion, and the priests look like sextons of a neglected graveyard. But here in Kyoto two of the largest temples were undergoing elaborate repairs, and in Tokio an immense new temple is being erected in the heart of the city. In Kyoto at the Temple of Nishi Hong Wangi I was present at a great seven days' religious festival. From nine o'clock in the morning until six o'clock in the evening the temple was perpetually thronged with people. I visited it in the afternoon. In one large room a priest was preaching. His congregation was largely composed of country people from all the districts round, who had journeyed in with their wives and families. There had been an abundant harvest, it was over and stored, and the people had come to give thanks. A great part of the congregation were blue-clad peasants with white handkerchiefs around their heads. Many of them had brought their children with them.

The priest preached sitting down, in a quiet conversational tone. From what a Japanese friend was kind enough to translate for me, there was nothing esoteric in the Buddhism he was teaching. It was simply plain lessons to the people, how to make good their simple lives interspersed with stories and anecdotes that occasionally amused his congregation. Following the crowd that kept streaming out from his hall towards the larger temple, I passed under a plain portico of huge wooden columns, severe and simple on the outside, but gorgeous with rich carvings of gold lacquer panels and hangings of richly wrought embroideries within. The entire floor of the great building was crowded, and the overflow of the congregation knelt upon the flags outside the door. With difficulty I picked my way inside. Two rows of priests in brilliantly coloured vestments were arranged on either side of the central figure of Buddha. Between them was the chief priest. Behind the altar screen was an invisible choir. In alternating numbers the solemn, supplicating chant was led by either row of priests. In a way it reminded one of the Gregorian chant one often hears in Catholic churches, but in this Buddhist chanting there was that curious Oriental strain of semi-tones that gave a strange and peculiar plaint to the chorus.

Faint blue columns of incense were streaming slowly from bronze censors towards the carved roof, and diffusing a delightful aromatic odour throughout the building. The congregation was composed of all sorts and conditions of the population, although the majority were peasants; there were a number of Japanese ladies who came accompanied by their maids, and here and there the brighter costume of a Geisha was to be seen among the crowd.

The series of services lasted for seven days. This was the fifth. Beginning at six o'clock in the morning, it went on till six o'clock in the evening. It was just at its conclusion while I was there. Mingling with the chorus from the priests and the choir ran a low murmur from the crowd. The old country men and women said their prayers aloud, and the refrain of "Namu Amida Butsu" seemed perpetually in one's ears. As the conclusion of the service approached, the voices of the choir, the priests, and the congregation increased in strength and volume, and ceased suddenly in a final chord of supplication. For a few moments there was stillness over the bowed heads of the congregation, and then the priests rose and the crowd began to stream down the great flight of steps. In the streets outside were rows of booths, where printed prayers and brightly embroidered triangular cloths, beads and images were being sold as mementoes of these services. The whole congregation, even old men and women, as they toddled down the steps at the base of which they put on their shoes, reminded one forcibly of a lot of children coming out from school. Laughing, chattering, and joking, there was a look of satisfaction and contentment on all their faces, returning homewards, as if they felt that in reply to their prayer, "Namu Amida Butsu," the compassionate Lord Buddha, had listened to their prayer, and whispered in answer to the heart of each, "Comfort ye, my people."

CHAPTER XXII

THE AINOS

A BOOK on Japan would be incomplete without some reference to the Ainos, that mysterious race found, and found only, in the northern island of Yesso. The Ainos have long been the puzzle of the ethnologist. Where the Ainos came from or to what other race they are akin are problems that have given occasion for much learned dissertation, but are still as far off solution as ever. Mr. Basil Chamberlain, all of whose writings upon Japan are replete with erudition and information, has observed that the Aino race deserves to be studied because "its domain once extended over the entire Japanese Archipelago," and also "because it is, so to speak, almost at its last gasp." Unfortunately the evidence for the latter fact is more conclusive than for the former. The Ainos are, it seems, to be no exception to that mysterious law of the survival of the fittest, which decrees that an inferior race shall go down before the superior, and in due course become merely a name. I have called this a mysterious law because such disappearance is not necessarily the result of conquest or of ruthless destruction. When the inferior race is brought into contact with the superior it seems, by some mysterious process, to be infected with the elements of decay, to be impregnated with the germs of annihilation. And, accordingly, it comes about, in accordance with the dictates of the law I have referred to, that although a society has been founded in Japan very much on the lines of our Aborigines Protection Society, an Aino Preservation Society, the Ainos seem doomed to extinction at no far-distant date.

Whether or not the Ainos once inhabited the whole of the Japanese islands and trekked north to get away from their conquerors, there can be no doubt of the fact that they are in almost every respect the very antithesis of the Japanese. The latter are a smooth-skinned race, the Ainos an extremely hairy one. The Japanese are essentially a clean, a scrupulously clean people, the Ainos just as essentially dirty. The long beards and general facial appearance of the latter are altogether in startling contrast to the physiognomy of the average Japanese.

When ethnology fails to place a race, philology often steps in with more or less of success. The Aino language has been profoundly studied by many eminent philologists, but I do not think the results have tended to throw much, if any, light on the mystery as to the origin and racial affinities of the Ainos. In general structure the language is not unlike that of the Japanese, but this might be expected as the result of centuries of intercourse between the two people.

The Ainos live almost solely by fishing and hunting. The Japanese laws, which have year by year been made more stringent, have somewhat interfered with the sporting proclivities of the people. Nets and fish traps are now forbidden, and fishing for the most part is effected by means of a spear or harpoon, either from the shore or from the somewhat primitive canoes used by the people.

Poisoned arrows were once largely used for the purpose of capturing game, but they are now forbidden by law. Originally the *modus operandi* in hunting was to set a trap with one of these arrows placed in it, and drive the game on to the same. The head of the arrow was only loosely fastened, and broke, leaving the poison inside even if the animal managed to pull out the shaft. The bear is found in Yesso, and that animal has entered very largely into every phase of Aino life, somewhat circumscribed though this is. That animal was, or used to be, the objective point of Aino festivals, and seems, to some extent at any rate, to have had a part in their crude religious ideas. Bears, are, however, becoming rare in Yesso, and the Japanese Government, which is paternal even in regard to the fauna of the islands, has from time to time interfered with many venerable Aino customs.

The religion of this interesting race is almost as mysterious as everything else appertaining to it. The Ainos have no idols and no temples, and their religious rites are of a decidedly simple nature. They, however, seem to believe in an infinity of spirits inhabiting various and varied things, and their pantheon is seemingly a crowded one. I have said seemingly, because the beliefs of a people such as this are difficult to get at, and even when one has got at them almost impossible to comprehend. One writer has termed the religion of the Ainos, "a very primitive nature-worship," and their gods "invisible, formless conceptions." Such definitions do not convey much information. Nature-worship is a vague description and "invisible, formless conceptions" of the deity or deities are not confined to the Ainos. Possibly, like all peoples but little advanced or developed mentally, their religious conceptions are of the vaguest and have assumed no definite shape. A fear of the unknown, a blind groping in the dark are, mayhap, all that the Aino possesses in reference to the spiritual world.

Although the religion of the Aino when living is somewhat incomprehensible his religious ceremonies in reference to the dead are of a somewhat elaborate nature. After life has become extinct the first proceeding is to light an enormous fire in the house. The corpse is then dressed in its best clothes and laid beside the fire, where are also placed dishes, a drinking-cup, and the implements of the chase. In the case of a woman, instead of these, her beads and other ornaments are laid alongside of her; for both sexes a pipe and a tobacco-box, so greatly used during life, are considered essentials when dead. Cakes made of rice or millet and a cup of saké, are also put upon the floor. A kind of wake or funeral feast follows, at which the mourners throw some saké on the corpse as a libation to its departed spirit, break off pieces of the cake and bury it in the ashes. The body is covered with a mat slung upon a pole and carried to the grave, followed by the mourners, each of whom places something in the grave, which, it is believed, will be carried to the next world with the spirit of the deceased person. At the conclusion of the ceremony the mourners wash their hands in water which has been brought for the purpose. This is then thrown on the grave and the vessel which conveyed it is broken in pieces and also thrown on the grave. The widow of the deceased shaves her head, while the man cuts his beard and hair, as outward symbols of grief. Many of these ceremonies, it will be seen, are such as are more or less common to all primitive races. There is, indeed, a marked resemblance between the habit of the Ainos in burying articles with the deceased for his use in the next world and that of the North American Indians. But I am not inclined to deduce any theory in reference to the origin of the Ainos from the existence of these customs. Mankind, in every part of the world, seems to have evolved his religious beliefs in very much the same way. His conception of the hereafter appears to have proceeded on precisely similar lines. The higher his scale in civilisation the more spiritual and the less material his conception of the future. The lower his scale precisely the reverse is the fact. The savage, which of course the Aino really is, cannot imagine a future state where there is no eating and drinking and hunting, and he, accordingly, thinks it incumbent on him, in order to show his respect for the dead, to provide the corpse with those articles which he deems essential in that unknown world where, according to his conception, eating and drinking and hunting will be as prevalent as in this.

The Ainos have a great respect for the graves of their dead, and Japanese legislation has taken the necessary steps to prevent any tampering therewith. Some years ago a few scientists from Europe went on an expedition from Hakodate with a view of obtaining information respecting the manners and customs of the Ainos. In the course of this expedition some graves were broken into and skulls and limbs extracted therefrom for the purpose of being taken to Europe for scientific research. This proceeding occasioned an angry outburst on the part of this usually placid people, and the Japanese authorities gave the necessary instructions to prevent the possibility of such an occurrence in future. I suppose the scientists, in the ardour of their enthusiasm, are hardly to be blamed. Science too frequently overlooks sentiment, which is, after all, one of the most potent forces in the world.

The dwellings of the Japanese are supposed to have been evolved from those of the Ainos. Both build their houses roof first, making the framework and placing the supports with shorter pieces for rafters, all being tied together with a rope made of some kind of fibre. Poles, 5 or 6 feet high at regular intervals are then placed in the ground, each pole having a fork at the top and short horizontal pieces from one to the other, the roof frame is then erected on and secured to the poles and subsequently thatched with straw. The floor is of earth, with the fireplace in the centre. As in Japanese houses, mats are used for sitting and sleeping purposes. The utensils of the Ainos are much more primitive than those in use by the Japanese people, and generally it may be remarked of the Ainos that their wants are few and that the people are content to live their own life in their own way and only desire to be severely left alone.

The dress is very similar to that of the Japanese peasant. The men, however, wear at certain seasons thick rain-coats made of salmon skin, as also leggings made of a fibre peculiar to themselves, and high boots constructed of straw. I am sorry to have to relate that the Ainos have a fondness for saké, and there is a good deal of intoxication among them. The climate of the island of Yesso, as I have already remarked, is extremely severe in the winter-time, and there can be little doubt that many of the Ainos suffer extreme privations. There have been a few cases of intermarriage between the two races, but unions of this nature are not looked on with any favour by either.

Attempts have been made by some of the missionaries

in Japan to convert the Ainos to Christianity, but I fear the attempts made in this direction have been attended with a very scant measure of success. A people such as this possesses minds of childlike simplicity, and to endeavour to get it to comprehend the abstruse doctrines and dogmas of Christianity is an almost hopeless task. The climate of Yesso is such as to render it possible for missionary efforts to take place only at certain seasons of the year, and I do not think there has been, so far as my information goes, any systematic propaganda of Christianity among this interesting race.

It is certainly a somewhat extraordinary fact that while the other islands of Japan have been rapidly assimilating and are being steadily influenced by the civilisation of Europe and America, the northern island appears to be, except possibly at Hakodate, in a state of complete isolation from all these influences and effects. Whether the Ainos have any conception of the influences at work in and the progress being made by the Empire of which they are subjects, I do not know, but to me it is both interesting and curious to regard this ancient and decaying race, either indifferent to or ignorant of all the bustle and hurry and worry of modern civilisation so close to them and yet so far removed from their childlike minds and ideas.

The question may be asked, How comes it that a highly civilised people such as the Japanese have been for many hundreds of years, have exercised practically no influence upon this subject race inhabiting a portion of their territory? A nation such as Japan, with a literature and an art of its own, with two highly developed religious systems, and with many of those other characteristics which are included in the term civilisation? How is it that neither art nor literature nor religion, nor any other characteristic of civilisation has, in the slightest degree, influenced this aboriginal race? Indeed, if the theories of ethnologists in regard to the Ainos be correct, and we are to judge by the ancient remains that have been found throughout Japan, the Ainos, when they were in undisputed possession of the Japanese Archipelago, were in a much more advanced condition of civilisation than they are to-day. The questions that I have put afford food for reflection, but they are difficult, if not impossible, to answer. I am certain, however, that the Japanese Government desires to, if possible, preserve the Aino race from extinction, and that it aspires to give this ancient people all the advantages of education and civilisation generally. Unfortunately the Ainos themselves are the obstacle to the carrying into effect of this project. They desire to live their own life in their own way. They have not only no wish to be, but they resent any effort to make them, either educated or civilised. They are what some people would term children of nature, out of place decidedly in a modern go-ahead eclectic Power like Japan, but an interesting survival of the past, and likewise an interesting reminder that the highly civilised races of to-day have, in their time, been evolved from very similar children of nature.

CHAPTER XXIII

JAPAN AS IT IS TO-DAY

"IN the Japan of to-day the world has before it a unique example of an Eastern people displaying the power to assimilate and to adopt the civilisation of the West, while preserving its own national dignity unimpaired," aptly remarks a modern writer. It is, indeed, in its powers of assimilation and adaptation that Japan, I think, stands unique among not only the nations of the world at the present time, but amongst the nations of whom we have any historical record. In one of his books on Japan—books which I may, in passing, remark give a more vivid insight into the life of the Japanese people than the works of any other writer—Mr. Lafcadio Hearn remarks that the so-called adoption of Western civilisation within a term of comparatively few years cannot mean the addition to the Japanese brain of any organs or powers previously absent from her, nor any sudden change in the mental or moral character of the race. Changes of that kind cannot be made in a generation. The Europeanising of Japan, Mr. Hearn in fact suggests, means nothing more than the rearrangement of a part of the pre-existing machinery of thought, while the mental readjustments effected by taking on Western civilisation, or what passes for it, have given good results only along directions in which the Japanese people have always shown special capacity. There has, in a word, he asserts, been no transformation—nothing more than the turning of old abilities into new and larger channels. Indeed the tendency of the people of Japan, when dispassionately investigated, will be seen to have been always moving in the same direction. A slight retrospect will, I think, clearly prove the truth of this assertion.

It is now about fifty years since Japan was first awakened, perhaps rudely awakened, from her slumber of two and a half centuries. When the European Powers and the United States of America knocked, perhaps somewhat rudely, at her door, it turned slowly on its hinges and creaked owing to the rust of many long years. How came it that a country which had imported its art, literature, religion, and civilisation, a country which until 1868 had a mediæval feudalism for its social basis, a country which until then was notorious for the practice of hara-kiri and the fierceness of its two-sworded Samurai should so suddenly take on Western attributes and become a seat of liberty and the exponent of Western civilisation in the Far East? All this is to some persons a rather perplexing problem. But the reasons are not, I think, far to seek. If we go back many centuries we shall find that Japan, though always tenacious of her national characteristics, never evinced any indisposition to mingle with or adopt what was good in other races. The national character for many hundreds of years has always displayed what I may term the germs of liberalism, and has not been influenced by narrow and petty national ideals concerning the customs, religion, art, or literature of other countries. As against this statement may be urged the action of Japan in expelling the Portuguese missionaries, destroying thoroughly Christianity, both buildings and converts, and effectually and effectively shutting the country against all intercourse with Europe and America for over two centuries. The answer of the Japanese of to-day to this question is simple enough. They point out that, although the object of St. Francis Xavier and his missionaries was essentially spiritual, viz., to convert Japan to Christianity, that of many of the foreigners who accompanied or succeeded him was not in any sense spiritual, but on the contrary was grossly and wickedly material. Accordingly Japan, having rightly or wrongly concluded that not only her civilisation but her national life, her independent existence, were menaced by the presence and the increasing number of these foreigners, she decided, on the principle that desperate diseases require desperate remedies, to expel them and to effectually seal her country against any possibility of future foreign invasions. I am not, I may remark, defending her action in the matter; I am only putting forward the views of Japanese men of light and leading of to-day in regard thereto.

When, many centuries ago, the Koreans brought to Japan the religion, laws, literature, and art of China, these were adopted and assimilated. Both Buddhism and Confucianism existed side by side in the country with the old Shinto religion. And, accordingly, during the many centuries which have elapsed since the religion of China and the ethical doctrines of her great teacher were introduced into Japan, there has never been a violent conflict between them and the ancient religion of the country. Had the Portuguese invaders confined themselves to a religious propaganda only, the Christian converts they made would not have been interfered with and the

Christian religion, strong and vigorous, would have existed uninterruptedly in Japan until to-day side by side with Buddhism and Shintoism. When St. Francis Xavier came to Japan Buddhism was the prevailing religion, and it undoubtedly had, as it still has, a great hold upon the people. But the preaching of the intrepid Jesuit and the missionaries he brought with him had an enormous success. The Christian religion was embraced by representatives of every class. In the year 1550 St. Francis, writing to Goa, placed on record for all time his opinion of the Japanese. "The nation," writes he, "with which we have to deal here surpasses in goodness any of the nations ever discovered. They are of a kindly disposition, wonderfully desirous of honour, which is placed above everything else. They listen with great avidity to discourse about God and divine things. In the native place of Paul they received us very kindly, the Governor, the chief citizens, and indeed the whole populace. Give thanks to God therefore that a very wide and promising field is open to you for your well-roused piety to spend its energies in." It certainly was a remarkable fact that a nation which had for so many centuries been under the influences of Buddhism should have welcomed these Portuguese missionaries. But it must be remembered that Japan had not that prejudice against foreigners which is very often the outcome of foreign conquest and foreign oppression. No foreign Power had ever conquered or indeed set its foot in the land. Both China and Korea had made various attempts on the independence of Japan, but unsuccessfully. Japan had never had to endure any humiliation at the hands of foreign invaders, consequently her nationalism had no narrow, selfish meaning, and accordingly she saw no reason for putting any obstacle in the way of St. Francis Xavier and his followers until she concluded, however much or little reason there may have been for her conclusions, that the incoming of these foreigners in some measure menaced her national existence. Before she arrived at that conclusion she was apparently prepared to welcome all that was good in the ethical teaching of the Portuguese missionaries, and, if a section of her population desired to embrace a religion to whose ethical teaching she had no objection; there was no reason, in her opinion, why that religion should not exist side by side with those more ancient religions which had lived amicably together during many centuries.

For nearly two hundred and fifty years Japan resolved to remain in a state of isolation. Then, as I have said, European Powers and the great Republic of the West came knocking and knocking loudly at her doors, and as a result thereof her thinking men came to realise that in a state of isolation a continued civilised existence is impossible. Accordingly Japan, tentatively at first, opened certain portions of her country to European intercourse, and as an inevitable consequence thereof found it necessary to adopt European ideas—and European armaments. The country had kept out the aggressor for some two thousand years or thereabouts, and Japan clearly saw that if the aggressor was to be kept out in the future, the near future, she would probably have to fight to maintain her national existence. The war with China was the outcome of the feeling that Korea under the suzerainty of China was a constant menace to not only the prosperity but the existence of the Empire. The same feeling undoubtedly led to the war with Russia, as Japan considered, and rightly in my opinion, that the possession of Korea by Russia meant the loss of national independence. That war was not as so many wars have been, the result of a racial hatred, the outcome of a spirit of revenge, or waged for aggressive designs. It was forced upon Japan, and was in every sense purely defensive. Japan waged it confident in her own strength from the fact that in the two thousand years of her history she had, in all the conflicts in which she had engaged, kept in view the one ideal—the conservation of the national existence, an ideal which she has consistently realised.

The position of Japan at the present moment is not only extremely interesting but extraordinary in a degree. She is the cynosure for the eyes of the civilised world, and for some years she has been subjected at the hands of experts and amateurs of all descriptions to the most minute investigation. Every phase of her national life has been rigidly scrutinised and exhaustively written about. The national character and characteristics have undergone the most intricate psychological examination, and if the world does not now know the real Japan it is certainly not from lack of material, literary material, whereon to form a judgment. Indeed the attention Japan has received has been sufficient to turn the head of any people. I am not sure that this large output of literature on matters Japanese has effected very much in the direction of enabling a sound judgment to be formed regarding the country and the people. Many writers who have dissertated upon Japan during the past couple of decades seem to have imagined that they had discovered it, and their impressions have been penned from that standpoint.

There used some years ago to be an advertisement of a "Popular Educator" in which a youth with a curly head of hair and a face of delightful innocence was depicted. Underneath the portrait the inquiry was printed, "What will he become?" And there was then given an illustrated alternative as to the appearance of this innocent youth at different ages in his career according to the path he trod in life. One alternative eventuated in the final evolution of an ancient and, from his appearance, very palpable villain, the other of a benevolent-looking old gentleman who quite evidently only lived to do good. It seems to me that a large number of persons in various parts of the world are to-day, as they have been for some time past, asking the question in reference to Japan, "What will she become?" It is without doubt a highly interesting inquiry, but the answer to it, so far as my knowledge goes, is not like the advertisement I have referred to, one of two courses—the one leading to perdition, the other to prosperity. On the contrary, the answers seem to be as numerous and varied as the answerers, and most of the answers would appear to have been arrived at simply and merely by the false premises and very often the entirely erroneous "facts" of the inquirers.

A favourite and fallacious method of dealing with Japan is that of regarding it as an Oriental nation, essentially Oriental with a thin veneer of Occidentalism. People who so reason, or occasionally do not reason at all but confine themselves to mere assertions, suggest that the difference between the Oriental and the Occidental is such that not a few years of perfunctory contact but centuries of time are necessary to bring about a real transmogrification. Persons who so think point not only to the difference in everything material in respect of East and West, but to a radical difference in psychology, an entire distinction in the mental outlook of each. They accordingly conclude that the differences so evident on all sides are not mere accidentals but fundamental, ineradicable. Scratch the

FIREWORKS IN TOKIO (SUMMER)

FROM A PRINT BY HIROSHIGE

Japanese, they in effect say, and beneath his veneer of civilisation you will find the barbarian, barbarism and Orientalism being with these persons synonymous terms. And if any incredulity in the matter be expressed they will triumphantly point to the recurrence of hara-kiri among the soldiers and sailors in the late war. A well-known writer on racial psychology has expressed himself dogmatically on this very point. I will quote two or three of his pronouncements in the matter.

"Each race possesses a constitution as unvarying as its anatomical constitution. There seems to be no doubt that the former corresponds to a certain special structure of the brain.

"A negro or a Japanese may easily take a university degree or become a lawyer; the sort of varnish he thus acquires is, however, quite superficial, and has no influence on his mental constitution. . . . What no education can give him because they are created by heredity alone, are the forms of thought, the logic, and, above all, the character of the Western man.

"Cross-breeding constitutes the only infallible means at our disposal of transforming in a fundamental manner the character of a people, heredity being the only force powerful enough to contend with heredity. Cross-breeding allows of the creation of a new race, possessing new physical and psychological characteristics."

Now, whether these views be correct in the main or partially correct as regards other races, I have no hesitation in describing them as inaccurate to a degree in reference to the Japanese. Not peculiar brain formation, but social evolution, environment, education are responsible for the traits which distinguish the Japanese from other Eastern nations. To assert, as do some psychological experts, that the mental constitution of races is as distinct and unchangeable as their physiological or anatomical characteristics is, to my mind, a fact not borne out by the history of the world. Physiological or anatomical distinctions are apparent, and can be classified; mental idiosyncrasies do not lend themselves to cataloguing. It is, I know, possible to draw up at any particular period a list of what I may term the idiosyncrasies of any race at that period. A writer in a London newspaper some little time back attempted to do so in reference to Oriental races generally. He enumerated the degraded position of women, the licentiousness of the men, the recognition and prevalence of prostitution, the non-desire of the youth for play, contempt for Western civilisation, and general hatred of foreigners. Admitting these charges to be correct, the characteristics detailed are, I may point out, merely ephemeral incidents. A contempt for Western civilisation and hatred of the foreigner, for example, which was certainly at one time pronounced in Japan, are rapidly passing away. The position of women in that country has also greatly improved, just as it has improved in Europe, while as regards prostitution and licentiousness Europe has, in my opinion, no need to throw stones.

There are undoubtedly a large number of persons who are convinced, or have been convinced, by the arguments of others, that the progress of Japan is a mere mushroom growth which cannot last. A few years ago one of the leading English papers in Japan attempted, to some extent, to voice this opinion in an article striking the note of warning for the benefit of the West against putting too much faith in those writers who had intimately studied Japan from within, and whose works were in general appreciation not only for their literary style, but for the vivid insight they gave into everything respecting the country. Quoth the journal in question:—

"In the case of such writers as Sir Edwin Arnold and Mr. Lafcadio Hearn, it is quite apparent that the logical faculty is in abeyance. Imagination reigns supreme. As poetic flights or outbursts the works of these authors on Japan are delightful reading. But no one who has studied the Japanese in a deeper manner, by more intimate daily intercourse with all classes of the people than either of these writers pretends to have had, can possibly regard a large part of their description as anything more than pleasing fancy. Both have given rein to the poetic fancy, and thus have, from a purely literary point of view, scored a success granted to few. . . . But as exponents of Japanese life and thought they are unreliable. . . . They have given form and beauty to much that never existed, except in vague outline or in undeveloped germs in the Japanese mind. In doing this they have unavoidably been guilty of misrepresentation. . . . The Japanese nation of Arnold and Hearn is not the nation we have known for a quarter of a century, but a purely ideal one manufactured out of the author's brains. It is high time that this was pointed out. For while such works please a certain section of the English public, they do a great deal of harm among a section of the Japanese public, as could be easily shown in detail did space allow."

I quite admit the fact that many Japanese themselves are quite convinced that there is a great gulf fixed between the ideas and the philosophy of Europe and those of the East, their own country included. In a book dealing particularly with the art of Japan, written in English by a Japanese, he attempts to emphasise this matter. He remarks: "Asia is one. The Himalayas divide only to accentuate two mighty civilisations—the Chinese, with its communism of Confucius, and the Indian, with its individualism of the Vedas. But not even the snowy barriers can interrupt for one moment that broad expanse of love for the Ultimate and Universal which is the common-thought inheritance of every Asiatic race, enabling them to produce all the great religions of the world, and distinguishing them from those maritime people of the Mediterranean and the Baltic who loved to dwell on the particular, and to search out the means not the end of life." Indeed, the writer of this book appears to be in a condition of transcendentalism in reference to the East. In another portion of it he waxes eloquent in regard to what he terms the glory of Asia, in language which I will briefly quote. He remarks:—

"But the glory of Asia is something more positive than these. It lies in that vibration of peace that beats in every heart; that harmony which brings together emperor and peasant; that sublime intuition of oneness which commands all sympathy, all courtesy, to be its fruits, making Takakura, Emperor of Japan, remove his sleeping robes on a winter night because the frost lay cold on the hearths of his poor; or Taiso of Tang forego food because his people were feeling the pinch of famine; . . . it lies in that worship of feeling which casts around poverty the halo of greatness, impresses his stern simplicity of apparel on the Indian prince, and sets up in China a throne whose imperial occupant—alone amongst the great secular rulers of the world—never wears a sword."

It were unkind to criticise eloquence of this description too seriously. The fact, if it be a fact, that the Emperor of China never wears a sword is in one sense interesting but it proves nothing. It is well to get down from eloquence of this kind to concrete facts, to come back to the point whence we started, viz., What will Japan become? What is her present condition? Any one who compares the Japan of to-day with the Japan of, say, thirty or forty years ago will, I think, impatiently sweep aside some of the absurd theories to which I have referred, psychological and otherwise. The unprejudiced man, letting his mind indulge in retrospect, and comparing that retrospective view with the present actuality, will, I believe, have no difficulty in determining that though Japan is and must remain an Oriental nation, what she has acquired of recent years is neither veneer or varnish, but has been assimilated into the very system of the people. Very probably Japan will never become thoroughly Occidentalised. There are many of us who hope she never may. I believe, however, that in adopting many Occidental customs and habits she will adapt and modify them to her own needs, and in due course evolve a race neither distinctly Occidental nor Oriental while retaining many of her past customs and her ancient characteristics. She will, in a word, be as far as possible an eclectic nation, and it is, so far as I know, the first time in the history of the world that an attempt has been made to develop such.

There are, I know, many people in Europe as well as in Japan who feel and express some apprehension in regard to what they term young Japan. This term, like many other terms, has never been accurately defined, but I take it to mean that portion of the country consisting of the young or younger men who have been educated according to Western ideas, have acquired Western modes of thought, and have developed—I do not use the word in an opprobious sense—a bumptiousness. It is assumed, on what grounds I know not, that this section—it must after all be a small section—of the population of the country has aspirations to make things "hum," if I may use an expressive bit of American slang. Young Japan, we are led to believe, is intensely ambitious and extremely cocksure. It cannot and will not go slow; on the contrary, it is in a fearful hurry, and is in reference to every matter political, commercial, religious, a hustler. It has no doubts upon any subject, and no difficulty in regard to making up its mind on any matter. This is what we hear and read. How much of it all is true I know not. I am very largely of opinion that this representation of young Japan is altogether a caricature. Youth we know in every clime is impulsive and impetuous. There is no need to go to Japan to convince ourselves of that fact. But youth, if it have these defects, also possesses enthusiasm, and I should be inclined to describe that as one of the most pleasing characteristics of the youth of Japan. After all, time will cure Young Japan of some of its defects. Young Japan will grow old, and if it loses its enthusiasm it will gain experience. I not only have no fear of these vivacious young men who love their country and are proud of it. I regard them not as a danger, but as a pleasing feature in the progress of Japan, and a potent factor in its future prosperity.

The writers and critics to whom I have referred in this chapter seem to be oblivious of the fact that progress is the law of nature. It has nothing to do with either climate or race. I admit that it may be affected by environment or other causes of a temporary nature. The Occidental visiting the East sees things that are strange to him—a people, the colour of whose skin and the contour of whose features are different to his own ; costume, style of architecture, and many other matters entirely dissimilar to what he has viewed in his own country. He accordingly jumps to the absolutely erroneous conclusion that these people are uncivilised, and that their lack of civilisation is due to some mental warp or some defect in either the structure or the size of their brain. Of course such a conception is entirely erroneous, and yet it is marvellous to what an extent it prevails. These people are for all practical purposes the same as himself, except that they have been affected by various matters and circumstances that I have called ephemeral. What a nation, like an individual, needs is the formation of a distinct character. Now, the character of a nation depends, in my opinion, on the high or low estimate it has formed as to the meaning and purpose of life, and also the extent to which it adheres to the unwritten moral law, which is, after all, something superior to, because higher than, mere legal enactments. I confess that as I wander about this marvellous country of Japan, as I mingle with its common people and see them in various phases of their lives I say to myself, as St. Francis Xavier said of them more than three hundred years ago, " This nation is the delight of my soul." The critic, the hypercritic, is everywhere. He suspects everybody and everything. He can find occult motives and psychological reasons for everything. I confess I am a trifle tired of the critic, especially the psychological critic, in reference to Japan. I view the people there as they are to-day, and I have satisfied myself that we can see at work in Japan the formation of a nation with a character. I care not to investigate the mental processes at work, or the difference between the brain of the Japanese and the brain of the European. I do see this, however, that the leaders of the people, the educated and cultured classes of the land, are intent on cutting out of the national character anything which is indefensible, or has been found unserviceable, and equally intent on adopting and adapting from any and every nation such qualities as it is considered would the better enable Japan to advance on the paths of progress and freedom, illuminating her way as a nation and as a people by a shining illustration of all that is best in the world, having sloughed off voluntarily and readily every characteristic, however ancient, which reason and justice and experience had shown to be unworthy of a power aspiring to stand out prominently before the world.

In Sir Rutherford Alcock's work on Japan, "The Capital of the Tycoon," published some forty-four years ago, a work which, as I have elsewhere said, is of undoubted value though somewhat marred by the prejudices of the author, he attempted a forecast of the future of the country, but, like so many prophets, his vaticinations have proved highly inaccurate. "Japan," he remarked, "is on the great highway of nations, the coveted of Russia, the most absorbing, if not the most aggressive of all the Powers; and a perpetual temptation alike to merchant and to missionary, who, each in different directions, finding the feudalism and spirit of isolation barriers to their path, will not cease to batter them in breach, or undermine them to their downfall. Such seems to be the probable fate of Japan, and its consummation is little more than a question of time. When all is accomplished, whether the civilising process will make them as a people wiser, better, or happier, is a problem of more doubtful solution. One thing is quite certain, that the obstructive principle which tends to the rejection of all Western innovations and proselytism as abominations, is much too active and vigorous in the Japanese mind to leave a hope that there will not be violent and obstinate resistance; and this inevitably leading to corresponding violence in the assault, there must be a period of convulsion and disorder before the change can be effected, and new foundations laid for another social edifice." Whether the civilising process will make the Japanese people wiser, better, or happier is the problem the answer to which can only be given in the future. Obviously we are not in a position to completely answer this question to-day. Indeed, before answering it at any time it might be advisable to invite the definition of wisdom and happiness. There were wisdom and happiness long prior to the time when the merchant and the missionary to whom Sir Rutherford Alcock refers battered and undermined Japan's feudalism and spirit of isolation. But, *mirable dictu*, Japan, instead of developing that obstructive principle which Sir Rutherford considered was so active and vigorous in the Japanese mind has, on the contrary, developed a spirit of adaptation and assimilation of Western innovations, and in so doing has in all probability saved herself from the cupidity not only of Russia, but of other Western Powers. Sir Rutherford Alcock was not a psychologist, but quite evidently he too misread the Japanese mind and its workings.

Truth to tell, Japan as it is to-day gives the lie to nearly all the prophets, and demonstrates that the psychologist is merely a charlatan. Her development, her evolution has proceeded along no particular lines. The fearful and awful rocks in the way, mediævalism and feudalism, were got rid of almost with a stroke of the pen, and everybody in Japan, from the Emperor to the peasant, has adapted himself to the changed order of things. It is the most wonderful transformation scene in the history of the world, and it is still in progress. What the end of it all will be I have, bearing the dangers of prophecy well in mind, attempted to show in a final chapter. But I may remark that nothing in regard to the forces at work in Japan of recent years, and the outcome of the same so far gives me at any rate more unmixed pleasure than the way in which the theorists have been confounded, those men who cut and carve and label human beings, whether individually or in the aggregate, as if they were mere blocks of wood. The Oriental mind, we have been told, cannot do this ; Oriental prejudices and idiosyncrasies and modes of thought and hereditary influences will not admit of that ; the traditions of the Far East, that mysterious thing, will prevent the other—we have been told all this, I repeat, and told it *ad nauseam.* Japan as it is to-day refutes these prophecies, these dogmatic pronouncements, psychical and ethnological. The Japanese race, when regarded from what I deem to be the only correct standpoint for forming a sound judgment as to the position it holds among the races of the world, namely, in respect of the size and convolution of the brain, occupies in my opinion a high, a very high place. All other factors, often given such undue prominence in forming an estimate as to the character of any people I regard as mere accidentals. The story of Japan during the last thirty or forty years affords ample proof of what I have said ; the position of thecountry to-day offers visible demonstration of it. Japan has reached and will keep the position of a great Power, and the Japanese that of a great people, just because of the preponderating mental abilities of the population of the country, its capacity for assimilation, its desire for knowledge, its pertinacity, strenuousness, and aspirations to possess and acquire by the process of selection the very best the world can give it.

CHAPTER XXIV

THE FUTURE OF JAPAN—PHYSICAL—MORAL—MENTAL

I KNOW by experience, even if the history of the world had not furnished many examples to prove it, that prophecy is risky. It is a fascinating pastime inasmuch as it affords the imaginative faculties full scope, but at the same time it is a mistake to let the imagination run riot. I have no intention, in considering the future of Japan, of depicting an Arcadia or a Utopia the outcome of one's desire rather than of the knowledge that one possesses of the possibilities of the country and the belief that in due course those possibilities will become actualities. Of course I admit that I may be mistaken in my estimate of the future, but I think an estimate of the future can only be based on a knowledge of the present, and it is upon that knowledge that I mean to attempt some forecast of what I believe to be the destiny of Japan.

"The Future of Japan" is a theme that has exercised the pens of many writers, who have given to the world many and most divergent views in regard thereto—the result, I think, of regarding the subject from a narrow or single point of view, instead of looking at it broadly, boldly, and dispassionately. In respect of a population of between forty and fifty millions in rapid process of transformation and taking on perhaps rather hurriedly, and, it may be, some superfluous or unnecessary attributes of Western civilisation, it is not only possible but easy to light on many ludicrous incidents and draw absolutely false conclusions from them. One visitor to Japan, for example, who wrote a series of essays on that country, since produced in book form, the laudable object of which was to present to the British public the real Japan with a view of counteracting the effects of those "superficial narratives to be found by the dozen in circulating libraries of the personal views and experiences of almost every literary wayfarer who has crossed the Pacific," has followed this bad plan in his remarks on "The Future of Japan." Imitation for imitation's sake is, or was, in his opinion, a growing evil in Japan. A certain gentleman, he relates, a wealthy merchant of Osaka, desired to celebrate the two hundredth anniversary of a copper mine coming into the possession of his family. The plan he finally decided to adopt was to present each of his three hundred employees with a swallow-tail coat. Another Japanese gentleman, who had fallen in with the habit of the New Year's Day call imitated from the Americans, improved upon it by leaving on his doorstep a large box with a lid and this notice above it: "To Visitors. I am out, but I wish you a Happy New Year all the same. N.B.—Please drop your New Year's Presents into the box." Over a well-known tobacconist's shop the writer of the book in question observed the following notice: "When we first opened our tobacco store at Tokio our establishment was patronised by Miss Nakakoshi, a celebrated beauty of Inamato-ro, Shin-yoshiwara, and she would only smoke tobacco purchased at our store. Through her patronage our tobacco became widely known, so we call it by the name of Ima Nakakoshi. And we beg to assure the public that it is as fragrant and sweet as the young lady herself. Try it and you will find our words prove true." Finally, over a pastry-cook's shop in Tokio he read and made a note of the following: "Cakes and Infections."

Now what do these several trivial, indeed contemptible, anecdotes prove? What arguments in regard to a nation of forty-seven millions of people can be bolstered up by instancing the imperfect acquaintance of a Japanese pastry-cook with the English language? The writer does not in so many words delineate the future of Japan as it appears to him, but he suggests it, and his Japan of the future is quite evidently to be nothing more or less than a kind of international dustheap whereon Europe and America have dumped all that is bad and rotten and deplorable in their modern social and political life. Here is the inferential forecast of the gentleman in question: "When Japan rings with the rattle of machinery; when the railway has become a feature of her scenery; when the boiler-chimney has defaced her choicest spots, as the paper-makers have already obliterated the delights of Oji; when the traditions of yashiki and shizoku alike are all finally engulfed in the barrack-room; when her art reckons its output by the thousand dozen; when the power in the land is shared between the politician and the plutocrat; when the peasant has been exchanged for the "factory hand," the kimono for the slop-suit, the tea-house for the music-hall, the geisha for the lion comique, and the daimio for the beer-peer—will Japan then have made a wise bargain, and will she, looking backward, date a happier era from the day we forced our acquaintance upon her at the cannon's mouth?"

A SIGN OF THE TIMES

Criticism of this kind, if it may be dignified by that term, no doubt affords opportunity for what is considered smart writing, and enables the persons indulging in it to air their witticisms and show their sense of the humorous, but it not only serves no useful purpose, but, on the contrary, is pernicious in its effects, inasmuch as it occasions, not unnaturally, a feeling of soreness on the part of those, whether individuals or a nation, who are made the subject of it. Japan has too often been the butt of the humourist. I have no desire to deprecate humour, which no doubt gives a savour to life, but that humour which is only exercised at the expense of others, in my opinion, needs reprobation. As I have said, Japan among nations has been subjected to too much of it, and it is to be hoped that in future writers about the country will endeavour to avoid making their little jokes, or serving up afresh the antiquated chestnuts of the foreign community.

The future of Japan may, I think, be considered under some half-dozen headings: The physical improvement of the Japanese race; Its moral advancement; Its intellectual advancement; Japan's national future; Her political future; and finally, The influence of the Japanese Empire on other Far Eastern races and on the world generally.

As regards the physical improvement of the race, I admit this is a somewhat difficult subject in regard to which to make any forecast. The stature of the Japanese is undoubtedly small, and the chest measurement small likewise. At the same time, any one moving about Japan must have noticed the fact that there are quite a large number of very tall men and women in the country, and that a goodly proportion of the inhabitants compare favourably in their physical attributes with European people. As I have observed elsewhere in this book, the dietary of the Japanese race has for many centuries back been almost entirely a vegetarian one. I know very well that vegetarianism has its advocates, and some of the arguments put forward in support of it are plausible if not convincing. At the same time, I think, it cannot be denied that those races which have been in the habit of eating meat for many centuries have, as regards physique, demonstrated that whether man was or was not intended to be a carnivorous animal, his development into a carnivorous animal has at any rate succeeded in enhancing and developing his physical powers. Of late years there has been possibly as the result of intercourse with Europeans, a large increase in the number of the inhabitants of Japan who eat meat. This tendency on the part of the population is growing, and I believe in the course of comparatively few years there will be a radical change in the dietary of the people. This change, if it be effected, must, I would suggest, have a material influence on their physique. We all know that food is essential for the building up of the human frame and its maintenance, and I think there are few people who would question the fact that the condition of the human frame, whether in individuals or the aggregates of individuals that we term nations, must be largely affected by the food partaken of. I, accordingly, look forward, not immediately of course, to a material change in the general physique of the Japanese people. I am not, as I know some persons are, of opinion that that change is likely to be brought about by intermarriage or unions of a temporary nature between Japanese and Europeans. There have been a few marriages, and there have no doubt been a good many unions, but the effect on the national breed has been small, and though it may be to some extent greater in the future, I do not look in this direction for any alteration in the physical characteristics of the Japanese people. That alteration will, in my opinion, be brought about by a change in the food of the people.

As regards the moral advancement of the Japanese race I shall say little, for the somewhat paradoxical reason that it is a matter on which so much might be said. Indeed, this is a subject on which a definition of the term moral might be advisable before entering into any prolonged consideration of it. I shall not attempt that definition, simply because I feel convinced that to do so would be to provoke controversy. As I have said in this book, moral, morality, and immorality are all terms that have to some extent lost their original meaning. I may say briefly in this connection that I use the term moral advancement simply and solely in respect of the practice of the duties of life from a high ethical point of view. That is, I know, a somewhat vague definition, but I think it will serve its purpose. Ever since Japan has been thrown open to foreigners we have heard a good deal about morality and immorality, both in the strict and the perverted sense of those words. The European who came there, male and female, was, or affected to be, shocked at the relations between the sexes he found prevailing. He saw prostitution recognised and regulated. He heard of, and in the old days possibly saw, something of phallic worship. He witnessed or heard of men and women making their ablutions together in public wash-houses, and he—sometimes it was a she—affected to be horrified at such a proceeding. Better, much better, it was inferred, the custom of the lower classes in England, never to wash at all, than this horrible outrage on public decency. And then the merchant or the trader who came to Japan, he also prated about commercial immorality, and the prevalence of untruthfulness among the Japanese with whom he did business. And in other directions too there were criticisms passed upon Japanese manners and customs, and many of these were condemned and denounced as immoral or wicked very often for no better reason than that they differed from those that obtained in Europe. However much or little ground there may have been for these charges against the Japanese people, I am not now concerned to discuss. One thing I will remark—that the Japanese possess two religions which, whatever their effects and no matter to what extent superstition may have been engrafted on them, have always held up a high moral standard. And if one dips even cursorily into the writings of the ethical teachers of Japan in the past, we invariably find the inculcation of an exalted standard of morals. Indeed, the practice of the Japanese people at the present time, as in all times in regard to the relations between parents and children, of wife to husband, of the people to the State, have been beyond criticism. In these matters Western nations have much to learn from them. Since the opening of the country to Europe, the Japanese Government has shown itself alive to European criticism on many points. It has effectually stamped out phallic worship; it has, in deference to European susceptibilities, abolished mixed bathing in the public wash-houses; and in various other ways it has striven in the direction of raising the standard of moral conduct throughout the country. That it has not attempted to put down prostitution, but, on the contrary, has recognised and regulated it, has been made a charge against it. The Japanese Government has most likely come to the conclusion that prostitution cannot be put down, and such being the case it has decided that, with a view of obviating those evils which are the outcome of it, the only alternative is to regulate it. I admit that in an ideal state of existence prostitution would not exist, but no country in the world has yet reached or approximated that ideal state. The evil of prostitution is just as flagrant in Europe as in the East, but Japan so far alone among the Great Powers of the world has seen fit to tackle this difficult and delicate matter, and to some extent regulate it. That her rulers look forward to the time when the Yoshiwara shall have ceased to exist I firmly believe, and I am convinced that they mean to do everything possible towards that consummation. But the rulers of Japan are not mere sentimentalists; they have to recognise facts, and recognising facts they have done what seems best to them under the circumstances.

As regards commercial morality, I believe even the European merchants and traders in the country admit that there has of late years been a marked improvement. In old Japan commercialism was looked down upon. Making a profit out of buying and selling was regarded as degrading; those who indulged in such practices were despised, and not unnaturally the trader, finding himself a member of a contemned class, lived down to the low level on which he had been placed. In old Japan traders, in the presence of the Samurai, were, when addressing him, required to touch the ground with their foreheads; when talking to him they had to keep their hands on the ground. Such a state of things, of course, has long been effete, but the influences thereof remained for a considerable time after the acts had ceased. There has now been effected a revulsion of feeling in such matters. Commerce is honoured, trade is esteemed, and the Japan of to-day is convinced of the fact that on her commerce, trade, and industries the future of the country largely depends. Men of the highest rank, men of the greatest culture, men of the deepest probity are now embarked in trade and commerce in Japan; the whole moral atmosphere connected with trade has changed, and there are at the present time no more honourable men in the whole commercial world than those of Japan. In this matter there has undoubtedly been an enormous advance in ideas and ideals. This advance, I believe, is destined to extend in other directions—indeed, in every direction. The Japan of to-day has, I think, so far as I have been able to gauge it, a feeling—a deep feeling, which perhaps I can best describe as *noblesse oblige*. It is sensible of the position the country has attained; it is full of hope and enthusiasm for the future thereof; it believes implicitly that it is incumbent on it not only to attain but to maintain a high moral standard in every direction. It has been urged as against the Japan of to-day by a writer on the subject that Spencer and Mill and Huxley have been widely read by the educated classes, and that Western thought and practice as to the structure of society and the freedom of the individual have been emphasised throughout the country. I confess to feeling no alarm in regard to the moral future of Japan because it has perused the works of the three philosophers named. It gives me no trepidation to read that Mill's work on "Representative Government" has been translated into a volume of five hundred pages in Japanese and reached its third edition. I am, on the contrary, pleased to learn that

Japan of to-day is concerned about culture, desirous of reading the works of those great philosophers whose names are among the immortal. There are no principles enunciated in any of the books of Spencer, Mill, or Huxley that, so far as I know, can undermine the moral character of the Japanese. On the contrary, I believe that a perusal of the writings of those great men will tend to assist the Japanese into a clearer understanding of moral principles, and in a desire to apply them to the duties of life. I look forward with great hope and a pronounced confidence to the moral future of Japan. Everything that I have seen in the country, everything that I have been able to learn respecting the people thereof—the ideas prevailing, the teaching given in its schools and universities, the whole trend of thought in the land, the literature read and produced, the aspirations, in fact, of the Japanese people to-day—lead me to think and to believe most firmly that in the Japan of the future we shall witness a nation on a higher moral plane than any of those with which the history of the world acquaints us.

Closely connected with the moral advancement of Japan is its intellectual advancement. I have referred to the statement made by a writer that the Japan of to-day is addicted to reading the works of certain English philosophers, and that one of these books translated into Japanese had run through several editions. This fact is typical of the intellectual ferment, the thirst for knowledge of all kinds that exists in the country to-day. That craving is not for philosophical works alone; it extends to and embraces every form of literature of an instructive or enlightening character. It is in evidence in the higher schools and the universities of the country; it is to be witnessed in the many periodicals which exist for the promotion of culture and the spread of knowledge. This intellectual ferment, as I have, I think, appropriately termed it, is extending rapidly, and is, I believe, destined to assume much greater proportions. The literature of the world is at the present time literally being devoured by Young Japan. I do not regard this literary voracity as the mere outcome of curiosity, or as in any way symptomatic of mere mental unrest. Young Japan appears, like Lord Bacon, to take all knowledge for its field of study, and in accord with the philosophical principles of that great man, the principles of utility and progress, to be concerned with everything that can alleviate the sufferings and promote the comforts of mankind. Of course, at the present time this condition of craving for knowledge is confined, from the point of view of numbers, to a small portion of the people. But the intellectuals of every country are in a minority—in some countries in a miserable minority—and the influence they exercise is never proportionate to their numbers. At the same time the intellectuals of Japan are, in view of the fact that the country has for some short time been open to Western influences, an amazingly large proportion of the population. I am of opinion that this intellectual movement in Japan is destined to widen considerably, and that its influence on the people will be immense. During the whole history of the world the potency of mind over matter has been the greatest wonder. In these present days this potency is even more pronounced, and mere brute force is nowadays only made effective when it is influenced and regulated and organised by mind. I regard the intellectual development of Japan as one of the most pleasing features that have accrued from its contact with Western civilisation. I do not mean to suggest that there was an intellectual atrophy in the country prior to those influences making themselves felt, but there was an isolation which is never good for intellectual development. The broader the sympathies of nations, as of individuals, the wider their outlook, the better for their mental progress. When Japan was in a condition of isolation the literature available for her people was limited both in style and quantity. Her people now have at their disposal the intellect of the whole civilised world, the great thoughts of the great men of all ages. And it is pleasing to be able to relate that no more appreciative readers of the world's classics are to be found than the young intellectuals of Japan to-day. I have said that I regard this intellectual enthusiasm as one of the most pleasing features of modern Japan. That it is destined to have great results I am firmly convinced. I believe, and I am not naturally an optimist, that in the Japan of the future, the not far-distant future, the world is destined to see a nation not only morally but mentally great, a nation which will develop in conjunction those high moral qualities which will give it what I may term a pronounced, a well-defined character, and an intellectual greatness superior to that of ancient Greece and Rome, because restrained and illumined by the predominance and potency of moral characteristics which those great nations did not possess.

CHAPTER XXV

THE FUTURE OF JAPAN—NATIONAL—POLITICAL—ITS INFLUENCE ON THE WORLD

I HAVE now come to my final chapter, in which I propose to offer some remarks embodying my opinion as to the future of Japan from a national and political standpoint, as also her influence upon the world generally. The theme is a great one, and would require a volume for its proper treatment. Obviously, therefore, it cannot be dealt with other than cursorily in the few pages I am about to devote to it.

Readers of this book will, I think, have had borne in upon them the fact that I am not only an ardent admirer of, but a believer in Japan and the Japanese. I utterly scout the idea put forward by some writers that what they have taken on of Western civilisation is either a veneer or a varnish, or that the advancement of the nation resembles the growth of the mushroom and is no more stable. I regard the Japanese as a serious people and the nation as having a serious purpose. If I did not there would be no need for me to dilate upon its future, for the simple reason that its future would be incomprehensible, and accordingly be absolutely impossible to forecast. As it is, it appears to me that the future of Japan is as plain as the proverbial pike-staff. I say this with a full knowledge of the dangers attendant on prophecy and the risk to the reputation of the vaticinator should events prove that he was mistaken in his prevision or erroneous in his conclusions.

I have traced in these pages what I may term the national development of Japan; how, after two and a half centuries of isolation, it, recognising the force of circumstances, determined to impose upon its own ancient civilisation all that was best in that of the West, and, having so determined, took practical and effective steps to that end. What is to be the result of it all, the result, that is to say, not upon a few thousands, or hundreds of thousands, of Japanese, but upon the nation as a whole? Will these accretions on the old civilisation of the land mould and influence and alter the people generally, or will the effect be circumscribed and merely develop a class standing out apart from the great body of the people and affecting a superiority because of its Western culture? In my opinion the result will be not partial, but universal, though not immediate. There are, of course, large portions of Japan, many millions of its population, upon whom the opening up of the country has, as yet had little, if any, effect. Many of the Japanese people have hardly ever seen a foreigner, or, if they have, have viewed him with no little curiosity. They certainly have not realised, and possibly have not suspected, the effect which foreign influences are likely to have upon this Land of the Rising Sun. But influences, we know, may be effective without being felt, and I am convinced, from what I have seen and heard and the investigations I have been enabled to make, that the Japan of to-day is not only in transition—in rapid transition—but that its evolution is sure and certain, and that the result thereof will be the ultimate development of a nation which will assuredly impress the world and will very probably have a much more potent effect upon it than mere numbers would account for. It is the building up of a nation such as this that I confidently look forward to in the future. We of this generation may not, probably will not, live to see it—we certainly shall not in its ultimate development—but we can already see at work the forces which are to produce it, and the eye of faith, of a reasonable faith, built not on mere surmise or ardent hopes, but upon the expectation of a reasonable issue to the factors at work producing it, assures us that the Japan of the future will, as I have said, be a nation whose light will shine, and shine brilliantly, before the whole world.

And as regards the political future of this wonderful country, I feel I can speak with equal confidence. What a marvellous change has come over this land, or our conception of this land, since the first British Minister resident there penned his impressions on approaching it. "A cluster of isles," he remarked, "appeared on the farthest verge of the horizon, apparently inhabited by a race at once grotesque and savage—not much given to hospitality, and rather addicted to martyrising strangers of whose creed they disapproved. Thus much stood out tolerably distinctly, but little else that was tangible. Severance from all social ties, isolation from one's kind, and a pariah existence, far away from all centres of civilisation—far beyond the utmost reach of railroad or telegraph—came much more vividly before me; and in Rembrandt masses of shade, with but one small ray of light, just enough to give force and depth to the whole—a sense of duty, a duty that *must* be done, whether pleasant or otherwise, and about which there was no choice. What a world of anxiety and doubt the consciousness of this saves us!" This exordium reads more like the utterance of a man being led out to execution than a Minister going to a country possessing an ancient civilisation—a civilisation which had had its effect on every phase of the national life. What would not many of us now give to have been in the place of Sir Rutherford Alcock, visiting this land shortly after it had been opened after 250 years of isolation! How we should revel in its artistic treasures, which had not then been dispersed all over the world; and what pleasure we should have taken in seeing feudalism otherwise than in the pages of history! And yet Sir Rutherford Alcock was only expressing the opinions of his time. He could see nothing in Japan but a grotesque and uncivilised people whom the Western nations had to deal with in a peremptory manner. What a change there has been in the intervening forty-four years! Japan now stands out prominently among the nations, her political future appears to be secure, and it is none the less secure because of the difficulties she has encountered and overcome in attaining her present position. I emphasise all the more readily her present and future political position since, as I have previously observed in this book, I believe that that position will be one exercised for the good of the world. I look upon Japan as a great civilising factor in the future of the human race because, strong though she is and stronger though she will become, I am positive that her strength will never be put forward for any selfish aims or from any improper motives. It is for this reason that I welcome the alliance with Great Britain. I hope that alliance will not be limited to any term of years, but will be extended indefinitely, because in it I see a prospect and an assurance for the peace of the world.

Inseparable from any allusion to the political future of

Japan is some consideration of the influence that she is likely to exercise upon the world generally. Any person taking up an atlas and looking at the position occupied by Japan must, if he is of a thoughtful disposition, be impressed by it. Take the question of the Pacific—one which, in view of the change in the policy of the United States of recent years, must assume considerable importance in the future. There are various factors which must be taken into account here. The construction of the Panama Canal is one, the completion of the Siberian Railway another, the development of Canada and the completion of the railway lines that now penetrate nearly every part of that vast dominion is a third. Japan is now, in fact, the very centre of three great markets—those of Europe, Asia, and America. In the struggle for the mastery of the Pacific, which appears certain to come, and will probably come sooner than many people suppose, Japan is certain to take a momentous part. Not only in respect of her own islands, but in reference to the great island of Formosa, ceded to her by China as the outcome of the war with that Power, Japan occupies a unique and a most important position in the Pacific. As regards the mastery of the Pacific, in reference to which so much has been written and so much speculation, a large amount of it unprofitable, has been indulged, I shall say but little. On the shores of the Pacific Russia still remains a power, which, though defeated by Japan, is still one of considerable importance. On the other side of the ocean there is the United States, which, as some persons think, has given hostages to fortune by annexing the Philippine Islands. England, moreover, claims consideration in respect not only of her possessions in the Straits Settlements, Hong Kong, &c., but by reason of her great Navy and, I may add, her alliance with Japan. Then, too, there are China, and, if of less importance, France and Germany. Of all these Japan, in my opinion, occupies the commanding position. She not only occupies the commanding position, but she is, I think, from various causes, bound to play a great part in the future mastery of the Pacific.

It is apparent that in the attainment and assertion of that mastery naval power must have a great and predominant part, and it is to the development of her naval power that Japan is devoting all her energies. Like Great Britain, from whom she has learned many lessons in this respect, she sees that an island empire can only maintain its position by possessing an overpowering naval force. As I have said before, I am fully convinced of the fact that in the development of her Navy, as of her Army, Japan has no aggressive designs. Her aspiration is the security and prevention from invasion of her island and the preservation of her national independence. At the same time, situated as she is in the great Pacific Ocean, she has palpably, from her position, rights and responsibilities and duties outside the immediate confines of her Empire. That, I think, will be admitted by any one. The phrase, "spheres of influcnce" has become somewhat hackneyed of recent years, and it has occasionally been used to give colour to aggressive designs. There may, too, be people who would say that spheres of influence is not a term that can properly be applied to a great water-way such as the Pacific. I am not, however, on the present occasion arguing with pedants. What I desire is to broadly emphasise the fact that in the future of the Pacific—those innumerable isles dotted here and there over its surface, Japan is a factor that cannot be left out of account. Year by year her position there is increasing in importance. Steamers ply to her ports weekly from Vancouver and San Francisco. The Japanese population are emigrating to the Pacific shores of America, the trade and commerce of Japan with the American Continent are growing and broadening. Everything in fact tends to show that within a comparatively short space of time Japan will have asserted her position, not only as a Great World Power, but as a great commercial nation in the Pacific. What is to be the outcome of it all? is the question that will naturally arise to the mind. I think that one outcome of it will be, as I have shown, the capture by Japan of the Chinese trade, if not in its entirety, at any rate in a very large degree. Another outcome will, I believe, be the enormous development of Japanese trade with both the United States and Canada. Some people may remark that these are not essentially political matters, and that I am somewhat wandering from my point in treating of them in connection with the influence of Japan upon the world generally. I do not think so. A nation may assert its influence and emphasise its importance to just as great an extent by its trade as by the double-dealings of diplomacy or by other equally questionable methods. Of one thing I am convinced, and that is that the influence of Japan upon the rest of the world will be a singularly healthy one. That country has fortunately struck out for itself, in diplomacy as in other matters, a new line. It has not behind it any traditions, nor before it prejudices wherewith to impede its progress. The diplomacy of Japan will, accordingly, be conducted in a straightforward manner, and its record so far in this respect has, I think, provided a splendid object-lesson for the rest of the world. The influence of Japan upon the other nations will I hope, as I believe, continue to be of a healthy nature. If that country sets forth prominently the fact that while aspiring to be great, it possesses none of those attributes that we have previously associated with great nations, the attributes of greed, covetousness, aggressiveness, and overbearing—an arrogant attitude in regard to weaker Powers, it will have performed a notable service in the history of the world. For myself I have no doubt whatever that Japan will teach this lesson, and in teaching it will have justified the great place that she has attained among the nations of the earth.

I have now concluded the task that I set before myself. My readers must be judges as to the measure of success, if any, I have attained in it. To attempt a survey of the past, present, and future of a great and ancient nation within the limited space at my disposal has been by no means easy. Every subject I have had under consideration has invited discursiveness, and tempted me to linger and dilate upon it, and it alone. The fascination of Japan must be upon every one, or almost every one, who writes about it, and that fascination is, I may observe, like the art of the country, catholic. Whether we deeply and exhaustively investigate one subject and one subject only, or take a hurried glance at every or almost every subject, we feel a glamour in respect of this wonderful country and its equally wonderful people. While I have endeavoured to prevent this fascination, this glamour, affecting my judgment, I am not ashamed to plead guilty to, but am, in fact, rather proud of it. Indeed, I shall feel gratified if a perusal of this book induces a few persons here and there to study still more deeply the history, the religion, the art of Japan, and the whole trend of events in that country during the past forty years. Every phase of the national life lends itself to investigation, and will, I feel sure, reward the investigator. He will, unless he be a person of a singularly unemotional disposition, utterly lacking in all those finer feelings which especially distinguish man from the brutes, hardly fail of being, before he has proceeded far in his investigations, quickly under the alluring influences of this Far Eastern land, entering heartily, zealously, and enthusiastically into its national life and the developments thereof in all their various ramifications.

The fascination that Japan has exercised upon writers such as Arnold and Hearn is what it does, though no doubt in a smaller degree, upon less gifted men. It is given to few to drink in and absorb the subtle charm of the country so thoroughly and express it so graphically and delicately, with such beauty and power and withal so much truth as have those brilliant men. I regard this great and growing fascination of Occidentals for this fair Eastern land and its inhabitants as a long step in the direction of the realisation of the brotherhood of man ; that ideal state of things which we hope for so expectantly, longingly, perhaps too often sceptically ; that happy time when national prejudices, jealousies, and animosities will have faded into oblivion, when nations by the simple process of studying one another, as Japan has been studied of recent years, will get to understand one another, when the literature and art of nations will be no longer merely national, but world possessions, when wars shall have ceased and the policy of aggression have come to be regarded as an evil thing, when, in a word, the brotherhood of man shall be no longer an idle dream, a mere speculative aspiration which no practical person ever expected to see realised, but an actuality within measurable distance of being accomplished. All these things may as yet be dreams, but let us dream them. The more they are dreamed, the more likely is the prospect of their realisation. One thing at least fills me with ardent hope, and that is the Japan, as I see it to-day, compared with the Japan of forty years ago. If such an upheaval is possible for one nation, who shall put any bounds to the potentialities of the world? So let us dream our dreams, and in our waking moments cast afar our eyes upon the land of the Rising, aye, now the Risen Sun, take heart and dream again in quiet confidence that some day, in some future reincarnation, mayhap, we shall witness the realisation of our hopes, and see that after all our dreams were merely an intelligent anticipation of the glad time coming.

INDEX

The Gresham Press,
UNWIN BROTHERS, LIMITED,
WOKING AND LONDON.